Times
Down Home

Times Down Home

75 Years with *Progressive Farmer*

Editor
Mary Elizabeth Johnson

Research and Narrative
Mary Jean Haddin

Oxmoor House, Inc.
Birmingham

Copyright © 1978 by Oxmoor House, Inc.
Book Division of The Progressive Farmer Company
Publisher of *Southern Living®, Progressive Farmer®,*
    and *Decorating & Craft Ideas®* Magazines.
P.O Box 2463, Birmingham, Alabama 35202

Eugene Butler   *Chairman of the Board*
Emory Cunningham   *President and Publisher*
Vernon Owens, Jr.   *Senior Executive Vice President*
Roger McGuire   *Executive Vice President*
Don Logan   *Vice President and Director of Book Division*

Times Down Home: 75 Years with *Progressive Farmer*

Designers: Steve Newman, Judy Hill, Phil Sankey, Steve Logan
Cover: Westgate Graphic Design, Inc.
Editorial assistance provided by John Logue, Candace C. Franklin, Fred Bonnie

Library of Congress Catalog Number: 78-59619
ISBN: 0-8487-0491-6   975.04

Manufactured in the United States of America
First Printing

1. Farm life – Southern States – History.
I. Haddin, Mary Jean.
II. The Progressive farmer.

Contents

75 Years of Progressive Farmer Mastheads

1903
Clarence H. Poe, Editor
J.W. Denmark, Proprietor and Publisher

1913
Clarence Poe, President and Editor; Tait Butler, Vice President and Editor; E.E. Miller, Managing Editor; W.F. Massey, Associate Editor; John S. Pearson, Secretary-Treasurer

1917
Clarence Poe, President and Editor; Tait Butler, Vice President and Editor; B.L. Moss, Managing Editor; W.F. Massey, Contributing Editor; John S. Pearson, Secretary-Treasurer; J.A. Martin, Advertising Manager

1919
Clarence Poe, President and Editor; Tait Butler, Vice President and Editor; G.H. Alford, Editor; B.L. Moss, Managing Editor; Mrs. W.N. Hutt, Editor, Woman's Department; John S. Pearson, Secretary-Treasurer

1930
Publishers: The Progressive Farmer Company; Clarence Poe, President; Tait Butler, Eugene Butler, B.W. Kilgore, Vice Presidents; John S. Pearson, Secretary-Treasurer
Editors: Clarence Poe, Tait Butler, B.W. Kilgore, W.C. Lassetter, Eugene Butler, Mrs. W.N. Hutt. Associate Editors: C.L. Newman, L.A. Niven, R.A. Nunn, H.L. Atkins, Ben Kilgore, Elise Phillips
Managers: General Business, John S. Pearson; Advertising, Fowler Dugger, J.B. Holloway; Circulation, F.W. Taylor, C.L. Dobson

1941
Officers: Clarence Poe, President; W.C. Lassetter, B. W. Kilgore, John S. Pearson, Eugene Butler, Vice Presidents; D.C. Husdon, Secretary
Editors: W.C. Lassetter, Clarence Poe, Eugene Butler, Sallie F. Hill. Managing Editor: Alexander Nunn. Associate Editor: L.A. Niven
Business Staff: General Manager, John S. Pearson; Associate, D.C. Hudson. Advertising: Fowler Dugger, Forbes McKay. Circulation: F.W. Taylor, R.W. Taylor

1946
Officers: Clarence Poe, President; Eugene Butler, John S. Pearson, W.C. Lassetter, Ben Kilgore, Fowler Dugger, Vice Presidents; D. C. Hudson, Secretary.
Editors: W.C. Lassetter, Clarence Poe, Eugene Butler, Sallie Hill. Managing Editor: Alexander Nunn. Associate Editors: L.A. Niven, Wm.C. LaRue, Joe Elliott. Art Editor: T. Wendell Godwin.
Business Staff: General Manager, John S. Pearson; Associate, D.C. Hudson. Advertising: Fowler Dugger, Manager; Associate, Forbes McKay; Eastern Mgr., H.E. Butcher; Western Mgr., Paul Huey (on leave; Lt. Col. U.S. Army); Acting Western Mgr., Oscar M. Dugger, Jr.; Circulation: F.W. Taylor, Mgr.

1961
Clarence Poe, Chairman, Board of Directors and Senior Editor; Eugene Butler, President and Editor-in-Chief; Fowler Dugger, Vice President-General Manager-Treasurer; J.D. Kilgore, Raleigh, N.C.; Alexander Nunn, Vice President and Executive Editor
Additional Directors: Oscar M. Dugger, Vice President and Director of Advertising; W.C. Lassetter, Memphis; Cordra York, Memphis, Tenn.; Charles A. Poe, Raleigh, N.C.; Eugene B. Butler, Secretary; Emory O. Cunningham, Vice President and Advertising Manager; J.L. Rogers, Vice President and Circulation Manager

1978
Eugene Butler, Chairman of the Board and Editor-in-Chief; Emory Cunningham, President and Publisher; Vernon Owens, Jr., Senior Executive Vice President; Roger McGuire, Executive Vice President; C.G. Scruggs, Vice President and Editor; Ed Wilborn, Executive Editor; Vernon Miller, Senior Editor; Bill Capps, Circulation Director; Eugene B. Butler, Secretary; James G. Nelson, Treasurer; O.B. Copeland, Assistant to the President

Color Plates   Page

Those of us who work for The Progressive Farmer Company know that it is dangerous to be sent into our archives on an assignment . . . We don't want to come out! No matter what subject we are supposed to be researching, we don't seem to be able to concentrate solely on it. There is just too much other material that is tantalizing. We linger over an ad for a 1906 washing machine that does the wash in six minutes, or a letter from a young man, desperate to find a wife who enjoys Shakespeare, and countless other items. We get lost.

We have finally concluded that there is just too much appealing material to leave it buried for only an occasional researcher to find and chortle over it. We have admitted that it needed to be gathered together to reach a wider audience. That decision was the germ of *Times Down Home*.

Our method has been simply to read through every *Progressive Farmer* magazine from 1902 to the present, concentrating more on the family and human interest items than on the professional farming articles. (These, too, however, were fascinating, particularly for the story they told of the attitudes of and toward the farmer in this country through the years. But that must be another book.) Our greatest difficulty has been cutting the original material. We were confronted by such a richness of informational articles, advice and letters to the editor. (One thing has been obvious: *Progressive Farmer* readers, both then and now, have considered it to be *their* magazine and have never hesitated to let the editors know just what they thought.) The passages finally selected for presentation in this book are given to you as they originally appeared in the magazine. The only writing we have done is for the introductions at the beginning of each chapter. You will begin to recognize the voices of some of the people described below.

We began with the "Home Circle," the women's section of 1902, presided over by "Aunt Jennie," who was the daughter of the first publisher, Col. L.L. Polk. In real life Mrs. Juanita Polk Denmark, "Aunt Jennie" inaugurated the letters column known as "Our Social Chat." The "Chatterers," as they called themselves, ranged over many subjects from compulsory school attendance to home remedies to the charms of bachelorhood, often answering each other by name (or pen name like "Mountain Hoojer" or "Brown-eyed Lula") as a real dialogue arose among these isolated farm people. (One audacious young man even suggested an exchange of pictures.) Aunt Jennie was expected to arbitrate, comfort and advise, much like an aunt or grandmother. The "Chatterers" expressed genuine worry when she became ill and eventually another woman took over as editor.

The *Progressive Farmer* made known its desire to serve its women readers as faithfully as it did its "friends of the sterner sex" in the introduction, in 1907, of its next women's editor. "Aunt Mary" (Mrs. Walter Grimes) was already known to its readers as the writer of a voluminous series of articles on "The Farm Home Beautiful," which included the grounds, outbuildings, and the gate, not to mention wall and floor coverings, furniture, and even pictures, books and piano. It was Aunt Mary who beseeched her readers to eschew "Nottingham" lace curtains at all costs.

In 1910, the Home Department became more scientific with Mrs. F.L. Stevens. (No more Aunts.) Trained in domestic science when there were very few schools offering that course, Mrs. Stevens offered a "Domestic Science Reading Course" through the pages of the *Progressive Farmer*—actual quizzes on various aspects of health and food preparation.

Mrs. W.N. Hutt arrived in 1913 to become the first full-time women's editor. She combined a broad knowledge of domestic science (she was introduced as one of the best-known lecturers at farm women's institutes) with a deep human sympathy for her readers, many of whom she knew were lonely and over-burdened. She made rural women's clubs her crusade, realizing the advantages to farm women of the exchange of knowledge and moral support. She also urged "demonstration work" for the female partner on the farm, which became a reality during her 17 years as editor of "The Progressive Farm Woman," as it was then called.

In 1930 Miss Lois Dowdle became Home Editor. She prepared the first distributed directions for making cotton (the Southern farmer's albatross during the Depression) into homemade mattresses, thereby using up thousands of bales of surplus cotton. When federal payments became available for cutting acreage, she urged their use in making homes more comfortable.

Miss Sallie Fletcher Hill became editor of the Home Department in 1933 and served in that position for 27 years, becoming Senior Editor following that. During her tenure a special "home cover" was introduced, making "The Progressive Home" a magazine within a magazine. Miss Hill combined practical articles with introductions to poetry and works of art. She started a correspondence course in home nursing which was completed by 5,000 readers.

A column entitled "Country Voices," published from 1943 to 1961, was a combination of philosophical acceptance with provocative opinions which brought forth hosts of letters from readers. *Progressive Farmer* inspired many latent writers, some of whom were excellent and a few of whom (among them, Jesse Stuart) went on to national literary prominence. The depth of feeling and attention to detail that comes out of these *Progressive Farmer* writings are enough to make one wonder if, indeed, life close to nature and supreme fact does not actually produce superior people.

It may be fair to say that without the *Progressive Farmer*'s chiding and cajoling its readers to be their best selves and be aware of the unique possibilities of their lives and region, our beloved Southland itself might not have quite as good a start on the progressive path. *Progressive Farmer* editorialized for running water and world peace; rural health programs, community spirit, and world peace; farmers' organizations and world peace; and above all—the wholesome country life and world peace.

Progressive Farmer went through the good times and bad times along with its farmer readers. Throughout much of its history, the editors (Clarence Poe, Tait Butler, Eugene Butler, B.W. Kilgore, and Alexander Nunn) were also among the owners of the magazine who worked to keep the *Progressive Farmer*, as stated in its masthead of 1903, "serving no master, ruled by no faction, circumscribed by no selfish or narrow policy." Throughout the years the magazine's publishing leaders, John S. Pearson, Fowler Dugger, and the current president of the company, Emory Cunningham, enabled and encouraged the *Progressive Farmer* to continue to "speak with no uncertain voice," to "fearlessly the right defend and impartially the wrong condemn."

One other part of our method perhaps requires explanation. We have divided the material into chapters that seemed to fit a theme cast by the material itself, but unlike most editors of books of "nostalgia," we have brought you up to the present day. We found that we just couldn't stop with the 1930's and 1940's. For the story went on and keeps going on. What has continued to interest us (and might be called the theme of the book itself) is that despite the phenomenal changes that have occurred in our outer lives over the cataclysmic years of our century, there is much of intelligence and much of the spirit that remains the same.

This book is intended purely as entertainment. We hope that you enjoy reading it as much as we have enjoyed the collecting, writing, and editing. While some of the recipes and remedies printed throughout these seventy-five years might work today, we warn you *not* to try them; particularly we warn against trying those that might physically affect you, internally or externally. We have *not* tested them. Our pleasure has been, as we hope yours will be, in the reading of them in the context of their own time and ours.

Turning the brown and crumbling pages of the old *Progressive Farmer* magazines evokes a picture of a whole region which has, perhaps more than any other region of our country, "never left home." It is like leafing through an old family photograph album, except that this one pictures a whole society. Charmed, we are glad to relinquish the intricacies of our own lives for awhile. Such is the lure of "nostalgia." It is peaceful to loll here surrounded by the past—the long, graceful skirts, the dear old one-room school. These were our "people," our mothers and fathers, our grandmothers and grandfathers.

One of the greatest pleasures of this retreat is a return to safety. We are transported home to that golden age of our childhood when the world was as it should be because our elders (omnipotent beings) made it so. That world had the authority and rightness—the perfection—of our childhood innocence. We love to rest there.

The other pleasure (and it does not bother us at all that this one is contradictory to the first) is that we can feel a trifle superior to those august figures of our childhood—our elders who always knew best. We can smile a bit condescendingly at their incredulity and delight in the telephone and the "water system." We can chuckle at their fifteen mile an hour speed limit. We can feel for a moment as if we were *their* parents, initiating them into the wonders of the modern world.

But if we pause long enough to become immersed in their daily living, to meet their personalities and beliefs, a different feeling grows. We surprise our ancestors in the midst of their lives as we are in the midst of ours—in the midst of getting and spending, trying and failing and trying again. We discover from our grandmothers that those quaint trailing skirts tired the hand with holding them up and made it impossible to carry bundles or children. We find that consolidated schools were long advocated to replace the "dear old one-room school" to allow the children both a broader and more specialized education. But lo and behold, when consolidated schools were an accomplished fact, many thoughtful people considered them a detriment to the education of the whole child. The long bus rides brought the children home too late to take part in the enterprise of the farm and farm home. In fact, if we pause long enough we do not derive our accustomed escape from nostalgia. For we discover our ancestors in the midst of lives neither wholly perfect, not wholly imperfect. We find them living in their time as we must live in ours—accepting it and resisting it.

But one theme of their lives especially grips us and forms a living connection—their high and solemn view of history and their part in it. Our grandparents lived with an eye to posterity. They considered each child born to them a charge against their immortal souls. They believed that they would be called upon, when the last trumpet sounded, to account, not just for their own lives, but for the upbringing and lives of their children. They lived daily with that mission: to raise their children into "men and women capable of thought and action, and worthy to make the future history of their beloved country."

We are surprised to find that nostalgia, by leading us into the past, has helped us to discover ourselves. Now we know where we have been, and where and who we are. We are those children, those men and women. We are the recipients of that care with the long view, that high and solemn duty. Nostalgia has brought us beyond retreat. For we are the parents now. The world we sanction will be our children's perfection. Here we have found our roots. In fact, we find that they have been with us all the time. They are inescapable. By accepting the chalice of responsibility from our ancestors, we have found ourselves rooted in the past and the future.

Now we understand why our longing for the past, our sense of "nostalgia," goes beyond "homesickness," its dictionary definition. Somehow we must have sensed the word's *own* roots, in Greek and Old English and Gothic: "to return home," "to survive," "to get well," and "be saved."

Doing a Week's Washing In 6 Minutes—Read the Proof

THIS woman is using a 1900 Gravity Washer. All she has to do is keep the washer going. A little push starts it one way— a little pull brings it back—the washer does the rest.

The clothes stay still—the water rushes through and around them—and the dirt is taken out.

In six minutes your tubful of clothes is clean.

This machine will wash anything—from lace curtains to carpets, and get them absolutely, spotlessly, specklessly clean.

There isn't anything about a 1900 Gravity Washer to wear out your clothes.

You can wash the finest linen, lawn and lace without breaking a thread.

"Tub rips" and "wash tears" are unknown.

Your clothes last twice as long.

You save time—labor—and money.

You wash quicker—easier—more economically.

Prove all this at my expense and risk.

I let you use a 1900 Gravity Washer a full month FREE.

Send for my New Washer Book.

Read particulars of my offer.

Say you are willing to test a 1900 Gravity Washer.

I will send one to any responsible party, freight prepaid.

I can ship promptly at any time—so you get your washer at once.

Take it home and use it a month. Do all your washings with it.

And, if you don't find the machine all I claim—if it doesn't save you time and work—if it doesn't wash your clothes cleaner and better—don't keep it.

I agree to accept your decision without any back talk—and I will.

If you want to keep the washer—as you surely will when you see how much time, and work, and money it will save you—you can take plenty of time to pay for it.

Pay so much a week—or so much a month—as suits you best.

Pay for the washer as it saves for you.

I make you this offer because I want you to find out for yourself what a 1900 Gravity Washer will do.

I am willing to trust you, because you can probably get trusted at home. And, if your credit is good in your own town, it is just as good with me.

It takes a big factory—the largest washer factory in the world—to keep up with my orders.

So far as I know, my factory is the only one ever devoted exclusively to making washers.

Over half a million of my washers are in use.

Over half a million pleased women can tell you what my washers will do.

But you don't have to take even their say-so. You can test a 1900 Gravity Washer yourself. Then you will know positively.

Write for my book today. It is FREE.

Your name and address on a post card mailed to me at once, gets you my book by return mail.

You are welcome to the book whether you want to buy a washer now or not.

It is a big illustrated book, printed on heavy enameled paper, and has pictures showing exactly how my Washers work.

You will be pleased with this book. It is the finest even I have ever put out. Write me at once.

Find out just how a 1900 Gravity Washer saves your time and strength—preserves your health—and protects your pocketbook.

Write now—Address—R. F. Bieber, Manager "1900" Washer Co., 355 Henry St., Binghamton. N. Y. Or, if you live in Canada, write to my Canadian Branch, 355 Yonge St., Toronto, Ontario.

Rafters of the Home—
Era 1902–1911

One of the most striking things about reading the *Progressive Farmer* of 1902 is how modern it seems to be! Many of the concerns that occupied the thoughts of the writers and readers of 1902 are still of importance to writers and readers of today. Each generation has a tendency to think that it is unique—that its problems have never been dealt with before. But there is comfort to be drawn from reading these excerpts from the old magazines . . . due in large part to the realization that we are *not* unique—that our grandfathers were already working on these problems and, as we turn to them today, we are not alone. True, our grandparents could not even have imagined the complications which would be brought about by what would seem to them magical mechanization and electrification. In fact, our chief concern today might be that while our *technology* has changed drastically, our *people* have not changed that much. We *can* identify with our ancestors of 75 years ago, even though our outer circumstances have changed so much as to be almost unrecognizable.

It is sustaining to us to know that even after all we have come through (life changes so great as to have turned us into a different species, it would seem), our overriding concern is the same now as it was then—how to raise our children to be happy and productive people. When we read the writers of 1902 decrying the "wave of public dishonesty sweeping the country" and the "subtle influences at work to destroy the home," we can either throw up our hands in hopelessness that after 75 years we haven't gotten any better, or we can feel comradeship with our grandparents and all humanity—that these are issues that men and women of good will may be working on until the end of time.

Two news items of this era seem especially prophetic—or rather the writer's responses to them seem prophetic. One, in 1907, was the race across the Atlantic ocean of the ship Lucania and her sister ship, the Lusitania. The editor's description shows the attitude of the times:

They are just two dumb things a-racing over the waves; they are more than dumb, they are dead things; they don't know anything, they can't feel anything; they are going to be driven hard across 2,800 miles of a wide, deep, unfeeling waste of heavy seas. One is going to win; but they are dead dumb things, and the one that loses will feel just like the one that wins. Yes. Ah, the gentle brotherhood of inanimate things, wherein there is no joy of one at another's cost.

Another prophetic response was John Charles McNeill's reaction to the Stock Law, which kept herds behind fences rather than wandering free:

. . . we will easily admit that in point of worldly affairs we are better off . . . For this advantage we have paid as purchase price the beauty and charm of that simpler, more primitive life; for the clink of coin we have given, as Tennyson hath

it, "The mellow lin-lan-lone of evening bells . . ." And the only question is, Was it a good trade? We pay for the enjoyment of other luxuries: Was the luxury of living in the old way too expensive for us?

Of course we have the woods still, but choice or laziness or other occupation may estrange us from them, while the old regime forced us into them daily and thus, perhaps unconsciously, brought to bear on our lives their wholesome influence . . .

This "wholesome influence" of nature was continually proclaimed by the *Progressive Farmer* in the early 1900's and throughout the years as one of the best reasons for living and raising children in the country. City children, to their detriment, had to be kept in an artificial environment, entertained and taken for walks in buggies, because they did not have the advantages that farm children had. The farm children could, from the time they could crawl, learn the lessons that Nature, the greatest teacher, taught, and could play with her, the most variable and responsive playmate, for which no manufactured toy could compensate. In this perfect educational setting, the country home's reason for being was to aid Nature in the production of self-reliant, cultivated, unselfish and beautiful people who would grace *any* environment. However, the peace and wholesomeness of their childhood homes would seem so superior to them that farm life would be their choice and they would *stay on the farm.*

Plainly, this proper nurturing of the nation's children was too important a job to be left entirely to the whims and inclinations of individual parents. The *Progressive Farmer*, as shown by the contemporary letters to it, tried to be both a guide and a friend. The country home must be tasteful outside and in, an inspiration to those who lived there and those who passed by. Its inhabitants must dress properly, cook, eat, breathe and sleep properly. The minor defects of country life—such as lack of good lighting, running water and excellence of formal education—must be recognized and remedied so that the children would have the advantages of city *and* country life and *stay on the farm*— the perfect home for all.

A major defect, tactily acknowledged, was loneliness, especially for farm women. The telephone was a hope and possibility and many pages were devoted to directions for setting up rural telephone lines. A blessedly accomplished fact was rural free mail delivery, bringing news of friends, relatives and the world. Improving roads became a political issue as better roads became vital to reliable mail delivery, for getting to market, and for consolidating schools. With better roads, of course, came that menace, the automobile: "There is undoubtedly strong feeling in all parts of the *Progressive Farmer*'s territory against reckless automobiling . . ."

As to regulation of speed the law provides that an operator shall not drive in the corporate limits of any city or town at a greater rate of speed than twelve miles an hour. Outside such limits a speed of fifteen miles an hour is

THE PROGRESSIVE FARMER AND SOUTHERN Farm Gazette

A Farm and Home Weekly for North and South Carolina, Virginia, Tennessee, and Georgia.

Vol. XXV.   No. 37.   RALEIGH, N. C., SEPTEMBER 17, 1910.   Weekly: $1 a Year.

Why Not Build a Telephone Line For Your Neighborhood?

WE have said so much about the convenience and the satisfaction which result from having a telephone in the house that we scarcely think it necessary to discuss that feature of the matter again. But we do wish to call your attention to the fact that you can build your own telephone line at a comparatively small cost—a wonderfully small cost compared to its value to you—and that this is a splendid season for you and your neighbors to get together and establish a telephone system of your own. You can then connect it with other lines, and be right in touch with the business and social activities of the world.

The Western Electric Co., issues a free booklet telling just how to go about this work, and the following details of construction are taken from it:

"A telephone line should run past or as near as possible to the buildings in which telephones are to be placed. It is not necessary, however, to run the main line past each of these buildings, as branch wires may extend from the main line to each building, saving wire and simplifying construction.

"For substantial and economical line construction poles of good stock, such as chestnut or cedar, are best on account of their lasting qualities. For a line of light construction a pole twenty-six feet in length and five or six inches in diameter at the top represents good practice and allows for re-setting if it becomes necessary through decay below the surface of the ground.

"The cross-arms familiar on all long distance lines are not necessary when one is considering the first principles of rural construction. Only two strands of wire are needed by such a system, and these are usually supported by twelve-inch painted oak brackets nailed securely to the pole before it is set into the ground. On each bracket should be screwed a glass insulator for attaching the wire, with a view to preventing leakage of current down the pole or from one side of the circuit to the other.

"Galvanized iron wire of No. 12 B B. gauge is most suitable for rural lines on account of its toughness and ability to withstand the action of the weather.

"The pictures show the method of attaching wires to the house and leading them in for connection to the instrument inside, and the method of connection from main line to house.

"Provided that the line is kept free from tree limbs and maintained in good condition, a large number of instruments may be connected on one pair of wires. It must be remembered, however, that the greater the number of telephones connected the less available they are at certain busy times. If calls are too frequent and the wires become heavily loaded—especially if there is a prospect of obtaining more subscribers—it may be advisable to run another pair of wires on the same set of poles. This not only lessens the call on the one wire, but it provides facilities for development and the handling of an increase of the number of subscribers. In case two sets of lines are used, a small switching station, located in some central house, must then be arranged, to allow for connection of one line with the other.

"The cost of one mile of line construction, exclusive of poles and labor, for a grounded system approximately twelve miles long and using thirty poles to the mile is about $7. For a full metallic system the cost is approximately $14. The cost of each subscriber's instruments and incidental equipment is approximately $13 more."

It will thus be seen that a telephone is easily within your reach, and once using it you will not be without it. Why not get busy and establish your line this fall?

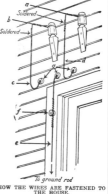
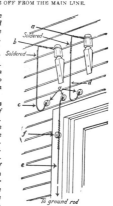

HOW THE BRANCH LINE RUNS OFF FROM THE MAIN LINE.

HOW THE WIRES ARE FASTENED TO THE HOUSE.

BUILDING A RURAL TELEPHONE LINE.

FEATURES OF THIS ISSUE.

permissible, except in going around curves . . . The driver must keep a careful look ahead for the approach of persons riding in vehicles or on horseback, and upon the approach of the same keep his machine under careful control, give ample roadway, and, if signalled by such rider or driver, immediately bring his machine to a full stop and allow ample room to pass; and, if requested to do so by said rider or driver, the driver of the machine, if a male, must lead the horse past the machine. at least, are not required to "lead the horse past the machine") we can identify also with their worries about smoking and drinking. Unlike the studies of today, which concentrate on physical health,

Our Lady Rural Carrier

Mrs. Alice Fowler, the lady rural carrier whose picture is given herewith, is said to be a fine manager of the two beautiful ponies that she drives, and they are greatly attached to her.

Senator Jas. F. Moore, of Pender, thus spoke of Mrs. Fowler in his July 4th speech: "Let me commend and compliment her for her bravery and progressiveness. •••I wish that all of our carriers were women. I am sure they would do the work effectively, and we country people would always be at the box to the minute to get the mail, and hear the news. •••You know, it is said that a woman can tell more in a minute than a man can all day."

As we, like our grandparents, try to keep our machines "under careful control" (feeling lucky that we, studies of these social problems in the early 20th century tended to

be more mental and moral. There was the study that showed that no college student who smoked ever amounted to anything. Letters to Aunt Jennie on the subject arrived regularly:

womankind bound, as the law now stands, by irrevocable ties to men who themselves acknowledge no master but who serve most assiduously King Alcohol, is worse than that of the African slave . . .

one who should have the trouble with the drunkards. If the law would compel the seller to keep all who drink his wine and whiskey with him and take care of them until they get sober, it would be a just law, and the seller would soon get tired of his business and quit.

The tobacco habit certainly does not in any sense make the homes happier, nor yet decrease the labor of keeping the house tidy. How pleasant it is to visit our neighbor who has a clean white hearth instead of one covered with dark brown spots . . . Tobacco dulls the mind . . . Young friends, do not let any one persuade you to begin the habit of smoking or using in any way this poisonous weed, tobacco.

As for "drink," drunkenness should

be made the first cause for divorce. There are few evils of which drink is not the father . . . Slavery has been abolished, so they say, but I tell you the truth when I say that the slavery of

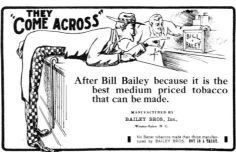

After Bill Bailey because it is the best medium priced tobacco that can be made.

MANUFACTURED BY
BAILEY BROS., Inc.,
Winston-Salem N. C.

No Better tobaccos made than those manufactured by BAILEY BROS. **NOT IN A TRUST.**

The following seemed a sensible suggestion:

Duplin County is now called a dry county, but there is as much drunkenness . . . now as there was when the barrooms were running . . . One part of the law provides that those who buy liquor . . . must not drink it at the place where they buy it . . . the lawmakers made a wide mistake, for in my estimation the seller of such drinks is the

We tend to think of our ancestors as better than ourselves, dealing with a simpler, purer reality. But our grandparents' burdens were no simpler to them than ours are to us. Few escapes from reality were available, and many people used patent medicines, often containing opium or alcohol, as panaceas. Here, as in other areas, the *Progressive Farmer* tried to educate:

The people want medicine for bald head and gray hair, to make fat and lose fat, to make them sleep and to keep them awake, to make them drunk and to sober them up, to revitalize and to devitalize. They take medicine to warm them up and to cool them off, to stay the ravages of age, medicine to take wrinkles out, medicine to make them tough and medicine to make them tender, medicine to sooth and medicine to stimulate . . . It is a fad as wide as the horizon of human hope. Rich and poor, wise and foolish, lean and fat, black and white, large and small, sick and healthy want drugs rubbed in and on them, with needles, injections, by the mouth, by plasters, salves, tablets, pills and tinctures . . . Finally I believe the world will be peopled by a race made up of copper stomachs on stilts, with spoons and troughs where they may stand from cradle to grave and guzzle and swill till kingdom come.

However, these evils were as much a part of city as of country life and we find ourselves agreeing

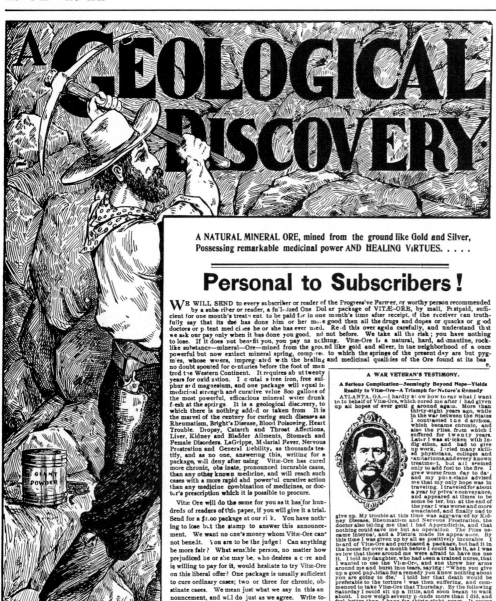

about the advantages of farm life. If the man in the country

lives what the world terms a small life . . . is apt to do the same things day after day and . . . is not apt to make a great deal of money . . . still if he is happy, there are those who will rejoice with him. If he suffers, men reach out their hands and touch him understandingly; his virtues, as well as his sins, are a matter of public knowledge . . . Old men and women stop him and bless him in memory of his father and mother; he knows a countless number of babies; and his neighbors' dogs come out and recognize him as a beloved friend. The joy of his acquaintances is so near to him . . . that he is gladdened with its radiance, and his eyes are wet in thought of their sorrow. He has time for reflection, and he learns to know his fellow man—know his strengths and weaknesses; learns to commend the one and condone the other. On weekdays he speaks to hundreds of people who call him by his first name; on Sundays he worships with a congregation that has known him since he was a babe in arms. When he is old he is not in the way, and when he dies men bring sympathy to his children and declare a common loss. Maybe he . . . has lived in a rut, but he has lived with his heart-side throbbing . . .

As we come to know this man and his wife—to know our grandfathers and grandmothers in a way we never did as children—we realize more fully that ours is a good heritage. We exult, as we read with them about the presidential campaign of 1904, that the country home was the nursery of the nation:

It has been said before that the plow boy is the leading figure of this blessed government . . . Unlike any other country in the world the American people go to the fields, and shops, and tanneries for their presidents. England is ruled by royalty—the United States by their plow boys . . . There the family makes the man, here the man makes the family.

This great and refreshing truth is strikingly illustrated in the nominees of the two great parties for President and Vice-President. Mr. Theodore Roosevelt is the one exception to the usual rule of country boys being called to the Presidential chair; but Mr. Roosevelt is a plain American without any frills about him. Judge Alton Brooks Parker was born on a farm . . . where he learned the necessity of honest labor . . .

Senator Charles Warren Fairbanks, the Republican nominee for Vice President, was born in a log cabin on his father's farm . . . Here he spent his boyhood, learning the large lessons that have fitted him for the exalted station he has filled so well . . . Henry Gassaway Davis found himself in his early teens a bread-winner for a widowed mother with five children . . . At nineteen years of age he obtained a position as brakesman on the Baltimore and Ohio Railroad . . .

Thus, with the exception of Mr. Roosevelt, all the candidates for the highest places within the gift of the American people, are men who in their youth went barefooted and fought for bread in hand-to-hand struggle. It is an inspiration to American youth that these are the boys who win the highest honors of the world . . .

Still exulting, let us turn to the pages of their daily lives. We can catch grandmother and grandfather immersed in hog-killing or in try-ing to figure out a water system. We may find them wishing for compulsory education or resisting it. These incidents and thousands more are the building pieces—the rafters of the home.

ROOSEVELT AND FAIRBANKS.

PARKER AND DAVIS.

The Farm Home Beautiful

It has been said that environment is stronger than heredity in character-building. And just in proportion as we make our homes beautiful and refined and attractive will our children . . . be, also refined and gracious and symmetrical of character, and the influence of such surroundings will reach out and restrain and shape and refine all along the journey of life.

Given a man and a woman who have a proper appreciation of the relative value of things, and understand the influence of the home upon everyday life and character, as well as the value of home missionary work in beautifying our home surroundings, and that man and woman will find a way of making the desert to bloom as the rose, and the influence of their work will radiate throughout the whole community and leaven a whole lot of rather slack and inert material.

The acme of living is love, the abiding place of love is the home, and the home-maker is woman. The more beautiful the home, the more proper the setting for love, and since each woman is by nature a home-maker, it is only when pursuing that occupation that she is at her best and so happiest.

I have little patience with those girls and women who, having no especial talent, go out into the world thinking to better themselves materially. Home is the place for every woman unless necessity demands that she seek employment elsewhere, and no home is more desirable than the country home . . .

You, the home-maker, should try in every way possible to have everything around you appear at its best, both for your own satisfaction and for the help and inspiration you will be to all with whom you come in contact. We of the South are peculiarly a home-loving

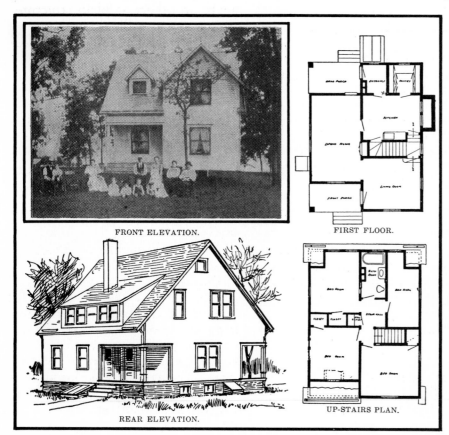

FRONT ELEVATION.

FIRST FLOOR.

REAR ELEVATION.

UP-STAIRS PLAN.

people, and nowhere can the home be more permanent than in the country.

Set to work to beautify your home and I'll warrant that you and your daughters will not lack for social pleasures. And even in these days of high-priced food, you, the farmer's wife, can have guests around your table when the city friend is pretending to enjoy a cereal and a cup of tea all alone.

You can be just as much in touch with the world, too, as you care to be. Rural free delivery and telephones are great, great blessings, and one of the first necessities of a modern home, whether in town or country, is the telephone. That is one thing which the home-maker must insist upon having, if possible.

All that is best in life lies within the country woman's grasp, your grasp—a real home . . . a house with sunshine, green grass and the shade of trees for your children to enjoy, vegetables, fruits, and flowers, fresh from the gathering, a table laden with as many delicacies as the thrifty home-maker cares to indulge in. No crowding nor haphazard living, but a bed, a chair, a plate for every one who comes within your borders, a haven for your growing boys and girls. Each night gathered around you are your loved ones . . .

An attractive farm home with neat well-painted buildings and well kept lawn and flower garden is a thing of beauty, and gives an added grace to the natural scenery, showing as it does the handiwork of man in harmony with that of the Creator. It speaks of the inner life of the occupants as well as the material toil of the wherewithal of life. It tells of intelligence and refinement and love of the beautiful, and presents to our inner consciousness a picture of a home life that is in tune with the Infinite.

The well should be near the house, the pump on the back porch, or in the kitchen if possible. The well-house or cover can be made very ornamental. Those made of different sized cedar branches, roof and all, are very attractive, and bits of lattice intertwined with vines lend a charming air to an otherwise plain structure. For a shallow well, there is nothing more picturesque than the old-fashioned sweep.

The more unpretentious the poultry house and coops are, the better. Cleanliness is the first requisite here. Lime should be freely used in the back yard, particularly if the yard be at all damp. All the outbuildings should be constructed in a thoroughly neat manner, grouped or placed so as not to be obtrusive, and painted or whitewashed.

If the back yard lacks shade, hasten to remedy that defect by setting out trees just as soon as possible, and place them where the building of future out-houses will not cause them to be felled. Fruit trees are excellent in the back yard, particularly the pear and the apple. The pear, as you know, is a very ornamental tree, and nothing is lovelier than the apple tree when in full bloom.

Keep the Barnyard at a Distance, and Do Not Crowd the Buildings.

Have the lot (barnyard), with its necessary objectionable features, as far from the house as is practical, and to the north or northwest if possible. The nearer the lot (barnyard) is to the dwelling, just so many more flies will the housekeeper have to contend with, and if it be poorly located the odors and noises will be very objectionable . . .

Are You "Living" On The Farm Or Just "Staying" There?

This picture shows a home with a water-works plant. But that is not all. The house is provided with heat from a warm air furnace and light from a private gas plant; and it has telephone, rural mail, and macadam road connections with the city, this making a place where a farmer can "live"—something "every American farmer is entitled to and what the great majority can have if they will make the effort." Read this water-works article carefully and begin now to make the effort to "live" on your farm instead of just "staying" on it.

An Inexpensive And Satisfactory Shower Bath

Messrs. Editors: I wish to commend the Progressive Farmer and Gazette for bringing before its readers plans for furnishing country homes with water and bath-rooms. Every plan yet suggested involves more expense than the average family can afford. I offer herewith a plan for a thoroughly satisfactory shower bath, the cost of which is within the reach of every one. The only outlay of money would be for a galvanized bucket, with metal spigot inserted in its side, near the bottom. The cost of this should not be more than $1 or $1.25. Any plumber can make it.

This bucket is placed on a shelf on the kitchen wall, about 5 feet above the floor. Next take a wash pan (an old one will do) and drive a dozen or more small nail holes in its bottom, and tack it to bottom of shelf with about two-thirds of it extending beyond shelf. On the floor under pan, place a large wash tub. Put about two and a half gallons of water in bucket, and you are ready for the bath. Get in the tub, turn the spigot slightly, and as the water trickles down, use soap and bath rag. After you have fully lathered and rubbed, turn on more water, and you have as clean and delightful bath as money can buy.

There are many people in the country who at a very small expense could have water in their houses. On some farms there are flowing springs where a hydraulic ram and a few yards of piping would carry the water into the house. We are apt to envy our city sisters, when often what they pay yearly for these conveniences would put the same into our country homes. If you have not access to a spring, and think you cannot afford a windmill, you can by means of a force-pump, pump the water into a large vat or reservoir placed in the garret and thus supply the bathroom and kitchen. This reservoir may be filled every day, or it may be large enough to hold water to last a week. If a bath-tub is needed anywhere, it is on the farm.

There is nothing better than a refreshing bath, a clean waist, and a pretty neck-ribbon to put a woman in the proper spirit to meet her family at the tea-table.

About that Well-House You Ought to Have.

In the south end of my well house I have a bath house and a bath tub in it. In the hot summer evening you may hear the water splashing and the glad laugh of the children as they enjoy their cool bath. There are shelves fixed up in this house, and wife's fruit jars, seeds and many other things too numerous to mention are kept.

Now if any one should say that this well house costs too much or they haven't time to build it I will describe the first milk house I built many years ago. Set up four posts six inches square and six feet high. Set them three feet apart one way and six feet the other way. Now put in a floor about three feet from the ground and from this floor board up outside and seal up inside and pack the walls tight with saw dust, leaving about half the front side unsealed for the door. This door is hinged on at the bottom and opens from the top, apron like, as old men's pants used to let down from the top, apron pants. Now this little milk house, after the water trough is put in and some shelves fixed around, is very convenient. It should be near the well under a shelter so as to keep the hot sun off.

Any one can make this out of any old thing. I keep mine whitewashed and everything keeps so very nice. Just try one and be pleased.

How to Beautify and Renovate an Old Home.

Messrs. Editors: While our neighbor is building his new house, we are doomed to this house built perhaps a quarter of a century, or it may be a whole century ago. Are we to let this discourage us? Not a bit. We did not start out to be discouraged. Maybe we have not learned to keep this yet, and do we appreciate the historic interests here?

To embellish this old home we will concede that this good man has it in repair: that the locks and hinges are all oiled, and that the window panes are in, and that the floors are oiled, and wiped up with water, for without this attention the woodwork will dry rot. And I would suggest a coat of linseed oil for the back of washstands and bureaus, for they, too, will go the same way.

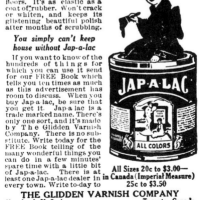

Begin on the Outside.

Reforms should usually begin in the lowest places: so we will take the back porch first. Everything not positively needed should be removed. And here we may begin with water, and work until every square inch is cleaned. Right here the farm boy will do some good work, on a warm rainy day when he cannot be out, and the experience will be a benefit to him. Give him clean towels, show your appreciation of his work, and he will begin to take pride, with the other keepers of the house. Tell him how Mr. Roosevelt had the White House washed outside the last time it was cleaned up.

But our work should not stop here, but rather go on to the guest chamber, which might be called the "index to the house," as well as an expression of the love of the family for their friends, and the stranger, that is sometimes within. So we will, like the woman of Shunam, prepare the prophet's chamber.

Of course it fared with the other rooms with the "spring cleaning;" now we have only to set it in order, and to make the job good. We should dust—in the drawers, under and above,—before we sweep, and again on completion. The colorings should be harmonious: where one color is selected it is carried out; but let me beg that the whole be soft and refreshing. My memory runs back thirty years, to a carpet that was woven in hard stripes, and it is not rested from it yet. So choose a carpet that will not detract from anything else. Green with red make good colors.

The bed should be of brass or natural wood, for beauty. Too much white looks blank. Brass curtain rods are, also, desirable.

And curtains made of bobonet which can be had ninety inches wide, are beautiful worked in some pretty pattern with thread, after the manner of the lace made twenty years ago.

Furnishing the Farm Home

The country home should convey a sense of breadth, stability, and kindliness, and even were they permissible elsewhere, such incumbrances as gilt chairs, onyx-topped, gilded tables and ornate lamps are out of keeping with the general atmosphere of a country home. In furnishing a home the interior painting and papering, the carpets and hangings are of more importance in obtaining a satisfactory result than the mere furniture.

. . . I do most emphatically wish to impress upon each of you who reads this article the real necessity of keeping for yourself and for the children to come after, any old family piece which may be in your possession . . . Do not let the agent sent out by some Northern or Western firm inveigle you into parting with any old piece of value. One or two pieces of old

AN INVITING CORNER FOR A SUMMER DAY.

Why should not more farm homes have liberal, well-shaded porches like this one? It is more beautiful and more comfortable than living shut up indoors. See what you can do about making such an addition to your house if you haven't one already.

furniture give an air to a room and breathe a sense of refinement and culture that many times the number of newly-bought, up-to-date articles of furniture fail to do.

Ornate furniture for any room in the house is undesirable; good woods and good designs are to be chosen before ornamentation every time. Most of the carving seen on furniture is machine carving glued on, not hand carving, as so many think . . . The plain, solid mission furniture is well suited to a country home. The solidity, the unpretentious shapes, the absence of glass all go to make up thoroughly desirable specimens adapted especially for hall, library and dining room. "A set of furniture," as we remember it only a few years ago, is now replaced by single pieces which harmonize, but are not of identical shape or upholstery. The purchasing of good furniture for a house or room thus becomes much easier by this good sense in fashion; a slim purse is not called upon to buy several pieces of furniture at one time, but one may gradually accumulate as desire prompts or necessity demands.

Let your living room be a living room, not a collection of stiff, uncomfortable furniture, worse than useless draperies and ornaments, that are neither a pleasure to the eye or a joy to the care-taker. . . . Ask yourself, when doing your planning, if the room is to be for your family or for your neighbors. Let comfort come first, and of course such beauty as that may include. Give the sunlight free entrance, not fearing the pattern on your dust-harboring carpets. Have no draperies which cannot be

The oil stove was a boon to farm wives. The old wood-burning range with its glowing firebox became a nightmare in summer heat. The only relief from it, before the oil stove, was to cook the breakfast the night before and keep it warm in the "fireless cooker," a large box or trunk packed with hay or newspaper. The caption for this 1925 ad for the Florence Oil Range read, "This flame heats the kettle, not the kitchen." Another relief provided by the oil stove was that chopping and carrying wood was no longer necessary.

washed and cherish fresh air as your dearest heritage . . . Avoid heavy upholstered furniture as hard to handle and collectors of dust and germs. Be as comfortable as you like with light cushions, which may be easily laundered, or often aired in the sunshine . . . A few words about sofa pillows: Do not buy the gaudy lithographed pillow tops, which have had such a vogue among the inartistic; neither make the pillow covers of velvet, satin or silk, unless the pillows are to be placed in a very handsome room . . . A delightful country woman of my acquaintance counts her sofa pillows by the score, and wherever a couch, a comfortable home-made couch, by the way,—may be placed, there you will find one banked with pillows, all for service. . .

The dining room should be made as attractive as possible. When the eye is pleased the digestion responds to the pleasure, and a successful meal is the natural consequence. All of us recognize this in the preparation and service of food, but all of us do not think of it as applied to the room in which the food is served. Beauty, as I have said before, does not of necessity lie in costliness, but it

In winter, the big, old, black wood-stove (which had to be regularly polished with stove-black) was a blessing—warming the whole kitchen and sometimes nearby rooms. "Brush the snow off, children," said this 1925 ad. "You can't hurt Mother's new Congoleum Rug."

does lie in harmonious suitability. And each of us can have a dining-room containing suitable furniture and furnishings and those in harmony.

Don't Have a Parlor.

But Lavish Your Joy Touches upon the Music Room, Living Room, Library, and Other Rooms.

A best room is necessary in every house, but the parlor is a room I do not care for at all; it is always inane, characterless, and absolutely unsuggestive of the inclinations or desires of the household. If you are fond of books, possess a few, and intend to increase the number, why not accumulate floor coverings, furniture and pictures suited to a library, and call it the library. If you are musical or have musically inclined sons or daughters, and possess a good piano, why not furnish the room accordingly and call it the music room? If of no particular inclination toward books or toward music, take some one color and furnish the room in harmony and call it the red-room, the blue-room, etc., as the case may be. This plan is much more attractive than mere parlor, a word suggestive of a heterogeneous gathering together of unrelated "dinky" sofas, frail chairs and bric-a-brac (mostly bric-a-brac), flimsy curtains, and much gilt.

Make "a Joy Forever" of the Living Room and Dining Room.

The Northern idea of a living room is excellent. I like the term

living room better than our equivalent sitting room; it is more comprehensive. Here comfort should reign supreme and no article of any great monetary value should be placed in this room.

Avoid Cheap Garishness in the Bedrooms.

In buying furniture for bedrooms here again we find the reign of "a set of furniture" is past. A metal bed with bureau and wash-stand of

oak, bird's-eye maple or mahogany is the preferred combination. The white enameled bed of simple design is the prettiest, the colored enameled bed is not in good taste, and particularly bad when combined with brass. The beds with brass knobs and railings have had their day, though an all-brass bed of simple design is beautiful but expensive.

WONDERFUL FURNITURE OFFER!

We offer 100 sets of beautiful White Maple Bed-room Furniture, consisting of one Dresser, one Washstand, one Table, one Rocker, one Straight Back Chair, one Double Iron Bed, one Double Wire Mattress, one Five-piece Toilet Set of White China, one Double Combination Felt and Excelsior Mattress, two Feather Pillows and two Bed-room Rugs for **$23.00** per set complete. All the articles are exactly as illustrated in this advertisement, and the furniture is constructed of beautifully finished and highly polished white maple, making it many times more attractive than oak and the daintiest bed-room suite imaginable. The regular dealer's price on this combination would be not less than $40.00.

We will sell any piece separately at the following prices: Rockers, $1.00; Straight Back Chairs, 75c.; Tables, $1.50; Washstands, $1.75; Dressers, $7.50; Bed Springs, $1.30; Double Iron Beds, $1.75; Five-piece Toilet Set, $2.25; Mattresses, $3.00; Pillows, each, 75c.; Rugs, each, 50c.

These Chairs 75 Cents Each. (Not Sold in Less Than Half Dozen Lots.)

These Rockers, $1.00 Each.

These Beautiful French White Maple Dressers, only $7.50 Each.

Double Iron Bed, $1.75. Double Wire Mattress, $1.30.

This Maple Washstand, $1.75 Each. The Five-piece White China Toilet Set, $2.25.

This Dainty Maple Table, $1.50.

This furniture is not listed in our general catalogue, as we have just purchased it, so order direct from this advertisement. Any or all articles may be returned, if not satisfactory or damaged, and your money at once refunded. We will ship the complete set on deposit of $5.00, you to have the right to examine same before paying balance, and we agree to refund your deposit and pay freight both ways, if the furniture is not entirely satisfactory to you when it arrives. As stated above, we will sell any piece separately, but strongly advise you to buy the complete set, as each piece is made to match each other piece and the effect of the whole set is wonderfully attractive. This furniture is on exhibition at our salesrooms, Shockoe Square, Richmond, Virginia, and all shipments will be made from there. We refer you to the Bank of Richmond, Richmond, Virginia, if you wish a reference regarding us. This is the most wonderful furniture offer we have ever made, and we heartily recommend our customers to avail themselves of it.

SPOTLESS COMPANY, Inc.,

103 SHOCKOE SQUARE, :: :: :: :: RICHMOND, VIRGINIA.

Let me advise against imitation woods. It is far more tasteful and refined to have oak, quartered oak preferably, than to have the so-called mahogany which is not mahogany at all, but some cheap wood painted, stained and grained in imitation. In purchasing mahogany furniture I have found that if a small part only of the article be

Improved Alliance SEWING MACHINE.

Delivered Freight Paid to any Railroad Station in North Carolina.
Warranted for 20 Years.

mahogany it is called a mahogany piece. This, of course, is deception. If you intend to purchase a mahogany piece have the dealer tell you what part is mahogany and what imitation. You'll be surprised at how little a part of what passes for a mahogany article is really mahogany. Solid mahogany is rarely seen nowadays; veneering is practically all one finds.

Books for the Farm Home Library.

Books, the delight of every balanced life! Oliver Wendell Holmes says that "above all things a child should tumble about in a library, for all men are afraid of books that have not handled them from infancy." You may have lacked these early advantages, but see to it that your children do not. What was an excuse for a paucity of books in years gone by is none whatsoever now, for many of the best works of the best writers, both of today and yesterday, may be purchased at very small cost . . .

A set of encyclopedias is greatly to be desired, especially for the library of a farmer, for a well-informed farmer is interested in divers matters. A set of standard encyclopedias will furnish information along any line which may become of interest to you or your growing children.

Great Books at Little Prices.

I append a list of desirable books which may be purchased for the small sum of twelve cents each; a better edition in every way may be purchased for nineteen cents: Aesop's Fables, Alice in Wonderland (Carroll), The Bondsman (Hall Caine), Children of the Abbey, Carnford (Mrs. Gaskell),

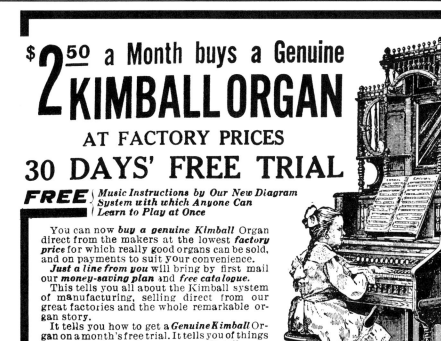
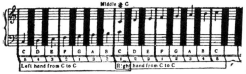

Fifteen Decisive Battles (Edward Creasy), First Violin (Fothergill), Gulliver's Travels (Swift), Fairy Tales (Grimm), House of the Seven Gables (Hawthorne), Idle Thoughts of an Idle Fellow (Jerome), Jane Eyre (Bronte), John Halifax, Gentleman (D. C. Murdock), Kidnapped (Stevenson), Last Days of Pompeii (Bulwer), The Light That Failed (Kipling), Little Minister (Barrie), Mosses from an Old Manse (Hawthorne), Robinson Crusoe (DeFoe), Scottish Chiefs (Porter), Swiss Family Robinson (Wyss), Tales from Shakespeare (Lamb), Tom Brown's School Days (Hughes), Tom Brown at Oxford (Hughes), Treasure Island (Stevenson), Vicar of Wakefield (Goldsmith), and a few of the works of George Eliot, Ruskin, Cooper, Hugo, Dumas, Henty, Holmes, Irving, Kipling, Longfellow, Robert Browning, Bryant, Dickens, Lyall, Conan Doyle, Scott, Carlyle, and Thackery.

Great Paintings You Should Know.

BABY STUART, BY VAN DYCK.

"Baby Stuart" without doubt is Van Dyck's most popular picture if not most representative of his style. Van Dyck was one of the world's great portrait painters. He not only painted a portrait but by adding to it brilliant decorative colors he made of it a picture as well. He was particularly happy, graceful and captivating in the poses of children as the illustration we have before us indicates. The artist was born at Antwerp in 1599. When but ten years old he showed remarkable ability and at nineteen he was installed in the studio of Rubens, one of the great painters of the day.

Pictures for the Different Rooms.

To Each Room of the Home Assign the Scenes and Subjects Most Appropriate to It

The charm of library, music-room or drawing-room is always enhanced by portraits in oil. The Coliseum, the Parthenon, the Campani, etc., cathedrals, and ruins, are all suitable subjects for hall pictures.

For the music-room choose likenesses of famous composers, singers, artists in any line, scenes from famous operas, particularly from those you have been fortunate enough to have heard, or from those of whose romances you are particularly fond; allegorical pictures bearing upon the subject of music; different conceptions of the patron saint of music, St. Cecilia, or any good picture having the slightest musical note. There, too, is the place for the dainty watercolor, a bit of scenery, of the whispering pine, of the sounding sea. In the living room, where books are in evidence at all times, especially where there is no library, hang family photographs, likenesses of one's favorite authors and heroes, views of places one has visited and especially admired, and if one be interested in anything particular, let the walls of this room tell of that attraction, be it horses, dogs, wild animals, the sea, ships, the woods, out of door life in any form, hunting, fishing, skating, coasting, for in the choice of pictures you stamp your rooms with individuality.

Pictures of cows standing in shaded waters, of sheep in some restful pasture, of birds, of poultry, a sketch of cornfield, such studies as "The Gleaner," "The Reaper," are all suited to the spirit of the dining-room. Do not have reproductions of dead game or of fish for dining-room pictures. Death in any form is gruesome: why unnecessarily place it before your eyes and particularly in the room where you take that which is primarily to continue the life that is within you?

Making One's Own Curtains.

Do not purchase a Nottingham lace curtain. Let me impress this upon you. There was a time when a lace curtain of this make was considered quite the proper thing, but now the edict of good taste forbids the harboring of a Nottingham lace curtain in any room in the house. There is such an element of imitation and pretense in these curtains, even the prettiest looking, that we of the twentieth century should pass them by with no sigh of regret.

Do not loop back your curtains. Some prefer the straight line from pole to pole with curtains just escaping the floor; however, from pole to window sill is the most approved arrangement. The curtain should never trail on the floor; if so arranged it serves only one purpose—that of dust—a poor purpose for a dainty curtain.

The Shade is for Service
Rather Than Ornament.

If possible, have every shade, every window of the house the same color. A very light tan, almost cream, is a good color to use.

White shades are preferred by most, but they become soiled more easily and the white light which they bring into the room is not so attractive as the mellow light the tan shade brings. If you have shades of different colors at your windows, take one color as basis and let all future purchases of shades be as near that color as you can get. Beware of a shade with fringe, for a shade is not ornament, but for service, therefore the less noticeable the better, and by all means taboo the red shade. If one cannot purchase both curtain

and shade, purchase the shade; curtain will be sure to follow.

Do not have fringe on your portieres; it cheapens the appearance of them. The bead portiere and the rope portiere are to be avoided. The rope portiere has no reason to be, a sillier catchpenny for the homemaker could not have been devised. If one were furnishing a house for summer use exclusively a bead portiere or two might not come in amiss, but in

the everyday life of the everyday family the bead portiere is practically useless.

The ubiquitous lambrequin was a fad of only a few years ago, but now it is seen less and less on mantel, chair, table, piano or picture, but if one be particularly partial to these smaller hangings the bedroom or living room may be decorated with simple bits of them on mantel, table or piano, but not on picture or chair. The prettiest mantel lambrequins are lengths of linen daintily embroidered; these are kept exquisitely neat by frequent changing. A simple strip of hemstitched linen is just as dainty though not so handsome. These lambrequins should hang only a few inches below the mantel shelf. I do not advise mantel lambrequins though, of any kind, for our Southern homes with their open fireplaces. The danger of fire from them is too great; a facetious gentleman of my acquaintance calls them home-burners.

Sofa Pillows, Etc.

In reference to sofa pillows, cotton, excelsior, small bits of cloth, all make fillings within the easy reach of the farmer's wife. I was once told by the extremely ingenius wife of a farmer that she gathered cat-tails, pulled them apart and sunned them till dry, and found them the best substitute for feathers in sofa pillows. Has anyone present tried the hanging gray moss of our eastern counties as a filler? I should think that would be capital.

But the first thing demanded by a sofa or couch pillow is the couch. These also can be manufactured at home. Those made to open with space to contain wearing apparel are, of course, more difficult to make and more expensive. I made one which did not open and found it very useful and attractive.

I am not an adept with a saw, but I can hammer all right, so I got a carpenter to make me a wide bench of two pieces of plank (one friend I knew made hers of a goods box). This I piled high with excelsior, tacked a piece of unbleached muslin across it, drawing the muslin just as tight as I could, then over that tacked blue denim, drawing the denim equally as tight. A pleated ruffle of denim reaching to

Making the Home Grounds Beautiful

Beautifying the home grounds!— What a beautiful subject.

First of all, have a good fence to keep out intruders. Then, if I had no trees, my first move would be to plant a few fine young white oaks and water oaks, and some of the choicest of flowering shrubbery, such as springa, snow-ball, artificials, white and pink, and lilac (oh, how I love lilacs!)

Next, vines—I would have an abundance of English ivy, and one honey-suckle bower—at the farthest corner of the ground, because

But most of all, roses, for the rose is the queen of the garden. I want roses all the year round— every color, and thousands of them—to give to the living and to lay on the dead.

I have a fine oleander a year old now. The cape jessamine also is easily grown, and the beautiful white flowers are worth very much to me, as they were my mother's favorite flower, and the same one that she loved and tended in life now flourishes on her grave.

Many of the annuals may be grown from seed, being hardy, and children enjoy their gay colors and sweet perfume, as much as that of the more expensive flowers.

the floor, tacked on with big-headed tacks, completed the settee and on it I placed pillows of dark blue denim worked in heavy white floss. This idea carried out in red denim for a red room or green denim for a green room would be very good. The plain couch covering is more desirable than the figured, as it gives a better background for the figured or embroidered pillows.

it spreads so badly it should never be planted where you wish anything else to grow.

I would have an arbor of victoria, and clematis on the porches. I would have a bed of pansies and one of hyacinths, a wilderness of violets and verbenas, and pink sweetwilliams and carnations.

Beauty and Convenience at Little Cost.

This bewitching little cottage cost very little—many of our humblest and ugliest farm homes cost more money—and yet by a little care and attention it has been made a veritable thing of beauty. Observe too, especially, the cheap but satisfactory wash-stand and bath-room—a thing every farm-house ought to have. Resolve now to have one this year, and couple this resolution with the more comprehensive one "More beauty for every farm home in 1908."

In laying out the lawn study broad effects. If the lawn is small, do not cut it up into flower beds and walks, for it will look yet smaller; and if it be large, many flower beds make it appear trivial when it should appear stately. Always take in consideration the lay of the land and cut the walks accordingly. In laying out your walks never sacrifice a tree; have the walk curve around it. . . . One never realizes the value of a tree until waiting year after year for one that has been planted to furnish just a tiny bit of shade.

In a growing family, a clever idea is to plant a tree upon the birth of each child, and when he becomes old enough to care of it, to give it into his keeping.

The trees in the old home yard have a powerful influence upon all who come in association with them. The boys and girls raised up under these shade trees will never forget them. They may forget many of their neighbors and associates, and many of their dear boyhood friends, but can never forget the beautiful yard trees under which they were reared. I have thought that boys and girls who were reared in a home surrounded by a beautiful grove were better and more refined and had higher ideals than those who were reared in homes which had no shade trees about them.

We have breakfast and supper out on a vine-covered porch and we eat strawberries and cream, and

Now, all these are for the sister who has time to cultivate and who has money to spend on her garden, but the rose is for all. Because the rich sister will give to the less fortunate cuttings and with a little labor she is abundantly rewarded with choicest flowers. I think I should like a bed of the old-fashioned hollyhocks—double ones of all colors. Also some ribbon and ornamental grasses. Let me say also a few evergreens, spruce pine, arbor, vitae, and weeping cedar.

If I could have just one of each choice plant, and all the roses I wanted, I would have a beautiful garden. Some prefer four-o'clocks, batchelor buttons, sunflowers, princess feather and gaudy zinnia, marigold and such, but I almost had rather have no flowers at all.

They are really but little better than weeds; and rather than plant these I will get golden-rod, purple aster, white ash and dog-tooth violets, for my flower garden.

When you come to think of it, a man is the only animal that calls attention to his dwelling place. Every bird, every beast, seeks to have his nest or den appear a part of the surrounding landscape. While fear is largely responsible for this, it is not wholly so, and we transgress the laws of our great teacher, nature, when we call attention with too loud a blast to our dwelling place. Simplicity and modesty, modesty and simplicity cannot be urged too strongly.

the mocking birds perch on the topmost branches of the nearest trees and, like "little Tommy Tucker," sing for their supper in the most entrancing way.

What does any human being want to exist in town for, when he can live, really live, in the country? The red raspberries are beginning to ripen, too—not enough to share with the family, but just enough to make it interesting to include the raspberry rows in my morning rambles. Then before they are gone the Lucretia dewberries will be so good that I shall just live to eat, and then there will be Japanese plums and figs and melons. I'm so thankful I'm living I don't know what to do. I don't mention cherries because that's a sore subject. I set out two cherry trees for myself and a service tree for the birds and the greedy things ate the cherries themselves and left the service berries for me, and small thanks to them for their gift.

We shan't have any Irish potatoes this year because they were planted the wrong time of the moon. Now I know that the scientific gentlemen who run this paper don't believe in the moon, but I do, and they are wrong and I am right. So please understand when I speak of successful farming, it is successful because it is strictly according to the moon. I've always agreed with the Irishman who said he loved the moon better than he did the sun, for the moon shone at night when you needed it, while the sun never did shine except in day time when you could get along very well without it.

DAFFODILS.

I WANDER'D LONELY as a cloud
    That floats on high o'er vales and hills,
    When all at once I saw a crowd,
A host, of golden daffodils;
Beside the lake, beneath the trees,
Fluttering and dancing in the breeze.

Continuous as the stars that shine
    And twinkle on the Milky Way,
They stretch'd in never-ending line
    Along the margin of a bay;
Ten thousand saw I at a glance,
Tossing their heads in sprightly dance.

The waves beside them danced; but they
    Outdid the sparkling waves in glee:
A poet could not but be gay,
    In such a jocund company:
I gazed—and gazed—but little thought
What wealth the show to me had brought:

For oft, when on my couch I lie
    In vacant or in pensive mood,
They flash upon that inward eye
    Which is the bliss of solitude;
And then my heart with pleasure fills,
And dances with the daffodils.
        —William Wordsworth.

The reason I made such a fatal mistake about the Irish potatoes was that some one told me the best time to plant for extra early potatoes, was in December. I'm always experimenting, and so I planted potatoes and tied up Christmas presents in tissue paper and red ribbon simultaneously, and my intellect reeled under the combination. I forgot all about the moon, with the results already noted. So I am still in the dark as to whether December is a good time to plant early potatoes or not. I don't much think it is, for we planted peas, too, and never laid eyes on them again.

Of course, beans are planted on Good Friday whether or no, but that's only the exception that proves the rule.

The True Home

Some women cling to their own homes like the honeysuckle over the door; yet like it, fill all the region about with the subtle fragrance of their goodness.

Maxims for the Married.

1. Since you are married you may as well make the best of it.

2. So make some maxims and try to live up to them.

3. And don't be discouraged if you fail. You will fail, but perhaps you won't always fail.

4. Never both be cross at the same time. Wait your turn.

5. Never cease to be lovers. If you cease, some one else may begin.

6. You were gentleman and lady before you were husband and wife. Don't forget it.

7. Keep yourself at your best. It is a compliment to your partner.

8. Keep your ideals high. You may miss it, but it is better to miss a high one than to hit a low one.

9. A blind love is a foolish one. Encourage the best.

10. Permanent mutual respect is necessary for a permanent mutual love.

11. The tight cord is the easiest to snap.

12. If you take liberties be prepared to give them.

13. There is only one thing worse than quarrels in public; that is caresses.

14. Money is not essential to happiness, but happy people usually have enough.

15. To save some.

16. The easiest way of saving is to do without things.

17. If you can't, then you had better do without a wife.

18. The man who respects his wife does not turn her into a mendicant. Give her a purse of her own.

19. If you save, save at your own expense.

20. In all matters of money prepare always for the worst and hope for the best.
A. Conan Doyle

A Man's Best Gift to His Family.

The country is full of men who are overworking, not because they care for money, but because they want to command the most comfortable conditions for their families; who, if they were told that they were shortening their lives ten years, would not hesitate to go on, accepting the sacrifice as part of their duty, and an opportunity to be welcomed rather than avoided. Those who know American men well know that there is a deep vein of idealism in the great majority of them in their attitude towards their families. It is here that they spend themselves lavishly; it is here that many give their lives without hesitation.

But the American father and husband does not always give wisely. In giving his means a man often gives himself, because he spends himself in order to acquire the means; but he ought to give himself in a higher way. It would be far better for many families if their conditions were not so easy and their family life richer; if the toiling man took more time to express his affection, to contribute his strength, to share his intellectual life, to enrich the breakfast and the dinner table and the evening with his large observation of life and knowledge of men, the varied experience which most men of affairs possess. If family life is to be put on the highest possible basis, there must be the giving of self. The lover who lavishes on the woman he loves presents of great material value degrades her if he does not share with her also the highest and best of his own life. And no matter what he gives her, if he withholds this, he leaves her unsatisfied. If she is in any sense worthy, and were compelled to choose, she would take the richer life and the poorer conditions rather than the richer conditions and poorer life.

After the quiet evening meal, my husband and I (for we live alone) sit together around a glowing fire. I have my music, both vocal and instrumental, and he keeps to the *Progressive Farmer,* *Southern Planter,* and lots and lots of Government bulletins; he gets a monthly report and keeps a stock of them on hand. And if I should tire of the piano, I get down one of Dickens and begin to enjoy Mr. Pickwick. Just as I am beginning to get well into the story, I must needs stop to listen to Mr. T., as he reads aloud something from the pens of either Professor Massey, Doctor Kilgore, or perhaps 'tis a fine cow that Professor Burkett has written about that in her record is ahead of even our own "Queen Victoria." Well, we will have to get Professor Burkett to tell us more about this fine cow. He reads

THE TRUE HOME.

THIS is the true nature of home—it is the place of Peace; the shelter, not only from all injury, but from all terror, doubt, and division. In so far as it is not this, it is not home; so far as the anxieties of the outer life penetrate into it, and the inconsistently minded, unknown, unloved, or hostile society of the outer world is allowed by either husband or wife to cross the threshold, it ceases to be home; it is then only a part of that outer world which you have roofed over, and lighted fire in. But so far as it is a sacred place, a vestal temple, a temple of the hearth watched over by household gods, before whose face none may come, but those whom they can receive with love—so far as it is this, and roof and fire are types only of a nobler shade and light,— shade as of the rock in a weary land, and light as of the Pharos in the stormy sea;—so far it vindicates the name, and fulfills the praise, of home.

And wherever a true wife comes, this home is always round her. The stars only may be over her head; the glow-worm in the night-cold grass may be the only fire at her feet: but home is yet wherever she is; and for a noble woman it stretches far round her, better than ceiled with cedar, or painted with vermilion, shedding its quiet light far, for those who else were homeless.—John Ruskin.

Woman's Work

The great and crying need of humanity today is for the broad, intellectual and progressive woman as a home-maker. And in no other place in the wide world is the influence of such a woman so potent for good as in her own home and in her position as wife and mother and home-maker.

Then who shall say that intellectual ability or refined and cultured womanhood is either restricted or degraded by the duties of housekeeping and home-making?

There must be some taint of inherent vulgarity about the person who considers household labor a drudgery. The cooking and dishwashing, the sweeping and dusting, the making and mending are all but the means to the end of maintaining a comfortable home and home life, and home is the haven to which all humanity turns for peace and joy and comfort and happiness.

aloud, and we comment together, and the evening with us is almost over.

For we must be up early, and out for a walk in the early dawning to enjoy the exquisite pleasures of nature and drink in the invigorating and refreshing breezes (nature's best tonic) and enjoy the soft, mellow light of the early morning and the beautiful panorama of nature's best theatrical performance. As we walk, we stop to observe, and now the dark blue curtains of heaven's vault are folding back and we observe the glorious orb and admire God's beautiful sun, as he emerges from the gilded gates of the east and comes slowly and deliberately, but never failingly, on the stage of action.

. . . Let me tell you men a secret: if you want your wife to wish herself home again, unfettered by matrimonial claims, you just stay in bed and let her get up in a cold room, go through several cold rooms to a cold kitchen: find no wood or kindling, and have to go to the back yard and bring it in all soaking wet, and try to cook . . .

Stay, stay at home, my heart, and rest,
Home-keeping hearts are happiest;
For they that wander, they know not where,
Are full of sorrow and full of care;
To stay at home is best.

The Way to Ennoble Housekeeping

To give all housekeepers a scientific training will give the work a much higher social standing. Giving those who engage in any calling a special education raises that calling to a higher rank—sometimes makes a profession of it . . . Giving nurses a special training has given them a new and an exalted position. So it will be with housekeepers. To the ignorant, untrained person all his work is drudgery, but give him a special education for his work and it becomes a joy and a pleasure. That is the difference between a rock breaker and a geologist; between the clod-hopper and the scientific farmer; between the scullion and the educated cook. The former goes through life like a tramp shut in a box car, the latter like an intelligent tourist in the look-out of an observation car. The occupation of the former produces narrowness, disgust and despair; of the latter a wider view, and an ever broadening hopefulness.

There are so many, many studies, and delightful problems in the home, in every day work, that a woman who is fully alive to

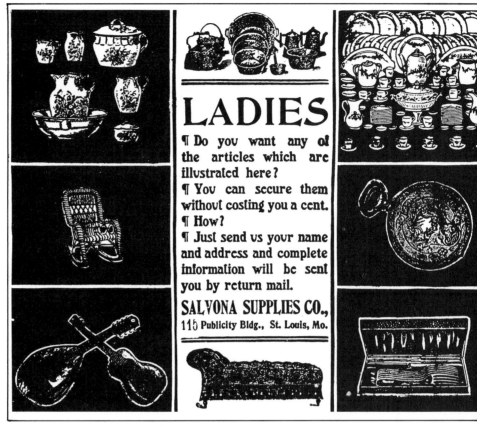

them need never lack for what is entertaining and valuable—valuable for her housekeeping, and valuable for her best and highest intellectual development.

Some of you might be interested in knowing of the new substitute for sweeping that is now being so much used in the large cities. It is a machine that sucks in, through a hose or pipe, all the dust and dirt on the surfaces over which the end of the tube is passed. It sweeps and dusts at the same time.

One of the most helpless human beings I ever saw was a bride who had never even made up a bed, and I witnessed her first effort. I was sorry for her, and at the same time felt a disgust unutterable. The idea of a seemingly sane human woman never having fixed the bed on which she slept when she had occupied space in the world for over twenty years made me ashamed of my sex. I was sorry for the young man, her husband, as he had a sensible mother and had evidently been captivated by a pretty face and superficial accomplishments. She declared to me that she had suffered from cramp in her arms caused by practicing on the piano several hours a day. Well, I wondered if she would have suffered in this way had she learned the calisthentics of the broom and thus strengthened her muscles. Wealth is all right provided it is coupled with good, common sense; but it is absurd to let a girl grow to womanhood and be of no more use in the world than a jelly fish.

One Woman's Experience with Poultry.

Dear Aunt Jennie: I am an Alamance farmer's wife and do a small poultry business. I do not raise poultry for the fancy of it, but I have some nice white W. D. Barred Plymouth Rock and Leghorns. I do not keep them in separate pens, but let them all run together, as the Plymouth Rocks are too large and the Leghorns too small, so I cross them and have what I think a better chicken than either of the pure stock. The Leghorn is a poor setter, but the Rocks enjoy sitting, but sometimes make poor hatchers, as they are too heavy and break their eggs.

The cross lays well, sets well, and make good mothers and are a nice size.

I commence setting my hens as soon as they want to sit in the spring on about 15 to 17 eggs. I like to have several to hatch about the same time so I can give each hen about 20 biddies and have some that I turn loose to go to laying again. I have a yard wired in and put them in coops for a few days, then turn them out in the lot. I feed the little chicks for several days on old bread moistened

  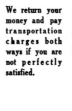

with water, then on wheat and cracked corn. When they are old enough I give them whole corn once a day. As soon as the young chicks can get along without the mother, I throw the old hen out of the lot and she soon forgets the biddies and goes to singing again and is soon laying. When my chickens are large enough to go about by themselves, I turn them out and let them go where they please.

I have no remedy when they begin to die. I would like to hear from someone else as how to manage, for I have not very much experience in the business.

How a Busy Woman Finds Leisure.

Dear Aunt Mary: I am taking my vacation now in a rather peculiar manner—that is, I am at home, and do all the house work, the cooking and washing for four, but I have eliminated everything but the essentials, and I do these in the easiest way.

I gather up the clothes and have them in the tubs the night before washing day and while I cook breakfast my husband pumps the water. After breakfast he sets the boiler on for me, and puts in the soap and as much paraffine shavings as soap. I then wring out the clothes and put them into the boiling water and boil the dirt out. I let them boil till I get the churning done and the dishes washed. Then I take them up and rinse them.

I wash in rain water whenever I can, for my clothes are then much

nicer and whiter. I do not do much ironing, in fact I never iron anything except the "Sunday clothes." I put melted parraffine in the hot starch and the clothes iron so nicely. I rarely make a fire in my wood stove except on wash days, but cook on an oil stove. It is such a saving of time and energy, and there is no heat, ashes or soot, and, most important, no going every few minutes to put in wood or to see about things. I use asbestos mats and it's a hard matter to scorch anything over one. I have double sauce pans and can cook two dishes over one burner.

I get all my work done in the forenoon and spend three or four hours of the afternoon in reading.

Since the last of June I have read "Scott's Poems," "Ivanhoe," "Guy Mannering," "Rob Roy," "Count Robert of Paris," "When Knighthood was in Flower," "The House of a Thousand Candles," "In Double Harness," "The Mystery," "Tom Sawyer, Detective," "The House Boat on the Styx," "The Pursuit of the House Boat," "Mrs. Raffles," "R. Homes & Co.," and "The Inventions of the Idiot."

When I have read all of Scott's works with a few others sandwiched in, I shall read Dickens again.

I surely am enjoying my vacation and if nothing happens to prevent, shall extend it through September.

Shall We Wash on Monday.

If Sunday is the best day of the week, is it not a pity that the day after should be called "Blue Monday?" Monday has never seemed to me the best wash day if only for the reason that very often the children could get another day's wear out of the apron or dress worn to church, if it did not have to be put in the tub that particular day. Some people prefer Saturday and some Thursday, but I like Tuesday best.

A Gasoline Flat Iron.

Dear Aunt Mary: I want to tell the ladies about my gasoline iron. It cost only $3.50 and gives the best of satisfaction. I get everything ready before I light it; and the ironing that took me a half a day by the old method, I can now

do in less than two hours. You get no time to rest while your irons are heating; never have to stop a moment to fix fires or clean irons. It is always clean and it takes so little time to start it. But you must always strain the gasoline or it will not burn well. It is the most economical way of ironing. Down here we have to do all our own work and are glad to find the easy ways.

Wash-Day Suggestions

Dear Aunt Mary: Machines are all nonsense. Let Tuesday, dear sisters, be your wash day. Monday afternoon gather up all your soiled clothes and assort them into three piles: The very soiled white ones and the not so very soiled ones and the colored clothes. Have the little boys to pump to two tubs of water for the white clothes, put in and soak well. Treat the colored ones the same way. Next morning have "John" to put a fire under your pot the next thing after the fire is put into the stove. Just as soon as you have finished eating your breakfast go wring out the least oiled ones, soap well and put in to the pot and mend up your fire. Now go to your dishes. By the time you are through with them your pot of clothes will be ready to rinse out and for the line. They will need no rubbing, if kept boiling briskly while in the pot. As soon as you lift out the first pot full have the other white ones ready to drop right in and treat the same way. If very soiled, add a tablespoonful of kerosene oil. They should be ready by the time you have the first ones on the line. As for the colored clothes, I never have very many of them, because it takes "elbow grease and back-aches" to clean them, for of course they can't be boiled clean. Sisters, use unbleached homespun for cook aprons, baby's every-day dresses and your own every-day dressing sacques. You might trim the little dresses and your waists with some fast colored finishing braid. You will have a few more pieces on wash-day, but will not even think of the number of them. And for the ironing: did you know little girls and often little boys, too, take great pride in ironing—"especially baby's starched clothes and something for mamma?" Always let the men folks do the drawing of your water—their backs are far stronger than ours.

Hoping that should this find its way to press some tired sister will try it and report. "Virginia."

When your iron gets rough and sticky rub it on a twig of cedar, and see how nicely it polishes.

The Help of the Washing Machine and the Ironing Board

You all know what I think of the farmer who does not buy his wife a good washing machine if he can afford it, so I shall not talk of that. A good ironing board is necessary to well-ironed clothes. A sleeve board is good for sleeves, gathers and small dresses or embroidered pieces. The best wringer is the cheapest, if the rollers are carefully wiped and loosened each time.

Economical House-Keeping Notes.

If you want to save numerous steps to the meat house, have a box with hinged cover in the kitchen with a week's supply of the different kinds of meat you use. Place several folds of old newspapers in the bottom to absorb the drippings, and in this box you can save every skin and scrap. The very fat pieces, which at times are not used, soak with the skins in a few changes of water, and fry out inside the stove. Nice enough for any use.

Make you a wash apron of an old gossamer skirt or piece of oilcloth. Have cook aprons with quilted lifters, for handling hot pans. Sew or pin the lifters on a band to attach to waistband of apron.

In this day when woolen blankets and light counter-panes may be had so cheaply, I think it is equally foolish to waste time piecing quilts and to waste strength in washing them. I like a good all-cotton or felt mattress and spiral wire mattress, with lots of blankets and feather pillows. I don't like quilts and feather beds. I guess they belong to the days when cooking was done on a pot-rack and in an oven and skillet.

When the nice muslin underwear gets stained or begins to show wear, I throw it into a good dark dye, and then use it for common wear. It lasts much longer, as it is not necessary to wash it, and then when utterly worn out is already colored for the rag carpet.

I do not wonder that so many women count among their hardships that of milking, when they must oftentimes wade through mud and slush half-shoe deep to get to the lot, and when they get there, have to stand in it, get the feet wet, milk in the open lot, no shelter, no umbrella, no help at all. Do you know that I think it presumptuous to expect a cow to give much milk if she is treated so indifferently, and it is cruel to expect any woman to stay in such a desperately cold and uncomfortable place until she drains the last drop into the bucket. Arrange things so that the cow and her milker will both be comfortable.

Ways to Grow Comely

It is an interesting moment in a woman's life when she is suddenly aware of the fact that she might improve herself. The possibilities of beautifying are beyond reckoning. From one improvement one drifts to another, and inside of six months any woman with the right kind of courage inside her chest can presto-change herself into a creature of loveliness. For loveliness is of many kinds, and if one sort cannot be acquired, another kind can.

How to be Beautiful.

If your mirror tells you that you are not beautiful, do not allow that to depress you. In our liberal interpretation of the meaning of the word "beauty," there are many degrees; and hopelessly homely, indeed, must be the woman who cannot be included within some one of them.

A pair of bright, speaking eyes, a sweet, lovable mouth—no matter whether it be large or small,—fine hair, a good complexion, or a graceful figure,—the possession of any one of these constitutes a claim to a certain amount of comeliness, the amount being altogether dependent on the determination of the possessor to make most of what has been given her.

How Not to Spoil the Hair.

Don't use a comb to spread the pompadour by pulling the hair forward over the forehead.

Don't comb the hair from the forehead over backward when ar-

SEWING MACHINE the CAUSE!

BEWARE OF SIDE NEEDLE SPINE

Physicians today recognize the sewing machine as being the basic cause of more nervous disorders, peculiar to women, than any other modern convenience.

Of all human inventions, the ordinary sewing machine does more to wreck a woman's health, by producing spinal weakness, causing nervous troubles, and lingering torturing internal displacements than any other cause.

The reason is plain—look at the construction of your sewing machine, on account of the needle being 4½ inches away from the centre, where it should be, you have to sit in a position with your body twisted out of plumb to operate it.

Think what this twisting of your spine and other delicate internal organs means, and you can't operate your machine with your feet on the treadle without this twist in your body.

Now compare this with a STANDARD CENTRAL NEEDLE MACHINE built to operate with the needle central, right in front of you and directly over the treadle

This construction enables you to sit straight and do your sewing without the least strain on your spine or any part of your internal anatomy. You can sew on this STANDARD CENTRAL NEEDLE MACHINE all day, without feeling tired or getting a pain in your back. You can sit in a natural position without undue strain on your stomach and nerves.

This new type of machine means freedom from suffering and ushers in a tremendous advance for health and happiness and freedom from disease. And this machine is easily within your reach—easy to buy and easy to operate, will save its cost in doctor's bills to say nothing of health.

If you value your health and the health of your growing daughters, write us today. We will send you by return FREE a book "A STITCH IN THE SIDE," which tells you the plain truth you and every other woman should know. This book is FREE. Yours for the asking. A postal brings it to you.

THE

STANDARD SEWING MACHING CO.

6449 Cedar Ave., Cleveland, O.

---

ranging to brush it. If the hair be long and heavy the strain comes on the front hairs at each stroke of the brush. If they do not fracture and fall out at once, they become loosened in the follicle, kink up, and fall out later.

Avoid vigorous brushing; bear in mind that one hair on the head is worth two in the brush.

Don't grasp the front hair by the points or ends and comb upward from points to roots, "roughing it" in order to make a full, round pompadour. This needless abuse destroys life and lustre, fractures the hair shaft, renders it knotty, and produces a frumpy, aged appearance.

Don't take everybody's advice and do all sorts of things to your hair and scalp.

Cleaning the Scalp.

For a number of years I was troubled with a fine white dandruff which formed on the scalp and would show all through my hair. I tried many remedies without success, such as cleaning with egg, washing with soaps that were recommended, and combing with a fine comb, but the more I combed the worse it got, and the washing only did good for a few days. A friend advised me to try using kerosene oil. I first gave my head a good washing, and then poured out a little oil in a dish handy to insert the ends of my fingers. The ends of the fingers were dipped into the oil and the scalp thoroughly rubbed with it. This burned and smarted for some time but it was just what was needed to get up a good circulation in the scalp.

After three or four applications, some time apart, the dandruff entirely disappeared, and never gives me any more trouble. The smell of the kerosene will disappear in a day or two.

(Ed. Note: We do not recommend that you try this. The possible hazards to health are obvious.)

How to Have a Fine Complexion.

"My dear, don't you know that the foundation-stone of beauty is laid in the stomach? It is. And hot water, either plain or with lemon or with salt, is the chief preservation of a healthy digestion."

"Take it—a pint of it—an hour before breakfast every day in the year, and the chances are that you'll need no other medicine."

The Art of Chewing.

Mr. Horace Fletcher has lived for five years on one-third the quantity of food eaten by a healthy working man. At the age of fifty-four and after this economic diet he can ride one hundred miles a day on his bicycle without fatigue. He began his experiments with food five years ago when he was refused life insurance on account of stomach trouble. He eats only what his appetite craves and he chews his food thoroughly. He averages thereby thirty-two chews to every mouthful of food. He frequently eats candy as a substitute for breakfast. A sample meal consists of baked brown potatoes and coffee which was four-fifths milk without trimming.

The Right Way to Sleep in Winter.

For the preservation of health, the cure of consumption and colds, it is not necessary to migrate to warmer climates, says a medical writer. Our crisp winter air is invigorating and as healing and truly balmy as the air on any sea-coast. Try it according to the following directions:
I. First, and very important, keep your bed and bed-room warm and dry during the day. An open window and a cold room will make the bed damp and cold, and will give its unfortunate occupant a severe cold at least, if not worse. A damp bed is a veritable brooding place of bacteria.

II. Secondly, all your clothing worn in the day-time, foot-wear included, open out and hang over chairs or on hooks near the stove or register to dry and air during the night. If you neglect this simple sanitary measure, your clothing

will feel damp and cold in the morning, because it still contains the evaporations from your body during the previous day, and after a while your clothing will have an unpleasant odor from these evaporations.

III. Thirdly, your bed and room warm and dry, have plenty of lightweight bedding. Then, just before retiring close the door and open a window from the bottom. Where more than one person sleeps in a room, the window must be raised higher. This will give an abundance of fresh air while you sleep. Place the bed so that the fresh air current will not strike you directly. Protected in your dry, warm bed—as cozy as a bug in a rug—the air, pure air, fresh, freighted with oxygen, a very elixir of life, will quiet your nerves, will rest you, will soothe you, and give you healing and strength. When arising in the morning, close the window quickly and let heat come into the room. Then, dressed in your aired and dry day clothing, you will feel clean, fresh, and vigorous.

Table Manners.

The writer of this recently sat near a young man who was, like himself, eating his mid-day lunch at a "lunch counter" in a large city. One could not believe from his clothes or his general appearance that he was not a well raised young man, and yet his "table manners" could not be described as anything else than those of a barbarian or a half-starved hog. He crowded big chunks of bread, almost a whole slice at a time, large sections of meat, large gobs of potatoes, gulps of coffee or water, et ceteras of vegetables, into his mouth so fast that practically he couldn't chew them at all. He wabbled things around in his mouth with his tongue a time or two and then forced them down his throat, much as a young turkey does a large chunk of bread, by getting it started and then crawling up on it.

As the Twig is Bent . . .

The Duty of Parents

Duty to children is not summed up in feeding, clothing and sending to a better or worse—at present usually worse—school. The parent's duty begins long before. It is as necessary that we should live healthfully and happily before our children are born, as that we should clothe them afterward. Only by being in the best condition ourselves can we give the proper heritage to a child. To bring a being into the world and handicap him by your own follies and negligences is a poor trick; and yet it is just the trick that nine-tenths of the parents play on their off-spring. Treat your child at least as well as you would a fellow-man, and be thoughtful of his future. Then, having once given him the good heritage, see to it that his home life shall be such that his mental and moral nature may be

rightly developed. Sick or weakly children will in their turn produce weaklings; halting, cowardly natures will have children who are dwarfed in the same way; and instead of the race being helped by these, its general average will be lowered. Consider, then, your duty to your children through yourself. Live in youth and manhood the sanest, cheerfulest and fullest life, and make your home reflect these virtues.

Confessions of a Father.

It seems very wonderful. Last week there were, in our little flat, just the two of us—my wife and I. And all of a sudden there is but one of us—the Baby.

I am a father—actually a father. Of course, that is a condition that arrives to most men, and I have always considered that it was a matter of routine, merely; simply an incident of married life, just as paying rent or settling with the dressmaker. But, heavens! It is no incident; it is an event like, in importance, to being married. When it comes, you go around feeling every moment that something has happened to you.

When I saw the Baby, it—he, I mean—somehow did not appear precisely as I had anticipated that a Jones would. He reminded me of a nest of mice that I once had uncovered in the barn, back home. He was so pink and wrinkly and squealy. Maybe I seemed a little disappointed, for I had been counting on a different result, he being mine and hers. But in a second, and just for a second, too, the sly rogue squinted up at me—he did!—and, by Jove, he knew me!

THE CHILDREN'S HOUR.

BETWEEN the dark and the daylight,
  When the night is beginning to lower,
  Comes a pause in the day's occupations,
That is known as the Children's Hour.

I hear in the chamber above me
  The patter of little feet,
The sound of a door that is opened,
  And voices soft and sweet.

From my study I see in the lamplight,
  Descending the broad hall stair,
Grave Alice, and laughing Allegra,
  And Edith with golden hair.

A whisper, and then a silence;
  Yet I know by their merry eyes
They are plotting and planning together
  To take me by surprise.

A sudden rush from the stairway,
  A sudden raid from the hall;
By three doors left unguarded
  They enter my castle wall.

They climb up into my turret,
  O'er the arms and back of my chair;
If I try to escape they surround me;
  They seem to be everywhere.

They almost devour me with kisses,
  Their arms about me entwine,
Till I think of the Bishop of Bingen
  In his Mouse-Tower on the Rhine.

Do you think, O blue-eyed banditti,
  Because you have scaled the wall,
Such an old mustache as I am,
  Is not a match for you all.

I have you fast in my fortress,
  And will not let you depart,
But put you down into the dungeon
  In the round-tower of my heart.

And there will I keep you forever,
  Yes, forever and a day,
Till the walls shall crumble to ruin,
  And moulder in dust away!
          —Henry Wadsworth Longfellow.

And he wasn't more than twenty or thirty minutes old! How's that for a Baby?

After they had hustled me out (as if I were a dummy, or a sack of meal!) I could hear him crying for me, which struck me as not very good for him, and made me mad at the cruelty of it. Poor little fellow, who wanted his papa!

When I went back to the store (having been given to understand that I was not of any use to anybody in any way) it took me only two strides to cover the three blocks to the car line. In the car I tried to keep from grinning, but the whole car full of people were grinning, and to this day I wonder how they knew! The news got through the city mighty quick. I bought a noon extra, and looked to see what was said about it— him—us, that is; but we must have got crowded out for some advertisement, at the last moment. These papers are run, not for news, but for money, and I am going to quit taking them.

At night I saw the Baby again. It had grown like the mischief. Its—his eyes are blue and watery. I do hope that they are not weak. They look weak. I think that he ought to be fitted with glasses, or at least be examined, but I shall not say so. Suggestions that I make are received with ridicule and contempt. Yet I am his father!

The instant that Baby saw me, he laughed. I read in the encyclopedia that normal babies do not laugh or take notice until about a month old. But Paul, my son, took notice when he was twenty minutes of age, and laughed when he was six and one-half hours!

They—the mother, the mother's mother, the nurse, the cook, and the neighbor women who have been in—have permitted me to hold it, once. I never had dreamed that a father must have permission from seven or ten women, and some of them outsiders, before he can handle his own offspring. I did not hold him long. The spectators pestered me so, and appeared so

THE STRANGE ADVENTVRES of the HOBBY = HORSE and the WOOLLY DOG.

Listen all and straight I 'll tell
Of strange adventures that once befell.

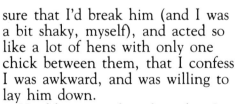

ONE night when the house was dark and still,
  These adventures did begin,
Of the hobby-horse and the woolly dog,
  And the trumpeter made of tin:
What time they went a-hunting,
  For to see what they could win.

Slyly through the door went they,
  Slyly through the house,
Hoping they might find a deer;
  But found, instead, a mouse.

" Now let us hunt!" the dog he barked;
  The hobby-horse ran fast;
The trumpeter raised up his horn,
  And blew a merry blast.

The dog he barked; the horse
    he ran;
  The trumpeter blew his horn;
And over the house they hunted the mouse
  From midnight until morn.

Through kitchen and through dining-room,—
  For woods they had the chairs,—
Through parlor and through hall they chased,
  And down the cellar stairs.

The hobby-horse knocked down
    a chair;
  The dog fell in a pail;
The trumpeter reached for the
    mouse,
  But only touched its tail!

They hunted the mouse all over the house,
  Until they nearly dropped:
They thought at last they had it fast
  When in a hole it popped!

    Then back to the nursery they crept,
      As the day was coming in —
The hobby-horse and the woolly dog
  And the trumpeter made of tin.

This is the tale I heard them tell
Of a strange adventure that once befell.

sure that I'd break him (and I was a bit shaky, myself), and acted so like a lot of hens with only one chick between them, that I confess I was awkward, and was willing to lay him down.

He felt very soft and mushy. I wonder if it is natural for a baby to be so jellyfish-like. He can't be a freak, with no back-bone or—or something. This troubles me, and if he does not harden after expo-

sure I shall have the doctor again.

Paul—we have named him Paul, as a compromise on Robert, which I wanted, and Launcelot, which his mother wanted, and Bartholomew and Jasper, which the grandmothers wanted, and Ned and Dick, which his grandfathers wanted, and Angus, which somebody else wanted, and Patrick,

which the cook wanted—Paul is to be a railroad president or a general in the army; whichever is his bent. The selection will be put to him, in due time, and he shall be educated with this single end in view. From all that I can tell, now, he would do well as either.

I already have spoken about him to Mr. Barrows, of the C. & O. K. I chanced to ride down town with Mr. Barrows, in the car, and

I asked him to bear Paul in mind, if there happened to be prospects of an opening in the head office. He laughed, as if I had perpetrated a joke!

Paul's grandparents are set upon having him a bishop! But one

FOR THE CHILDREN

thing he shall not be, and that is, a grocer. No, sir!

Now, I've got to tell you about that Baby. He isn't like other babies. Bless you, no! So I have no fear of boring you. I recollect how I used to go out of my way to avoid Jenkins, when he had his—I mean, when they had their first child. He was always inflicting upon me what it said and did, and nothing out of the common run, either . . . But my son! It's a different proposition.

From experience I have found that there is nothing that gives a child more real pleasure than taking him for a walk through the woods. The trees are a particular delight to him in the fall. There is something about the beautiful, vivid coloring of the leaves that seems to have a peculiar charm for him; so now is a good time to teach him the names of different leaves. Let him gather the leaves

for himself and compare them, putting those of the same shape and those of the same color to themselves, and then tell him the names of the different leaves and it will make a lasting impression on his mind. It is also interesting to

have him collect as many different kinds of seed as he can find. Tell him that the seed vessels are called cradles, then he will be interested in how the babies are tucked away and cared for and how many different kinds of cradles there are and how they differ in size, shape and color. All this teaches the child to think and observe.

I do not believe in paying children for every little thing they do, for I think they ought to help about whatever needs to be done without thought of reward, but they must have something of their own to take interest in and also to bring in a little money. One has chickens, one a pig, another a calf, another a corn patch, etc. My children all have their bank account in the savings department. I never tell them they can't spend their own money, but I encourage them to save it.

Whenever my children need punishing, I do it myself—and at once. I do think it a great mistake to wait until father comes home to tell him about it and let him do it. It makes the children dread to see him, and makes his homecoming unhappy. I confess it takes a good deal of resolution to do this. I don't believe much in whipping.

Last, but not least, don't be afraid of loving them too much. Today my little four-year-old said, "Mamma, you could not do without your little girl, could you?—for I loves you and you loves me."

While the tasks alloted country children oftentimes seem too hard for their little hands to do, theirs is the easiest life after all. They know no such thing as restlessness and discomfort because of having too little to do. City children are oftentimes miserable because their little hands have so few tasks to perform. The place of all places to raise children to be noble men and womanly women is in "God's country," as one writer aptly expresses it."

The Greensboro Record is exactly sane in its opposition to the stilted pride and the folly-born notions of "style" which keeps little children, boys and girls alike, primped out in shoes and stockings all summer. To deny their little feet this annual escape from prison, to deny them the freedom of the summer's air and earth, and the strengthening growth which nature gains for foot and ankle and

leg and the whole body by reason of the romping freedom which the barefoot child enjoys, is a wrong against the children, a sin against the next generation. Boys thus

pampered and petted will become the sickly dudes of the next generation and the little girls, if they live, will grow into women as weak in mind as in body, who will walk with a hobbling, wooden-leg gait, instead of the graceful, rhythmic movement which nature loves to give them when left alone. The human body cries out for freedom from those artificial hamperings of fashion and folly. Away with the shoes and stockings and let Dame Nature have a chance. She has more sense than anybody about raising healthy children.

Amusing Small Children.

Dear Aunt Mary: Is it permissable for a "mere man" to come into the circle and tell the mothers his experience about amusing small children? I have two little boys, whose mother is more or less an invalid, so it has often fallen to me to play nurse for them. I have been wonderfully successful in keeping them quiet and satisfied—quiet was necessary when their mother was sick. I will tell you the things that they seem to like best.

On rainy days, I give them a small supply of soap and water and let them blow bubbles. If you give them too much water they will get themselves and everything around them very wet, but with just a little, in a big bowl, they keep dry. One of the advertising pages of a magazine torn out and rolled sidewise makes the best sort of "bubbler." I also have a little box of harmless water-color paints and they love to paint the illustrations of any old papers or magazines I will let them have. These paints are not expensive, and keep the boys busy for a long time.

When it is not raining I like to have them out of doors, so in one corner of the yard, where there is a big oak tree, I have put a wooden packing-box where they can keep the dearest of their belongings. One day I suggested that they "play house," and showed them how to convert the little spaces between the tree-roots into roofs, with rocks for table, acorn cups for table-ware, little plants stuck in the crevices for trees, etc. They soon got tired of this, but a little girl who had come over from the next farm to play with them spent the entire day collecting various household goods of similar fashion, and cried when her mother took her away from them that night, so I offer this suggestion especially for the little girls. My wife says that a doll to live in the house would make it more attractive; one of those small dolls, all china, whose body will stand every sort of weather.

If any of the mothers will tell me in exchange for all this valuable information what to do with a very loving small boy who insists on waking up every morning before the first peep of dawn and coming into his father's room to be entertained, I will be very glad.

A Girls' Tomato Club.

For this summer our clubs are limited in scope, providing only for raising of tomatoes and cucumbers and canning and pickling fruit raised. It was thought we might possibly secure 100 girls in the two counties. No more were desired because the work was started so late it would be difficult to secure tomato plants. We have now about 200 girls and have had to stop applications.

The girls are, if there is time, expected to plant the seeds for tomatoes, raise plants, and transplant them, taking entire care of plants till fruit is ripe. Then the Department of Agriculture will send a canning outfit into the district and show girls how to can properly. After this is done a market is found for the canned goods.

The only conditions of membership are that after the first hard work is done, the girls herself must do the rest under directions, and she must have all the proceeds to do with as she pleases.

"Neither young men nor young women," says Dr. Sylvanus Stall, "can afford to read fiction before they are twenty-five years of age. There is too much that is indispensable for intelligence, for laying of foundation principles for study, for business, health and morals, that need to be read first. If fiction is read before a correct taste is formed and foundation principles laid, the best books will never be read at all."

The Sweetest Harvest on the Farm

Valentine
This is the time for birds to mate;
Today the dove
Will mark the ancient amorous date
With moans of love;
The crow will change his call to prate
His hopes thereof.

The starling will display the red
That lights his wings;
The wren will know the sweet things said
By him who swings
And ducks and dips his crested head
And sings and sings.

They are obedient to their blood,
Nor ask a sign,
Save bouyant air and swelling bud,
At hands divine,
But choose, each in the barren wood,
His Valentine.

In caution's maze they never wait
Until they die;
They flock the season's open gate
Ere time steals by.
Love, shall we see and imitate,
You, love, and I?

John Charles McNeill, in "Songs, Merry and Sad."

This ad in 1922 for the Colgate "Beauty Box" was one of the first color ads run by the Progressive Farmer. *Since the process for reproducing color preceded color photography, the 1920's were a golden age for illustrators, who could evoke a mood by subtle blending of color and shape.*

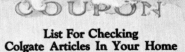

Give the Girl a Cow Before She Marries

Almost every farmer gives his daughter a cow when she marries; but let me insist that he give it to her before then so she won't be striving to get married just to come into possession of her cow. Let her have it while she is enjoying single blessedness and she will realize a handsome profit if milk and butter are properly kept and marketed. Then, too, an occasional calf for the market adds something to her pin money. In many instances a girl treated this way will enjoy her profits and remain with her parents till she has better judgment in deciding matters pertaining to a lifetime contract.

They Wouldn't Hear Him.

Angie invited her young man to supper. Everything passed off harmoniously until the seven-year old brother broke the blissful silence by saying:

"Oh, ma, you oughter see Mr. _____ when he called to take Angie to the drill. He looked so

In this 1924 ad, the lady seems to feel as proprietary toward her Ford as she might about conveniences more commonly within women's province, such as her precious oil stove or her bathtub. Women were urged to "know something about the car even though you do not run it." One man described standing in front of his car to crank it, with his wife and baby inside. The car started suddenly and moved backwards. When the man shouted to his wife to turn off the engine, she fumbled about and turned on more gas. Since a steep embankment was behind the car, tragedy was only averted by an alert spectator who jumped on the running board and managed to turn off the engine.

nice sittin' longside of her with his arm _____"

"Fred?" screamed the maiden, quickly placing her hand over the boy's mouth.

"You oughter seen him," continued the persistant informant after gaining his breath. "He had his arm _____"

"Freddie!" shouted the mother, as in her frantic attempt to reach the boy's auricular appendage, she upset the contents of the teapot.

"I was just going to say," the half-frightened boy pleaded, between a cry and an injured whine, "he had his arm ____"

"Fred," thundered the father, "leave the table!"

And the boy did so, exclaiming as he went, "I was only going to say Mr. ____ had his army clothes on, and I leave it to him if he didn't."

Are Old Bachelors Happy?

Dear Aunt Mary: The bachelor problem discussed in the Home Circle is a subject worth consideration and careful thought.

In my travels I meet with them most every day and the average bachelor is more or less careless or rude in his manner. Now what causes this? Simply because they have no wife or family to spend the evening with and therefore they are always out on the streets or some other place, gossiping or telling jokes and tales, and they really get led off in that way.

Now just think a little on the other hand: if they had a wife and children to spend their evenings with in talking and reading of something useful, their lives would surely be led into a better way. Man becomes like his surroundings and lives like his associates.

Here at the boarding-house where I am stopping for a few days, we have four old bachelors boarding, three of them are county officers and the other a lawyer, and they are from forty to sixty years old, all drifting through life by themselves, making good money, but in my opinion without much real pleasure.

One of these old bachelors was sitting out on the veranda yesterday evening and as some birds went flying around he remarked if a man was as happy as one of these birds he would be getting something out of life. Poor man!

Who, by the way, is more enterprising than the country widower? Now if the majority of bachelors had one-half of the affection and persistence, or perhaps I should say

Choose Jewelry as a Present

perseverance of the old widower, the heart of many a girl, of many an old maid, of many a widow would be made to rejoice.

But of all utterly selfish beings on earth, the Southern bachelor is in the lead. I heard one say not long since: "I had rather have a full dinner pail and no wife." His heart is evidently in his stomach and so nothing touches it except his food. As a rule women are not to blame at all for the present craze for single life.

Women Do Not Wish to Give Up Their Independence

Dear Aunt Mary: So Henpecked thinks there are so many unmarried women because they have never been asked to marry men that drink or that do not drink.

I do not agree with him and can show him the real reason if he will only be frank enough to "fess up."

Here is an example which can be duplicated almost anywhere: Mary has a good position, she pays her board, buys her clothes, and still has a little money to spend as she pleases. And oh, how happy a few dollars does make some of us feel when we can do absolutely as we wish with it! Once a year she has a little outing to the mountains or seashore. Now John comes along, offers his heart and hand: what is it that causes her to hesitate—for he does not drink?

The girls of today are very fond of ease and luxury, and reason thus: John's salary is not much more than mine, he has nothing saved and I have nothing. Can I give up my freedom, wear last year's hats and do my own housework; be tied down to a life of poverty just to become Mrs. John?

It is not necessary for a man to drink always in order for our girls to hesitate, although I am proud to say most of the girls I know would hesitate if he drank—for the average girl of today looks at marriage from every point of view.

I am not saying that the girls are doing the wisest thing by remaining unmarried, because old age will come and a home and children are not to be despised.

But certainly it is not because they can't marry; don't you see, Henpecked?

Our grandmothers married young because there was nothing else for them to do. They could teach the "young idea to shoot," but that was outside of her home. Now there is not a calling open to man that a woman can not fill, unless it requires a great deal of physical strength.

Woman's place is in the home, and most men know it. A sunny smile at the breakfast table and a proper interest in the work of the husband are prized infinitely more than a long dissertation on a meeting of the Woman's Club of the night before and the wife's appointment as chairman of a committee to investigate the food of the babies of the city. Most babies make their own wants known in this respect.

Men like natural women. It isn't what a woman says, but how she says it; not what she wears, but how she wears it; not what she does, but how she does it. A woman needs to know how and when to flatter; how and when to sympathize; how and when to be jolly or serious; how and when to talk and when to keep silent. Men care for little things,—little looks, little words, little thoughts of kindness and interest and comfort. The brilliant, sparkling, pretty woman is a very acceptable thing to a man until matrimony is mentioned, and then he grabs his hat, jumps out of the window and runs to the good-hearted, big-souled, generous-minded, modest little woman, be she ever so humble or homely.

School Work That Fits For Life's Duties

What is education? The baby lies in the cradle; it does not know anything. At the other end of life is the man who weighs the stars and bridges oceans, and rules and directs the destiny of an empire. The difference between the helpless, ignorant babe and a Newton, a Fulton, a Gladstone, is education.

Education includes the whole development of the whole man. Nothing deserves the name which does not include the development of his conscience and of his affections. Do not let us repeat our blunder in a vain attempt to make education apart from religion. As Professor Huxley has truly said, education without religion will do nothing but make of the gutter-snipe a beast of the field, and we know what came of that experiment a long time ago.

Nothing is education but that which out of a boy or a girl makes a man or a woman with wisdom to see the truth, with conscience to enforce duty, with inspiration to service, with manhood within because God is within.

Parents Should Co-operate with the Schools

It would be well if all the parents of boys and girls attending the

DR. WALTER J. QUICK,
The New Dean of the Agricultural Department and Professor of Agriculture in the Virginia Polytechnic Institute.

public schools—and for that matter, private schools also—would do some severe and honest thinking and self-examination and analysis at the beginning of the coming school term and would make some very strong and definite resolutions and stick to them. One vice of the public school system is the temptation it offers parents to shirk their responsibility and to unload the whole burden of management, training and instruction of children on the public school system and teachers. The schools cannot be made effective and cannot do the work they are intended to do without the cordial co-operation and earnest help of the parents of the pupils.

Compulsory Education

No one has yet, as I remember, claimed that it would not make for better citizenship and more useful lives. No one has denied that such laws are to be found in the most highly advanced States of the Union and in the freest and most progressive foreign countries. No one has attempted to show that it would injure the children. The opposition seems to be based, as I have said, almost exclusively on the theory that it is an interference with the rights of the parent to compel him to send his children to school.

It seems to me that our friends who take this view are looking at only one side of the question. The parents have rights beyond all question; but have the children none? Is it not the duty of the State to see that so far as possible each child has a fair chance in the struggle of life? And can anyone say that the child who has been allowed to grow up in ignorance, whose early life has been spent at work instead of in study, has a fair chance in the competition of the modern world?

Environment is more potent than we sometimes think. It is probable that the antipathy to farm life is formed before the child is able to reason on the subject. An inviting school house and attractive play ground will do more than a profitable corn or cotton crop to keep the child on the farm. Children cannot be forced to like school. They like it only when it is worth liking. Bare, harsh, cheerless, immodest,—these are the conditions that prevail in too many rural school houses and grounds.

A Marysville schoolma'am was teaching her class the mysteries of grammar.

"Now, Johnny, said she, "in what tense do I speak when I say, 'I am beautiful?'"

The little fellow answered, quick as a wink, "The past."

Before and After Taking.

LOOK ON THIS PICTURE—

The cuts above show the old school buildings in Cedar Falls and Franklinsville districts, Randolph County, N. C., before taking consolidation and local tax.

AND THEN ON THIS—

The two cuts below show the new buildings in these same Cedar Falls and Franklinsville districts after taking consolidation and the local tax.

"GO, AND DO THOU LIKEWISE."

When I took charge of the Eagle Rock school in September last I found a house in the midst of a large yard grown up in briers, weeds, and broom sedge. Just in front of the door was a road made by drivers taking a short cut from one public road to another.

The interior of the house was no more inviting, containing only desks and two small blackboards, the floors and walls being much discolored. I had to begin with small things. I found two nice, large calendars, and hung one in each room.

But the yard gave me the horrors. I laid the case before the children and called upon them for help toward a new order of things. Then I appointed December 13 as work day on the yard, and sent requests to several patrons to be there on that day, and in the notes specified the tools each should bring.

When I drove up with my wagon load of tools and workmen on the 13th there were waiting for me a strong force of hands and eight horses and mules. They plowed, and chopped and dug, and harrowed, and laid off walks, and when we left things were marvelously changed.

The following Friday was appointed Arbor Day, and all the people of the community, whether patrons or not, were invited to bring trees. Nature recognized her friends, and gave a lovely day, and the people came. The children rendered some appropriate selections. Miss Royster followed with an address, and then we went out and planted the trees. There were forty-seven planted, mostly elms and maples.

One gentleman sent word that it was impossible for him to be there then, but to have three places marked, and when I began the new year his trees would be there. They were. He named one for me, one for my assistant, and one for the preacher. The preacher—ungrateful one—has died, but the teachers, as was to be expected, are holding their own. Out of the fifty trees forty-six lived.

Education and Housework

There had been a domestic crisis in the Weeks family. The maid of all work had been ill; company had arrived unexpectedly, and the weather was very hot. But Florence Weeks had just come home from college, and proved a reinforcement that saved the day for the tired mother.

When the skirmish was over her mother said: "Florence, I believe you sweep and dust and cook and wash dishes better since you studied calculus!"

"Why not mother?" answered the girl. "Isn't that what calculus is for?"

To be able to do what needs to be done, and to do it at a minute's notice, is to be the most perfect product of modern education. A woman is urged to it not alone by religion, as in earlier times, but by every social consideration as well. That a woman can read Greek or calculate an eclipse makes her more, not less, ready for service in an emergency in kitchen or laundry or dining room. That she knows how to use her head and her hand for large matters is ground for expecting her to be skillful in small ones when occasion requires.

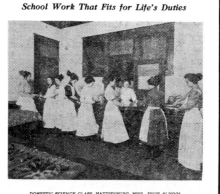

School Work That Fits for Life's Duties

DOMESTIC SCIENCE CLASS, HATTIESBURG, MISS. HIGH SCHOOL.

"What greater service can a school render to the State than to send forth a number of girls cultured and refined in body, mind and spirit, and trained in the real art of home-making?"

I have heard the question asked—Where there is a boy and a girl, and just one of them is to be educated, which should have the education?

I say the girl. A boy with an ordinary education can be a carpenter, farmer, or almost any old thing. What can a girl do without an education? She can't do anything.

Some people say the boys should be the best educated because they have to take care of the girls. This might have been the case 30 or 40 years ago, when a girl remained with her parents until she was fifteen or sixteen, and then married the first man that "popped the question." Not so with the independent girl of today. If she doesn't marry, she is not ashamed to be called an "old maid." Men do not care to go to the altar with a pretty, blushing sixteen-year-old girl now. They want a woman, not a mere girl. Any girl should be in school at sixteen and not think of marrying. There are thousands of positions open to the educated girl. If she is educated she can make her own way and not worry for support.

Common Sense and Education

You'll find that education's about the only thing lying around loose in this world, and that it's about the only thing a fellow can have as much of as he's willing to haul away. Everything else is screwed down tight and the screw-driver lost.

There are two parts of a college education—the part that you get in the school-rooms from the professors, and the part that you get outside of it from the boys. That's the really important part. For the first can only make you a scholar, while the second can make you a man.

Education's a good deal like eating—a fellow can't always tell which particular thing did him good, but he can usually tell which

one did him harm. After a square meal of roast beef and vegetables, and mince pie and watermelons, you can't say just which ingredient is going into muscle, but you don't have to be very bright to figure out which one started the demand for pain-killer in your insides, or to guess, next morning, which one made you believe in a personal devil the night before. And so, while a fellow can't figure out to an ounce whether it's Latin or algebra, or history or what among

the solids that is building him up in this place or that, he can go right along feeding them in and betting that they're not the things that turn his tongue fuzzy. It's down among the sweets, among his amusements and recreations, that he's going to find his stomach-ache, and it's there that he wants to go slow and to pick and choose.

It's not the first half, but the second half of a college education which merchants mean when they ask if a college education pays. It's the Willie and Bertie boys; the chocolate eclair and tutti-frutti boys, the la-de-dah and the baa-baa-billy-goat boys; the high cock-a-lo-rum and the cock-a-doodle-doo boys; the Bah Jove! hair-parted-in-the-middle, cigareete smoking, Champagne-Charlie, up-

all-night-and-in-all day boys that make 'em doubt the cash value of the college output, and overlook the roast-beef and blood-gravy boys, the shirt-sleeves and high water-pants boys, who take their college education and make some fellow's business hum with it.

A Duty to Dress Becomingly

The Clothes a Woman Wears

A woman well-dressed is appropriately dressed. A woman appropriately dressed is well-dressed. The nurse's costume is a good example of suitability. It is of wash material, and therefore as sterile as boiling and hot irons can make it. No ruffles, lace or embroidery bedeck it. The cloth is strong, yet thin enough for summer wear. Its lines are straight, simple and becoming. The dress could be of unbleached cotton and serve the purpose just as well. It might be of flaming red, have stripes three inches wide or spots as big as saucers. Instead it is neither sombre nor too light. It makes everyone, whether tall or short, black-haired or goldi-locked, look her best, and shocks the sensibilities of neither the sick nor the well.

From the dress of the nurse to that of the housewife is but a short step. The germ in the kitchen is scarcely less important than that of the sick room. It is not only the cause of most of our sickness but also is the cause of the spoiling of our foods. Therefore, where once we wore our cast-off skirts and old waists now we wash them, make them over for the children, and have our garments for the kitchen

simple, easily laundered, without frills and buttoned together at the waist.

I do not think there is anyone so old, so young, so pretty, so homely, so thin, fat, disfigured or comely that she can afford to cease striving for the beautiful. Everyone of us makes the world a little brighter to someone by looking our best, and even if there be no one at all to see us, we have the pleasure of giving satisfaction to that most important being in the world—ourself.

Fortunately, there is in us a love for the beautiful. It is that instinct which makes the little girl pull down her mother's head and tuck a flower in the thinning locks or that causes her to bedeck herself with daisies or clover blossoms.

Expense and beauty do not necessarily go hand in hand. A 12-cent lawn comes in as pretty colors as do more costly materials.

Every woman longs for a really good dress. She sees her more prosperous neighbor with a silken gown and longs for the time when she may have one also. It matters not that it is not appropriate, that the children will soil and rumple it and that the dust of the roads will make it dingy. Reason tells her that it is not the thing for her and still she wants it, and she should have it, too, if her husband can afford it. Her reason for wanting it is beyond the comprehension of man's mind, just as his reason for spending enough on tobacco to buy five gowns is beyond the intricacies of her mind. In buying her that dress he purchases for her, not so many yards of material, but peace, satisfaction and a sense of self-respect, the cause of which can be found only in our primal natures.

Buying the "Good" Dress

Nowadays dress-making is a comparatively simple affair, with patterns for everything from a baby's bib to the most elaborate gown. It is simply a question of obeying the markings. The choosing of the material, color and style is our own affair.

In deciding on a suit, it is hardest to choose. Serge catches dust, smooth cloths—like broadcloth—show the spots, cashmere and henrietta are too thick for summer, too thin for winter. A brilliantine for summer and a cheviot for winter are perhaps as satisfactory as anything.

Color is a thing to be chosen with care. The tone that will make the skin look the clearest can be decided only by holding different colored materials to the face and noting effects. As a rule, grays, blacks and whites look well on the elderly, blue on the fair, and pink on those with a hint of cream and red in the skin. Red and purple should be avoided by the large or florid. Nature never made a mistake, and if the color of the hair or eyes is carried out, the effect is sure to be pleasing.

Lines and general style mean much but the effect is lost without good, well-made corsets. The very slight person can seldom disregard them because she must avoid slovenliness, and the woman of excellent development must certainly give them serious consideration. Have corsets comfortable above all things and do not pull in the waist at the expense of the bust or hips. A snug, well-fitted underwaist is a

great help. Slim people usually err by having the clothes too full, while stout people accentuate their size by wearing those that lie too flat to the skin.

Shirt-Waist Suits

The shirt-waist suit is more popular than ever. Dots and stripes and checks in foulards will be seen on every side, and also the Dresden effects in soft taffeta and louisine silk. The shirt-waist suit has made a record for itself and needs no recommendation, but the black and white checks, as well as the narrow stripes with the wide stripes, will be new comparatively. One of the most attractive models is of spring-green Madras, made with groups of tucks in both waist and skirt, and straps of the same goods stitched between the plaits. Then there is plaid gingham made entirely on the bias. The skirt yoke is the same as illustrated in the bridal toilette in this issue, and the skirts laid in plaits from it, the plaits stitched to the knees and from there left to flare. Straps of white linen finish the seam at the yoke in both waist and skirt, and also shirt-waist suits in lace-striped and dotted mohair. One of these gowns made of Wedgwood blue is likely to be becoming to the woman with dark-blue eyes.

A Fashion Show

A novel exposition occupies Madison Square Garden, New York, the first half of September, a "fashion show," the first of its kind in this country. Its purpose is to set styles and establish a unity of ideas in the making of gowns between American and European modistes. The latter have contributed to the exposition 150 gowns of every style, and a large number of American makes are shown. Handsome girls wear the different styles on a stage, and Delegate Otto Adler delivers addresses on European fashions. Every style of garment for outdoors, social functions, etc., are shown, also the making of various articles, the dressing of hair in accordance with style of gown, etc. There is also a large millinery exhibit.

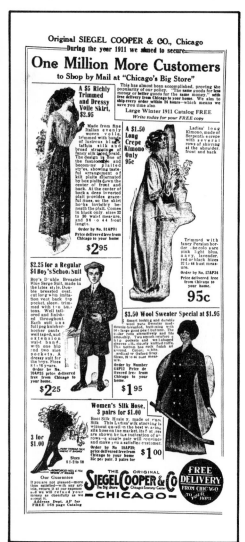
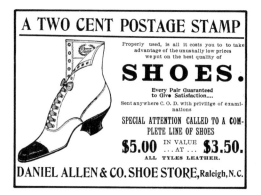
The Spring Skirt

One feature of the spring skirt is that it is short. In fact, the number of short sensible skirts one sees nowadays would lead one to think that the feminine apostles of Fashion had defied her mandates. But not so, for the smart skirt which clears the ground has the stamp and approval of the powers. The trailing skirt is reserved for house wear, a neat scheme which encourages every woman to replace her walking skirt for another one, thus scoring a point for the street skirt which fulfills its destiny best when it is brushed and hung away ready for the next time.

What Neckwear May Do for Your Looks

Necks change with age—some have double chins, while others become long and stringy. The only safe thing to do is to cover them with collars well up under the ears. A fluffy bow under the chin is always becoming to the thin woman, but the fat woman with a short neck must eschew the bow.

The tall, slender woman may wear the wide girdle of her youth if she cares to, but the stout one should have a narrow belt, preferably of black if she cannot have one the color of her dress. The buckles may be as handsome as one chooses in either case.

Wear Gloves That Fit

Gloves should fit well, and as it is possible nowadays to find many different models, there is no necessity for packing fat fingers and plump hands into gloves intended to cover long slender ones, with the result that they bulge here and puff out there, thereby only emphasizing their unshapeliness. Thin women can always find gloves to fit them.

If your fingers are fat, wear few rings and always remember that a superabundance of jewelry bespeaks ill breeding. Bracelets look well on slender wrists, but not on stout ones.

The handbag should be selected with the same care and if you can have only one, let it be black, then when it gets "rusty" give it a generous coat of shoe polish. Black kid gloves and black belts can be treated in like manner. Dainty handkerchiefs are every woman's right, but the elderly woman will prefer fine quality to novel effects, and neat white embroideries to patches of color. Many ladies prefer home-embroidered or home-made handkerchiefs and this work when well done lasts longer and bespeaks individuality, besides beguiling many otherwise lost moments into producing many beautiful and useful articles.

Eating is the First Activity of Living

Many wrecked homes, many divorces, many crimes have been traced directly to a bad digestion, the result of wrong methods of cooking.

Science in the Kitchen

While the women of to-day are rejoicing that this is the "woman's century," and while we pride ourselves upon our emancipation from many an old-time creed and custom, it is well, sometimes to ask ourselves if we, as women, fully comprehend the greater responsibility which the enlightenment of the age and the assuming of its privileges entails, and are willing to avail ourselves of these privileges to enlighten ourselves and then to make a practical use of this knowledge for the benefit of our families.

It is often easier to get into a rut and stay there than to exert ourselves to get out upon a higher plane of thought and action. It is easier to prepare the same food in the same manner as it was prepared by our mothers and grandmothers, than it is to make a careful study of the relation existing between bodily health and strength

and the digestion of food. But, until we fully comprehend this important principle, certain it is that there will always be more or less human suffering and unhappiness.

This is an age of activity; a time of great mental and physical effort, and it is necessary that our minds and our bodies should both be nourished to the highest degree of perfection. And how shall this be done unless the professor of housewifery shall acquaint herself with the needs of the human organism, and be able to supply those needs in a scientific manner?

Eating

Eating is the first activity of living. Hunger is the deepest rooted of all the senses. The desire to eat created the mouth, and the nose, its guard. The eye was made by the same instinct, it is hungry for light; touch is closely related to the neutrative. The hands are food-gatherers. Hunger is the cause of activity.

Food Preservatives are Injurious

The Bureau of Chemistry of the Department of Agriculture announces that it has decided that the use of preservatives, such as sulphuric and boracic acid, in foods, is injurious to the health of consumers. The general public had already reached this conclusion through the more direct road of common sense, but it is reassuring to have its opinion fortified by the dictum of science.

What Shall We Eat in Hot Weather?

Dr. H. W. Wiley, chemist of the Department of Agriculture, answers that question in the following interview, in which he takes occasion to express his opinion of soda water and iced tea as sure means to an early death. We quote:

"The devil lurks in the soda water fountain, and iced tea is simply suicide. If persons would only use precaution there is no reason why one should suffer more with sickness in summer than winter."

Asked if meat was unhealthy in hot weather, he said: "Meat is much more easily digested than starchy vegetables, and is both nutritious and condimental. Vegetables are watery, and furnish little nutriment, their qualities being condimental and mechanical. Meat, good bread, potatoes and milk free from germs is the diet to be relied upon at all times for good health. Good bread should be the foundation of every meal, and too much care cannot be given to its preparation. Bread should be at least a day old before it is eaten, if not older."

I have seen many a woman that could bake a loaf of bread that was divine, and she didn't think that amounted to anything. She thought if she could be president of something and read a report she would be "hot stuff." She never dreamed that to bake good bread was doing a divine thing. But to bake a loaf of bread right, you know, is a thing that you can go before God with and be just as good and as great as you can when you are praying.

Our First Canning Article

Dear Aunt Mary: According to your request of last week, I will give to your readers my method of canning fruit in glass cans.

I use the Mason cans and always try to have good rubbers, and if they are not good ones, I use two rubbers on one can. Then, too, if my lids have become rough or bent I buy new lids.

Now as to the canning. First, I have my cans all washed well and turned down to drain on a table, but my lids I put near the stove so as to have them thoroughly dry. Then I put on my fruit in a granite kettle with just enough water to start it boiling; then I stir the fruit often but very carefully, so as not to tear up the fruit, until it nearly reaches the boiling point. Then I put a lid on my kettle and let the juice of the fruit boil up just a minute; next slip the kettle to the side of the stove where the fruit will keep warm but not boil. I then wring a large coarse towel out of cold warm water and wrap the can entirely in this and then proceed to put in the fruit. I pack the fruit some as I put it in to exclude the air, and when I get the can about full I put on the rubber and then fill the can just as long as I can make a piece lie on top. This excludes all the air that may be in the lid and as you screw down the lid, the juice will run over on every side but your towel will catch it, and so will not burn your fingers.

Aunt Jennie's Letter.

I find it less trouble to cook things for canning while dinner is on the stove and the fire is going and, too, if you have only enough to fill a few cans it is soon done and you do not miss the time. I always can tomatoes then. Don't wait for a bushel of anything before beginning, but just put up the quarts as you can get them and you will soon find that it is like earning pennies, and you will have more than you thought. If you put

the material in the can boiling hot, the jars are perfectly clean, and the rubbers good, then store them in a dark closet you will be glad that you exerted yourself even if the days were hot.

How to Pack Eggs for Long Keeping

The yolk of the egg spoils much quicker than the white. For this reason it is important that the yolk should be surrounded with a layer of the white. If the egg is placed on the side or large end the heavy yolk will settle to the bottom and

come in contact with the shell, which admits the air. If it is placed on the small end it will always have a layer of white between it and the shell. Eggs absorb odors easily, therefore only odorless material should be used when packing them.

Suggestions for a Thanksgiving Dinner

Be sure to kill and dress the turkey at least two days before Thanksgiving and hang it in a cool place. If you can provide wild turkey you will have a treat indeed, but most of us are truly thankful for the home-grown article, and for all the boasted superiority of the strutting gobbler, a hen turkey is to be preferred.

Some of the present-day culinary authorities object to the stuffing of a fowl; but for those who prefer the toothsome stuffing, the following simple recipes will be found excellent: (1) A good stuffing is made of bread-crumbs rolled fine, moistened with butter and two eggs beaten slightly, seasoned with salt, pepper, and parsley; some add a little sage, thyme, or sweet marjoram. (2) To a generous cupful of bread-crumbs allow a tablespoonful of sausage meat, season with pepper and a little minced parsley; moisten slightly with milk. It is best to have the sausage meat partly cooked before using. (4) To the ordinary bread-crumb stuffing moistened slightly with either melted butter or oyster liquor, add two dozen small oysters chopped fine.

Put the stuffing loosely into the turkey; do not crowd it in. While roasting do not forget to baste the turkey frequently, allowing fifteen to eighteen minutes per pound for roasting. When done, place on a large platter and garnish with small cakes of sausage or small links of sausage, fried oysters or crisp slices of bacon.

A Last Year's Ham, and Oysters

One of last year's hams boiled the day before, should grace the table, and if necessary, it may be sliced, though remaining in shape, to help in the ease of service during the dinner. When oysters form part of the dinner they may be stewed as the first course or scalloped, and served with the turkey and ham.

Delightful Dishes in Dear Old Dixie

As true Southerners, we'll want rice and sweet potatoes. If you have a double-boiler you'll find little trouble in having delicious rice, each grain standing to itself. Don't have a gluey mass. Wash a cup of rice in at least two waters, drop it slowly into about two quarts of salted boiling water. Cook about

thirty minutes, not stirring once during the cooking, then set the vessel on back of stove for a few minutes in order that the rice may dry out thoroughly. Turn the rice out into an uncovered dish and serve steaming hot.

Candied potatoes are easily prepared. Parboil the sweet potatoes in their skins, peel and slice. Butter a baking dish, put in a layer of sliced potatoes, sprinkle with sugar, bits of butter, and a small pinch of mixed spices. Fill the dish in this manner, then pour in about one-half cup of warm water, cover and bake about a half-hour. Uncover and brown.

The large Spanish or Bermuda onions are best for boiling. Wash and peel, changing the water at least three times during the boiling; always adding boiling water. When done, drain thoroughly and place in serving dish, seasoning with salt and pepper and pouring melted butter over them.

Now for the Sauces and Things

With the turkey should be cranberries, and let's add slaw. To make nice cranberry sauce, remove all soft berries, wash thoroughly, place for about two minutes in scalding water, remove, and to every pound of fruit add one-half pound granulated sugar, more if you like the sauce quite sweet, and one-half pint water. Cook over a moderate fire; be careful to cover and not to stir the fruit, but occasionally shake the vessel, the berries will thereby retain their shape. Boil for about seven or eight minutes, remove from the fire, pour into a dish and set aside to cool.

There are numerous recipes for slaw. I think that you'll like this one. Shred sufficient cabbage to make one quart. Heat four tablespoonfuls of vinegar, one level teaspoon of salt, one of pepper, two of white sugar, two of prepared mustard, one tablespoonful butter, the yolks of two eggs beaten thoroughly; put all into an enameled bowl, set in a kettle of hot water, sirring constantly till it thickens; then stir in the shredded cabbage, mixing thoroughly. When cabbage is well heated, pour out into a bowl and let remain until thoroughly cold before serving.

For Dessert—the "Pre-eminent Pie."

For dessert, to carry out the true Thanksgiving flavor, we must have the "pre-eminent pie"—pumpkin pie and apple pie.

For the pumpkin pie try this— mash very dry two cupfuls of stewed pumpkin, well sweetened, stirring in gradually while still warm three well-beaten eggs, one tablespoonful sifted flour, the grated rind of a lemon, a pinch each of powdered cinnamon, allspice, and mace, two tablespoonfuls of butter and about a cupful of rich milk, or enough to form a thick batter; beat well, folding in one cupful of chopped figs, and one-fourth of a pound of seeded raisins cut in halves. Fill into pastry shells and bake a golden brown in a moderately heated oven.

The following recipe is a particularly nice one for an apple pie: Line a pie tin with any good pastry and fill it with peeled and quartered apples. When full add bits of butter, one-half cupful of sugar,

into which has been stirred one heaping teaspoonful of flour. Over this grate half a nutmeg and add enough water to cook the apples. Bake until it is done and the apples can be pierced with a straw. Set away to cool. Whip one-half pint of cream and pour over all.

To Drink—Hot Spiced Cider and Coffee

Hot spiced cider makes an excellent beverage to serve with the Thanksgiving dinner. To prepare it get good fresh cider and boil it three minutes with a small bag of cloves and allspice, two large sticks of cinnamon, and a very little sugar. Strain and serve steaming hot. For those who do not care for the spiced cider provide good strong coffee. We'll want a few salted peanuts too, and these are easily prepared. Shell, and blanch the peanuts by pouring boiling water over them; let them stand for a few minutes, the skins are then easily removed. Dry the nuts between the folds of a clean napkin and put them in a baking pan

with a tablespoonful of melted butter, shake well that each nut may be coated; set the pan in the oven, shaking the pan frequently that the nuts may brown evenly. When browned sufficiently, strew thickly with salt, and when cold remove to the serving dish.

This is the Way it Would Look at the Big Hotel

When written out in the form of a menu-card, the above suggestions for the Thanksgiving dinner will have this appearance:

Stewed Oysters	Crackers
Pickles	Salted Peanuts
Roast Turkey	Boiled Country Ham
Cranberries	Slaw
Boiled Rice	Candied Potatoes
Boiled Onions	
Pumpkin Pie	Apple Meringue Pie
Cheese	
Spiced Cider	Coffee

And before we sit down to our Thanksgiving dinner, no matter how bountiful or how frugal, not one of us should fail to give thanks to Almighty God for his manifold blessings and benefits.

Christmas Recipes

Dear Aunt Jennie—As Christmas is so near I thought that the following recipes might help some one. There is so much in knowing how to do things, and if we have reliable guides there is no danger of mistaken roads. The following recipes have been tested, and I can commend them to your readers:

Mincemeat for a Small Family— Left-over pieces of meat from either roast or steak may be used for mincemeat. For two pies make one cupful of finely chopped, cold, cooked meat. Add two tablespoonfuls of sugar, two of chopped suet, half a cupful of raisins, half a cupful of currants, two tart apples, chopped fine, half a teaspoonful of cinnamon, a saltspoonful of cloves, the grated rind and juice of one lemon, and half a pint of boiled cider.

Peanut Brittle—Shell and remove the brown skins from two quarts of peanuts; roll until the kernels are broken to the size of half a pea. Sift, saving the siftings to dust over a board when you are rolling the candy. Put one pound of granulated sugar in an aluminum or iron saucepan over the fire; stir until the sugar is melted and a light brown. Be careful not to burn. Mix in quickly half the nuts and turn at once on the board that has been dusted with the fine nuts. Roll without delay into a very thin sheet. Then with a large knife mark into squares. In a few moments break apart. You may then melt the second pound of sugar in the same way.

Egg Bread

Fine egg bread may be made in this way: ½ qt. meal, 1 scant teaspoon of soda, 3 eggs. Mix up with whole clabber, that is, clabber with all its natural cream, or with good, thick butter-milk—rather soft—using lard and salt to taste.

The Best Breakfast Food

Hasty pudding—that is the name they give it "up North" In our part of the world it is "mush." The Boston Herald and the New York

Sun have been bemoaning its disappearance from the modern bill of fare. A correspondent of the latter paper well expresses the prevailing sentiment when he speaks of this dish and "also of corn cakes, corn bread, and all the marvelous products of corn" as food for which our souls and our hearts and our stomachs and our bowels yearn. It is really to be deplored that an ingredient of daily food made so familiar and so essential to our fathers by necessity should now, after having demonstrated its exceptional worth, be in a fair way to disappear. Let us get back to the food of our fathers and to their manly physical vigor. . . . The "corn dodger" and the "hoecake" are the

most primitive bread forms; and made right and of the right grade of fresh meal, probably they are still the best forms. But "egg bread," "batter bread," corn cakes (fried) and other varieties are quite worth while. (The sweetened cubes of cold meal offered one at the average hotel as "corn bread" are not. Who ever could have invented that stuff?) But most of all, our affections cling to "mush" or "hasty puddin'." Your meal must be fresh, ground slowly and coarse. If kept more than two or three weeks it loses its flavor. If crushed in rollers, it is heated and spoiled. If ground fine, it is not good. It must also be from selected white Southern corn. Then stirred carefully but not rapidly, into boiling water (the correct combination is a hickory paddle and a thick iron pot) so that it may be thoroughly scalded and yet not allowed to gather into lumps, it makes the best "breakfast food" ever invented. It is equally good with milk and sugar, with milk alone, or with butter and salt. And if generally and regularly used, it would go far to correct the indigestion, defective teeth, constipation, headaches, and so forth to which our generation is heir.

There is a reason and a tolerably good one, why the inhabitants of cities and large towns have ceased to relish corn bread, and that as the disastrous change that has taken place in the manufacture of meal. Instead of the leisurely grinding by means of mill-stones run by water-power we have the product of the steam-driven mill, and the Farmer can say with truth that the result is not fit for man or beast. In the steam-driven mill, the meal is heated to a temperature that is destructive of the life and flavor of maize; it will not respond to the efforts of the most experienced cook; it is soggy, musty and indigestible. But if I had my way a course in water-ground corn meal would be a part of the education of every school child.

How to Make Lye Hominy

Hard wood ashes should be used, those from burning hickory being best. Select good corn, seeing that kernels are uniform size. In making a quantity of hominy, use one quart of ashes to eight quarts of corn. Sift out all the coarse cinders from the ashes and tie the fine ashes up in a cloth of closely woven texture. Place the bag of ashes in a large kettle with the corn and cover with water. More water should be added as it boils away. Continue boiling until the hulls will slip from the corn, then drain and remove the bag of ashes. Wash the corn through several waters to remove all the lye, and rub well to remove the hulls. The hulled corn should then be boiled till tender. It may be canned in the usual way of canning fruits and vegetables.

Do set out some mint and try flavoring your iced tea with it during the long July and August days when it's too hot to eat. You put two or three sprigs in the tea when it's hot—just enough to give it an odd taste—and then when you pour it out in glasses arrange a few sprays on top of the lemon and ice so they will stand up like a flower garden—it's both pretty and good.

The men always look disappointed when they first taste it, but that makes no difference. This is a world of disappointments anyway, and one more won't matter.

How many of you like persimmon beer with a nice juicy sweet potato? When making the beer don't forget to add a few locusts, if you can get them, and note the difference.

A Cool Summer Drink

Raspberry Vinegar—Put three quarts of ripe raspberries into an earthen bowl; pour over them a quart of vinegar; at the end of twenty-four hours press and strain out the liquor and turn it over another three quarts of fresh, ripe berries. Let it stand another twenty-four hours; again express and strain the juice and to each pint add a pound of sugar, and boil for twenty minutes. Turn it into bottles and cork when cold. When used dilute the raspberry vinegar with three parts of water.

Home Made Flavoring Extracts and Food Colorings

Not only is it a matter of economy to make, at home, the flavoring extracts one uses in the kitchen, but it is also possible, in this way, to be quite sure of their purity.

Coloring matters especially should be made at home because it is the only way to be quite sure they are harmless.

Lemon extract is made by grating off the yellow rind of a lemon, using great care to reject every bit of the white, which is very bitter.

Put the grated rind into a bottle and cover it with alcohol. Cork tightly, and set away for three weeks, when it will be found ready for use. To make the extract extra strong, drain the alcohol from the rind after three weeks, and pour it over freshly grated peel, rejecting the first rind; cork tightly as before and after a few weeks, strain from the grated rind and use like any lemon extract.

Vanilla extract is more expensive to make than the others, but it is also much more difficult to purchase pure vanilla flavoring; a very little of the home made flavoring will flavor a pudding, cake, or a freezer of cream, and when it is once used, one soon sees the advantage in making it at home.

Purchase of a druggist, one fourth of an ounce of vanilla beans, one-half ounce of tanka beans, and one-half pint of alcohol; boil and cool one-half pint of clear water, and put it, with other ingredients, into a bottle and it is ready for use. Use only a little at first until, by using it, one finds out just how much should be used.

The different coloring matters are very simple, and nothing adds more to the Sunday evening tea table than a cake with frosting delicately tinted.

By bruising the leaves of spinach, it is possible to secure a pretty shade of green which can be pale or deep green, as seems desirable, by adding more or less of the juice, from the spinach leaves. The leaves can be placed on a plate, and squeezed with the potato masher, the juice being allowed to run off into a spoon as fast as it gathers. Pistachio, or almond flavoring are suitable for green icing, but one can use anything there is at hand for flavoring.

A delicate rose pink can be secured by using the juice of fresh or canned red currants. Rose flavoring is appropriate for pink icing, and if a child's birthday chances to come in the time of roses, lay a rose on the cake, as it is placed on the table, or adorn the cake and plate with as many pretty buds (previously washed and examined for insects), as there are years in the child's age.

The Joys of a Country Meeting

"Lay by Time"

Lay-by time! Ah, what a host of memories the words recall. Seining parties, melons and grapes and peaches; nights of brilliant moon-light and love-light; days of visiting and day-dreaming; thrumming of an old banjo, the rollicking song of the violin and the amorous strains of the wooing guitar! "And the boys, the stalwart boys, who are in love from the cradle up;" merry mocking maidens, manly men, and matrons, grandfathers and grandmothers—all join in the carnival of rest, at lay-by time.

Boys and girls and babies revel in the glad midsummer dream. The honeysuckles twine around the old homestead door, perfuming all the air in honor of the festival of leisure. The sunflowers gleam like fabled crowns of gold, in the

simmering August sunshine. The bluejays and woodpeckers are at leisure, too, and make the landscape flash with their joyful wings. At night the whippoorwill calls out in plaintive love, as if some needed task were left undone.

Camp-meetings are an institution of lay-by time, when all the toilers cease, and meet together to praise the Lord of the harvest. It is the Beulah Land for lovers, this old camp ground. Up with the lark, out in the sparkling dew at sunrise, go to the morning prayer. A country girl in pink calico is the most beautiful thing that earth has ever possessed. And the long buggy rides between sermons! How much can be said in the silent forest drives?

SUMMER LIFE IN THE COUNTRY.

Going Swimming

The choicest stream for the purpose is one that has wound its way through the filter of the sandhills, having its head at a shady spring with white sand dancing at its bottom, and coming clear and swift and cool into the flat loam lands. It should not be more than thirty yards wide, so that the afternoon shadows may extend across it; it should have a gravel bed; it should be crooked and capricious, so as to challenge the swimmer for something of a tussle; on its farther side flags and rushes should wade out knee-deep and stand there in a green line: above these flags and rushes should hang thick black-gum boughs whereon should ripple and shimmer the water-lights. The spring-board ought to be at the head of a bluff, just below a dark eddy with bugs and spiders on its surface and a wasp nest barely out of the way of high water.

I say, at a bluff. For complete enjoyment, swimmers ought not to have to sqush through mud to reach the place and then hang their shirts and trousers on ironwood bushes. They must go to a bluff, where they can throw their clothes on good green grass and make a clean run for the jump. Now give seventy-five yards of straight stream below the spring-board, before you get to the bonnets and trailing water-grasses at the next bend, and I'm with you at that place every day in the summer, except dog days.

So much for the place. The best time is laying-by time. Peaches and apples are ripe; watermelons and— but let the cider pass. If I were to mention it, though, I might say that a good gourd of it smacks right fine. After you get your siesta and wake up to meditate upon the delicious truth that there is not a thing to do, you go out on the front porch, blow your fist for the neighbors and their dogs, and set out through the tasseling corn for the creek.

We boys used to think it fine fun to go a mile or so up stream and set

some old log adrift and ride her down to the landing. This is the greatest breeder of trickery in the world. When your prospective circus-rider stands up on the log and begins to walk it, be sure that some one will snatch it from under him: and, once dislodged, he must overcome the combined resistance of his companions to crawl back upon it. I have laughed and shouted enough on these excursions to balance a sea of tears. Yet it is rather dangerous because of lurking snags. Many a time, since growing old and sober, have I been thankful that my lungs and liver are still safe within my hide.

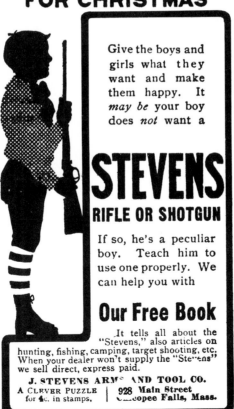

Fishing

A shady stream that is crooked; a boat of some kind; a gourd of bait; a line and pole of the same length, fitted with jack-hook, jug-cork, and two buckshot,—and there is nothing else, except a square of tobacco, low water, and an early start, that any angler can desire. Human companionship is not necessary.

Just before the conquering sun gets his knee upon the eastern wall and begins to shower his arrows athwart the world, you seat yourself in the tail-end of your skiff and shove off. You make a bend and there, with mellow-bugs swimming upon it, shade all across it, a dark tract in the middle where the lily-pads give out,—there is your trout pool. Ah, it looks good! You drift past it on the opposite side and then cautiously turn your boat's nose across and upstream, stealthily making your way within casting distance.

You gather a handful of long lily-stems and sit on them as an anchor. You take a good chew of tobacco. You cast your eye about for copperheads. Thunder! What's the hurry? You have got all the time there is. There is plenty of time on the river.

If a woman can mount a horse and ride away over hill and dale, she can defy time and trouble. There is nothing equal to it! Motoring? No! The best automobile is a dead thing (built for lazy people), even though at times it can respond in an almost life-like, intelligent way. But a good horse—friend and companion who can be tried and trusted—ah! The delight of a ride upon such an animal is indescribable!

In the fall, visiting is a delight to the men of the family. In winter when they must be shut up a whole day with "the women folks," they are apt to regard visiting as a nuisance, but when they can wander over fields and woods looking at livestock and exchanging ideas about farming, it is a different story. The warmth of the sun lures even the women out of doors, and a long afternoon spent in the mellow sunlight under the trees is an experience long to be remembered.

The good old fashion of taking a roll of sewing or fancy work along when visiting is being revived, and there is nothing that so adds to the happiness of any woman as to be the first in the neighborhood to bring out a new quilt or bit of drawn work. Talk about the dreariness of country life! Did you ever see a little group of women under a tree or on a porch intent on some new pattern in lace or patch work? If you did, you know that the country has charms city people never dream of. A chicken dinner, congenial friends, light work and merry conversation make up the sum of living when country people go visiting. Could any one ask more? Harmless gossip, neighborhood news, patterns and recipes are all exchanged before the horses are brought out for the homeward

Thanksgiving in the Nursery.

Oh, for an hour in that dear place!
Oh, for the peace of that dear time!
Oh, for that childish trust sublime!
Oh, for a glimpse of mother's face!
—*Eugene Field.*

trip, and hostess and guests are alike profited.

It does most women a great deal of good to get away from home as often as possible. The majority of them go home thinking their children a great deal better than the children of their neighbors, and their homes far superior in every way to the homes they visit. The little deficiencies they may have fretted over in the past all disappear, and they are sure no house, no children and no husband can compare with their own precious possessions.

The Lawn Swing—Get One for Your Family

One of the most satisfactory and comfortable seats for the home yard is the lawn swing, now so common in both country and city. We know of no contrivance giving more pure enjoyment and rest during the hot summer months, than one of these swings, located underneath a large shade tree in one's door yard. More pleasure can be gotten for the nominal outlay in money for this swing than from almost any other piece of furniture ever devised.

Only those who possess the swings and have used them for several seasons can really appreciate them.

The tired wife and mother on the farm can profitably spend an hour or two each day when her work is done, upon this gently vibrating swing chair and return to her household duties rested and refreshed.

The noon-day rest hour of the farmer and his sons can be also made far more enjoyable when one of these swings is at hand. Then, too, the children will come in for their share of the enjoyment, and many an hour will be spent by them in swaying back and forth in the old lawn swing.

Entertainments for Outdoors and Indoors

Campfire entertainments for the moonlight nights of the autumn are always enjoyable. I remember a "corn roast" that was given with great success. The green corn in the shuck was roasted in a huge campfire, and with a generous supply of sandwiches furnished the refreshments for the evening. Later sitting about the great campfire, each guest was requested to tell his favorite story. A small prize was offered for the best tale. Fish roasts or melon parties could be easily carried out in the same manner.

Hallowe'en

No more attractive place can be found at a country home for indulging in Hallowe'en sports than a new barn or other out-building decorated profusely with autumn leaves, boughs of evergreen and jack o'lanterns.

Now for the sports: all should relate in some way to the mysterious future, for to-night one has a lurking idea that what happens has some significance "sure enough." Three small bowls or saucers are placed on a table, one contains clear water, one soapy water, one empty. The girls, blindfolded, are led to the table with instructions to dip the left hand in one of the bowls: if in the empty bowl, no marriage at all; if in the soapy water a widower; if in the clear water a young bachelor. Then the boys have their turn: the empty bowl, no marriage; the soapy water, a widow; the clear water, a young girl.

Another pleasant form of amusement consists in a tub or large basin filled with water, upon which one tries his fortune by means of fairy boats. These boats are made from the half-shell of an English walnut in which a tiny taper has been fastened by its own wax. Make a wish, light the taper, then set the little boat sailing across the tub or bowl by lightly blowing against it. If the bark capsizes, or if the light goes out, the wish will not be granted, but if the boat reaches the other side of the basin without a mishap, or if the taper burns down entirely the wish will come true.

The Joys of a Country Meeting

Dear Aunt Mary: I am on a little pleasure trip to Statham. The lodge to which I belong (the Athena Rebekahs) were invited to visit Paradise lodge here, and of course we accepted. The people here are living examples of our much boasted Southern hospitality. Nobody seems a stranger; all were dear friends from the beginning. We met at Midway Chapel, a small Christian church, to which most of the people here belong, and we there had the pleasure of listening to several interesting speeches and fine recitatiors.

And the dinner—fried chicken by the peck, potato custards by the dozens, the most delicious varieties of cakes all iced, and each one a masterpiece, pickles of many kinds, egg custards and pies galore, fig preserves, tubs of lemonade, and an abundance of barbecued meats, with enough left after the feast for another spread.

Bevies of pretty girls were there, and handsome young fellows just reaching manhood. It was good to see their thorough enjoyment; stalwart young farmers were there, too, with their sweet little wives. And babies!—dear little wiggly, new babies on their first outing, the central attractions for the mothers and grandmothers. The little toddlers were there, too—the darling three-year-olds, just on the borderland of knowledge, getting their first memorable impressions.

Mark Twain As An Agricultural Editor

Mark Twain never really edited a farm paper, but he wrote a story, just the same, telling of an imaginary experience along this line.

The editor of the paper was sick and wanted a vacation. Mark agreed to fill his place while he took a rest, and the editor jumped at the offer.

Of course, being a humorist, the new editor had to be funny, so he handed out to his readers such valuable misinformation as this:

"Turnips should never be pulled; it injures them. It is much better to send a boy up and let him shake the tree."

"The guano is a fine bird, but great care is necessary in rearing it. It should not be imported earlier than June or later than September. In the winter it should be kept in a warm place, where it can hatch out its young."

"A CARICATURE, MARK TWAIN." BY DENYS WORTMAN, JR., AGE 16. (GOLD BADGE.)

"Concerning the pumpkin—This berry is a favorite with the natives of the interior of New England, who prefer it to the gooseberry for the making of fruit cake, and who likewise give it the preference over the raspberry for feeding cows, as being more filling and fully as satisfying. The pumpkin is the only esculent of the orange family that will thrive in the North, except the gourd and one or two varieties of the squash. But the custom of planting it in the front yard with the shrubbery is fast going out of vogue, for it is now generally conceded that the pumpkin as a shade tree is a failure."

Fancy Work

I see that at least one noted physician is prescribing fancy work as preventive and probable cure for nervous affections. By doing light fancy work the patients are led to think of other things than themselves and are greatly benefited.

Christmas Gifts of Home Manufacture

As you have time, help the small folks to make clothespin dollies to ornament the Christmas tree and gladden the hearts of the wee maidens who may receive them. If one person can mark the face more successfully than the rest, let the work be divided, one member of the group cutting out the Red Riding Hood cape and bonnet, while another sews on the straight piece that pasted together serves for a skirt, and the others sew and paste while the artist makes the face.

A serviceable pillow for lounge or chair seat can be made from old kid gloves. Cut squares from the back and wrist, and sew together checker board fashion.

There are so few things we can make for the men folks that they really appreciate. If we trouble to embroider a lounging robe, or even a smoking cap, they do not care to wear them, for we fail in some way to take them feel comfortable, I fear; although the dear fellows do not tell us that that is the reason they fail to wear them. A whisk broom is one of the most appropriate presents for a gentleman friend that you can possibly buy, unless it be a clothes brush, but the broom is cheaper and you can make such pretty covers for it. They may be fashioned of any material you prefer, but dark blue velvet embroidered in forget-me-nots makes an especially pretty cover. Collar and cuff boxes may be made at home, provided you are deft with your needle, and you can use your paint brush for a design on side and cover. Pen wipers prove a convenience for the friend who writes.

Now since veils are so much worn, another present for a fastidious friend is a veil case. Procure a

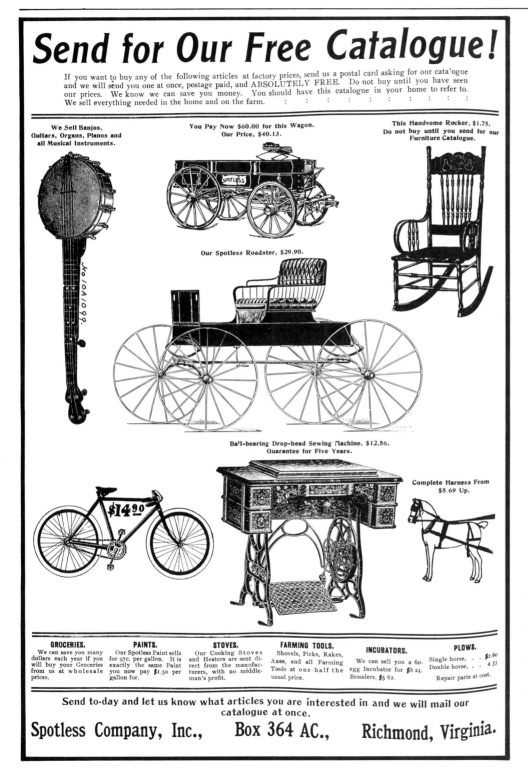
small round stick a half yard long: cover it with a thin roll of perfumed wadding. Cover with linen ornamented with embroidery or ribbon. Ribbons are placed at each end to tie the case.

An acceptable and inexpensive gift for a careful woman, young or old, traveller or stay-at-home, is a set of a dozen dress-wrappers. Get good quality cheese cloth. Cut it in lengths of a yard and a quarter. Feather-stitch a half-inch hem all around with bright-colored silk. Work initials in one corner in simple outline-stitch. These wrappers will be found most convenient for folding about dress-waists to be kept in drawers.

Not long ago I saw a comfortable bed shoe made of white wool, the entire shoe done in double crochet. The shoe was begun in the center of the sole, starting with a chain the length of the foot, and worked round and round, shaped like a foot, coming well up around the ankle, where it was secured by a crocheted cord and tassel. A gift of this kind would be thoroughly appreciated by an invalid. A pretty and attractive device is a crocheted cover of bright wool for a hot water bag. The one I saw had the initial done in contrasting color on the side. This would make an exceedingly attractive gift for the young girl away at boarding school.

The plain linen handkerchief may be adapted to many uses. An exceedingly dainty baby cap may be made from a single handerchief. Fold one edge back to form a finish about the face. Finish with

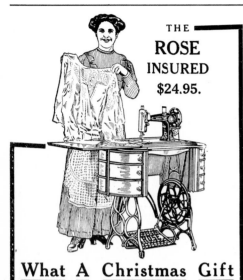

seam at the back of the head, al-lowing remaining two corners to fall at the back, and by means of buttonholed eyelets around the neck a ribbon is drawn which brings the cap into shape.

Three handkerchiefs will make a unique corset cover. Use one each for the front and back and a half for each under-arm piece. Join the pieces with insertion, gather in at the waist and finish the top with insertion, beading, and lace.

A Sofa Pillow

Dear Aunt Jennie—If the house-wife has not learned the art of fine embroidery, but wants a pretty pil-low cover, she may utilize her silk scraps for this purpose in making one of the biscuit covers now so popular. The pieces are cut in squares three inches each way, then there is a lining two inches square which is cut from calico or cambric. Each square of silk is basted to a thin lining, a box-pleat laid in the center of each side to make the edge the exact size of the cambric lining. Baste three sides, then, before basting the fourth, fill with cotton batting, baste down the edge and this will form a puff. Cut a lining as large as you want the pillow cover—a good size is to allow fifteen blocks each side. The blending of colors may be varied to please the maker's fancy, but where one has a variety of pieces, the best way to arrange them is like patchwork, al-ternating the light and dark colors. One can soon have enough filling for at least one pillow by saving the feathers when dressing a chicken or turkey. Dry the feathers and put them in a bag; then de-vote some idle hour to stripping these feathers, throwing away the quills and putting the down in an-other bag, and the feathers, mixed with small bits of cotton, make a good filling for sofa pillows.

Chest Protector

For the one who has to take long drives in the cold, a knitted chest protector will be appreciated. This may be made from the good parts of old woolen underwear; cut it the size you want, being sure to get it large enough so that it will come well over the chest and if the piece is large enough cut the neck part right with the other, then overcast or hem with a very fine hem and crochet a row or two of scallops around it. The neck part must be long enough so that there will be two or three thick-nesses of the goods over the neck and so it may be pulled well up over the chin. It is all open in the back, being fastened in the back at the neck with the snap fasteners that women use to fasten their dresses in the placquet hole. When it is all completed, color it some nice dark color, if it is not already dark enough, and it cannot be told from new, but will represent a lot of loving thought.

This kitchen of 1927 shows many of the tangible improvements the Progressive Farmer had been urging for a generation: an enamel-topped, easily-wiped table, an oil stove, and running water in the shining white sink. The illustrator produced also a sense of the intangible advantages—the airiness and tranquility—of the farm home.

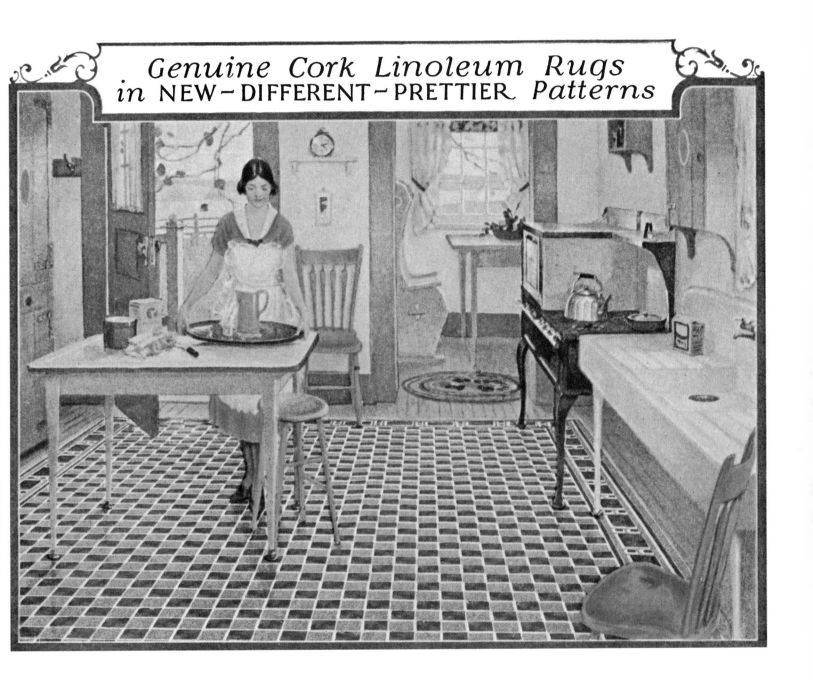

Genuine Cork Linoleum Rugs
in NEW - DIFFERENT - PRETTIER *Patterns*

—and Baking Powder does the rest

CALUMET
THE WORLD'S GREATEST
BAKING POWDER

Profit by the experience of others and use the leavener that has given unfailing and economical satisfaction for thirty-five years.

Bakings made with Calumet are uniform, sweet and wholesome. Use it for your children's sake because perfectly raised bakings are easily digested—and that means health.

There is no Substitute for Calumet

EVERY INGREDIENT USED OFFICIALLY APPROVED BY U. S. FOOD AUTHORITIES

SALES 2½ TIMES THOSE OF ANY OTHER BRAND

A Few Home Remedies

Remedy for Poison Ivy

A far better remedy than sugar of lead for poisoning by "poison oak" is the juice of the Impatiens fulva, commonly known as "lady's slipper," "touch-me-not," "snap weed," "silver leaf," etc. The plant grows along the banks of streams, or in very wet places, is from 2 to 4 feet high, stem almost translucent with very large joints, delicate pale green leaves which look silvery on the underside when put in water, small yellow flowers, seed pod snaps when touched, throwing the ripe seed several feet.

To use, mash the stem and leaves and apply the mass to the poisoned spot. There will be little or no smarting. May be applied to the face without danger to the eyes. Two applications of 3 to 12 hours each usually cures the worst cases.

It will also cure snake bites, if applied to the wound. I have cured two cases of moccasin bites on horses with it. Also cures spider and bee stings.

A Bite From a Mad-Dog

If, unfortunately, it should chance that any one is bitten by a dog that is said to be mad, it is

---

Baking powder was one of the earliest cooking aids. The 1924 ad shown here indicates that Calumet Baking Powder had been in production since 1889. Surely in 1889, and apparently in 1924, as now, children were eager for the results.

worth while to chain the animal up, instead of shooting it instantly; for if it should turn out that it is not mad and a false alarm is frequently raised—the relief to the minds of all concerned in indescribable.

A Scratch From a Cat

A scratch from a cat is sometimes not only painful, but difficult to heal. When this is the case the limb should be bathed with a hot fomentation of camomile and poppy heads, and a hot bread-and-water poultice applied, to be renewed with the bathing every few hours.

Grazing of the Skin

If the skin is raised, wet it, and put it in its place. Cover it with the thin skin taken from the inside of an egg, a little goldbeater's skin, a cob-web or a piece of thin silk dipped in oil. Tie a piece of tape or ribbon round it, and leave it undisturbed for two or three days.

Have you caught cold?

At night get a good stiff brush, a horse brush if you can get nothing better, and curry yourself thoroughly, just as you would curry the horses, then dash cold water over yourself, rub, and go to bed.

Helpful Hints

Camphor put in drawers or trunks will keep away mice.

Rub hinges with a feather dipped in oil, and they will not creak.

SICK MADE WELL WEAK MADE STRONG.

MARVELOUS ELIXIR OF LIFE DISCOVERED BY FAMOUS DOCTOR-SCIENTIST THAT CURES EVERY KNOWN AILMENT.

Wonderful Cures Are Effected That Seem Like Miracles Performed—The Secret of Long Life of Olden Times Revived.

The Remedy Is Free to All Who Send Name And Address.

After years of patient study, and delving into the dusty record of the past, as well as following modern experiments in the realms of medical science, Dr. James W. Kidd, 100 Baltes building, Fort Wayne, Ind., makes the startling an-

DR. JAMES WILLIAM KIDD.

nouncement that he has surely discovered the elixir of life. That he is able with the aid of a mysterious compound, known only to himself, produced as a result of the years he has spent in searching for this precious life-giving boon, to cure any and every disease that is known to the human body. There is no doubt of the doctor's earnestness in making his claim and the remarkable cures that he is daily effecting seems to bear him out very strongly. His theory which he advances is one of reason and based on sound experience in a medical practice of many years. It costs nothing to try his remarkable "Elixir of Life," as he calls it, for he sends it free, to anyone who is a sufferer, in sufficient quantities to convince of its ability to cure, so there is absolutely no risk to run. Some of the cures cited are very remarkable, and but for reliable witnesses would hardly be credited. The lame have thrown away crutches and walked about after two or three trials of the remedy. The sick, given up by home doctors, have been restored to their families and friends in perfect health. Rheumatism, neuralgia, stomach, heart, liver, kidney, blood and skin diseases and bladder troubles disappear as by magic. Headaches, backaches, nervousness, fevers, consumption, coughs, colds, asthma, catarrh, bronchitis and all affections of the throat, lungs or any vital organs are easily overcome in a space of time that is simply marvelous.

Partial paralysis, locomotor ataxia, dropsy, gout, scrofula and piles are quickly and permanently removed. It purifies the entire system, blood and tissues, restores normal nerve power, circulation and a state of perfect health is produced at once. To the doctor all systems are alike and equally affected by this great "Elixir of Life." Send for the remedy to-day. It is free to every sufferer. State what you want to be cured of and the sure remedy for it will be sent you free by return mail.

A small bag of sulphur kept in a drawer or cupboard will drive away red ants.

Boil three or four onions in a pint of water, apply with a soft brush to gilt frames, and flies will keep off them.

A spoonful of vinegar put into the water in which meats or fowls are boiled makes them tender.

Equal parts of ammonia and spirits of turpentine will take paint out of clothing, no matter how dry or hard the paint may be. Saturate the spot two or three times, then wash out in soap-suds.

A little charcoal mixed with clear water thrown into a sink will disinfect and deodorize it.

The odor of sweet-peas is so offensive to flies that it will drive them out of a sick room.

Dear Aunt Mary: Silver may be easily and nicely cleaned by rubbing it with a piece of Irish potato dipped in common baking soda.

A cheap furniture polish that will keep tables, etc., in good condition can be made of equal parts of spirits of turpentine and olive oil. Apply with a piece of flannel, afterwards polishing with a dry cloth.

Safe method of fastening on loose lamp tops: Mix plaster of Paris into a soft mass with warm water and put on quickly before it hardens.

A cheap cement for mending stoves, stopping rat holes, etc., can be made by mixing equal parts of nice red clay, sifted ashes, and salt. Stir together well, mix up soft, and apply smoothly.

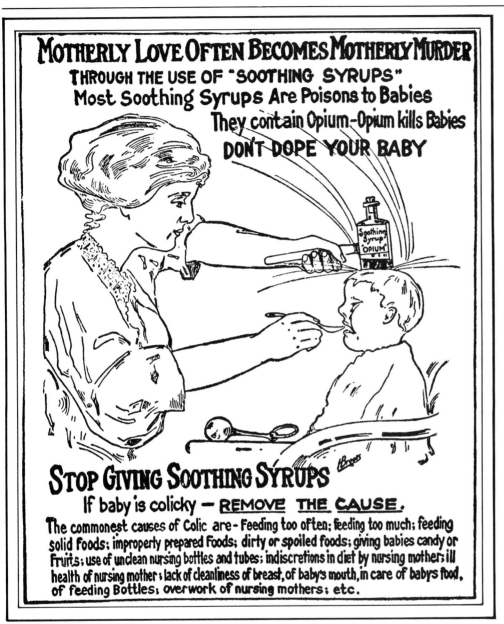

MOTHERLY LOVE OFTEN BECOMES MOTHERLY MURDER

THROUGH THE USE OF "SOOTHING SYRUPS"
Most Soothing Syrups Are Poisons to Babies
They contain Opium – Opium kills Babies
DON'T DOPE YOUR BABY

STOP GIVING SOOTHING SYRUPS
If baby is colicky – REMOVE THE CAUSE.
The commonest causes of Colic are – Feeding too often; feeding too much; feeding solid foods; improperly prepared foods; dirty or spoiled foods; giving babies candy or fruits; use of unclean nursing bottles and tubes; indiscretions in diet by nursing mother; ill health of nursing mother; lack of cleanliness of breast, of baby's mouth, in care of baby's food, of feeding Bottles; overwork of nursing mothers; etc.

The Long Promise: Science in the Home

The farm home, at the beginning of our century, may seem to us almost as natural as its setting. It seems almost as if, amid the grass and trees, a farmhouse had sprouted with inhabitants and a cycle as natural as that of a rabbit and its burrow. We may wonder if the inhabitants of the farm home themselves did not feel governed (such was their constant contact with nature and their lack of control over it) by natural law as immutable as the setting of the sun. Certainly most of the solutions they offered to problems involved primarily changing themselves, rather than changing the environment, as if the environment were a given. Thus, a solution to a long walk to the well was not to shorten the walk but to have a cheerful spirit. As one woman wrote: "In reviewing the long years of labor . . . I am convinced that the one thing that saved me from total wreck and ruin was that I did not look upon my work as drudgery."

The feeling that life is all a piece, fore-ordained and immutable, is as foreign to us today, as our many-facetted lives would be to our grandparents. Far from being whole and unchangeable, our life, we may feel, is the opposite. It has too many pieces which are changing too fast for us. Unlike our grandparents, we are accustomed to seeing our lives in terms of their external pieces; sometimes

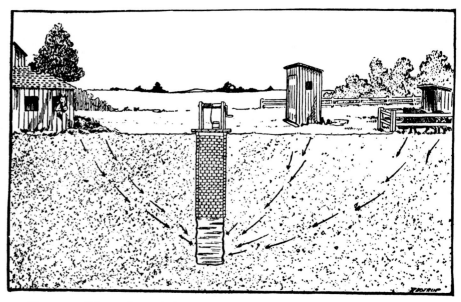

HOW IS YOUR WATER SUPPLY?

If your well is so situated that you get the seepage from stables and other polluted places, do not blame the Almighty when members of your family get sick. Either move your well or move the centers of pollution.

it may even seem as if the puzzle does not fit together—as if there were no internal organization—no force (human or divine) on the inside. To discover what we are all about we examine the parts of our lives. We read articles about them. We watch TV programs about them. We take surveys to determine what "we" think about them. We examine our political lives, our economic, religious, social, marital and sexual lives—our physical, mental and moral lives—our lives as parents, students, bread-winners, food—and—goods consumers, TV watchers, etc. This very examination would seem to point to our belief that, if labelled and studied, parts of our lives can be changed if we exert some external force upon

them. And to the belief that we have some chance and also some responsibility to change them.

The difference between our attitude of locating the cause of the problem and finding an external solution to it, and the farmer's wife seeing her walk to the well as part of an immutable whole and trying to find an internal solution, has a great deal to do with the growth of science in our lives. Though there was no cut-off point at which one attitude turned into the other, we find in the *Progressive Farmer*, beginning about 1912, a burgeoning of scientific articles and charts to help in locating problems and finding external solutions to them. For several years, science had been offering improved implements and methods to the farmer. Now science was poking into others facets of farm life. It had discovered a way to make voices and light travel on wires and a machine to suck up dust. It was discovering germs and their relation to illness and sanitary conditions.

Was illness, then, not a punishment for sin but rather a punishment for ignorance? Correction of sin was a chancy business and difficult to lay hold on. Sympathy toward the afflicted might be the only decent course. But ignorance could be rectified by known rules, if only one could find them. The *Progressive Farmer* set about finding the rules and disseminating them. When illness appeared, it insisted, "instead of laying it all on the Lord . . . look into the drain pipes, the cellars and back yards, and find where the germs come from." Submission (a trait in which the farmer's wife had been trained) to immutable forces (either human or divine) was suddenly inexcusable. The farmer's wife should no longer "bear and forbear." Now that it had been proven possible to act in favor of one's destiny, the farmer's wife was expected to do so and culpable if she did not.

But the farmer's wife had had very little training in action on her own behalf. Her training had all been in submission to others' needs. To change her—and even more difficult, her husband's—life habits must often have seemed a challenge greater than wrestling with sins. And yet, as she realized

ANTY DRUDGE

Mrs. Corntassel: "Oh, dear! Just look at this! And smell it! John caught a skunk in the hen house last night—and his shirt and trousers are ruined. He didn't know what it was in the dark. I'll *never* get the smell out."

Anty Drudge: "Well—I don't know. That's one thing I've never meddled with. But if anything will bring out both stain and smell, it's Fels-Naptha Soap. Let's try it, anyway. I see you have a box. That's right. I always tell everybody to keep plenty on hand."

that "instead of laying it all on the Lord," science had given her weapons to use in favor of her children's health, Science itself must have seemed a god. But it was a god of light and compassion, sweeping out the old guilts and fears as an electric light swept a

room of shadow. With what zeal many determined to learn the new rules is shown by requests sent to *Progressive Farmer.*

But for personal contact and moral support, another aid appeared—women's clubs. Women's clubs multiplied rapidly during this time, filling both the need for knowledge and for moral support. At club meetings women could learn what action to take to get rid of flies, to plan nutritious meals, etc. And perhaps most important of all, they could exchange their feelings and needs, their hopes and fears with, not just relatives, but peers. Accustomed as we are to having been members, since our early school days, of organizations to fit our every interest, it is hard for us to imagine the impact of women's clubs. Here is one woman's experience:

From Christmas to our meeting (July 15) I had not been off our farm . . . One day a neighbor about a mile away came and brought me a piece about cheap and pretty curtains and told me to practice it for I was to read it the next week at the meeting. I said I could not, but she came for me, as she has a horse for herself, and carried me there. When I went to read I just broke down and cried and all the rest cried with me, and they petted me and told me I was brave just to try. Mrs. —— coaxed me to try again and I did and read it right to the end. When I was young I used to recite so next time I am going to recite 'The Curfew Shall Not Ring Tonight.'

Southern farm people were beginning to feel some control of their personal destinies. In 1912

the South got a chance, in the person of Woodrow Wilson, to control the destiny of the country. The *Progressive Farmer* was jubilant, for it was "the first time in more than sixty years (that) the United States has elected President a man born south of Mason and Dixon's line." Other factors also were expected to lead to a new blooming of the South, chief among them being the imminent opening of the Panama Canal, "probably the most important change in the physical earth since the Almighty finished the work of creation." The *Progressive Farmer* predicted

a shifting of the world's trade currents, and the South being nearest to the Canal, should profit mostly largely by it. Railroads that have heretofore run east and west—from San Francisco to Chicago and St. Louis and from St. Louis and Chicago to New York, Philadelphia and Boston—these will begin to turn more and more toward Galveston and New Orleans and Mobile and Savannah and Charleston . . .

The editorial concluded:

Splendid, indeed, is the opportunity ahead of the South. It would seem to lack but one thing to become one of the most interesting and promising sections of the whole world—the thorough education of its people . . .

This education, with the changes it would bring, the *Progressive Farmer* had, since its inception, been urging upon its readers, in line with its definition of conservatism: "the advocacy of things and measures we are certain are practicable, economical and useful."

"The Woman's Betterment"

A Club of Genuine Usefulness

Our regular day is Friday, as that was the most convenient for the majority. The first Friday we each take our fancy work, spend the time in talking, perhaps have a bit of music, and each member is expected to contribute some little item for the general good—that is, on household matters, or some way of making the work easier. For instance, in the spring it may be about housecleaning; in the summer, on canning; or before Christmas, something on making articles suitable for presents. It is wonderful, too, the many helps each of us get this way.

The next week is our literary meeting. Each member is responsible for one day's program in the year. And every member is supposed to take some part, no matter how small. This gives each woman a chance to have the subject she is most interested in.

Each member is entitled to one afternoon's work from the other eleven; that is, one meeting each month we help each other. Generally we plan it to have the one who is to have the work done entertain the club that day. Sometimes we do button-holes, sometimes plain sewing; once we cut and sewed silk rags for curtains; and since the craze for rag rugs has come in, we have more of this work than anything else.

Our last meeting for the month is for charity. At this time we each bring with us whatever clothing we can spare that can be fixed over and used, to help others. We cut over stockings, make over garments of all kinds and in this way really get a great deal to give away. Our president has a large trunk into which all these garments are put and are given away as needed. Any left at the end of the year go to the Salvation Army.

We co-operate, too, on a small scale. Each of us takes a magazine. On these we get club rates and they range in price and character to suit the subscriber's taste and purse. These we pass around. We also bought a large-size ice cream freezer and a vacuum cleaner (a hand-power). These we each use in turn, and so far we have planned it so there have been no clashes, but harmony in their use.

Here is a man who makes the delicious remark that he does not believe in women going to meetings because they always come home and want to change things.

Put Your Money In The Bank

There Are Two Classes of People: Those Who Keep Their Money In A Bank and Those Who Do Not.

We women are queer folks in money matters. We might be divided into two classes. Some of us, the majority perhaps, take their chicken, their garden, egg and honey money and tuck a little here and hide a little there. A few pennies are taken out for one thing or another, and the agent sometimes tempts the rest of it to our sorrow.

The wise ones of us take the money we earn, and keep out ten cents for Maggie's hair ribbon, five cents for beet seed, six cents for a spool of white thread number sixty, the four pennies being saved for the children's Sunday school collection, perhaps twenty more for the moving pictures, and then we put the rest in the bank where it is safe and sound. The house may burn; but it is unchanged; agents may come and agents may go, but it remains inviolate.

Why do not more of us put our money in the bank? Because we are scared, just plain scared. We do not know just how to put money in the bank. Who are we that we should walk in a great door, go up to a strange man in a cage and say, "Will you take care of my money until I want it?" even if the sign on the window does say "Bank?" This may sound silly but anyone who has yet to de-

Agricultural Building

The Clemson Agricultural College

South Carolina's School of Engineering and Agriculture.

One of the largest and best equipped Agricultural and Mechanical Colleges in the South. 1,544 Acres of land. Value of plant over $1,300,000. Over 90 teachers, officers and assistants. Enrollment, 834. Every county in South Carolina represented. 12 Degree courses. 4 short courses. 26 Departments of instruction. New and modern buildings, equipment and sanitation. Over $100,000 expended in public service.

Location and Environment.

The College is located in Oconee County at the foot of the Blue Ridge Mountains, on the homestead of Jno. C. Calhoun and later of his son-in-law, Thos. G. Clemson. The College is over 800 feet above the sea-level and the climate is healthful and invigorating. Temptations to dissipate or to spend money foolishly are reduced to a minimum.

The students are under military government and every effort is made to train up manly young men who will reflect credit on the College and on the State.

Religious Influences.

The College contributes to the salary of four resident ministers who conduct divine services and do pastorial work at churches and among the cadets in barracks. There

with a salaried Y. M. C. A. Secretary, who lives in the barracks.

Requirements of Admission.

No student will be admitted to the Freshman Class who is not at least 16 years old at the time of entrance.

An honorable discharge from the last school or college attended is required.

The College no longer maintains a preparatory class.

Student Activities.

Clemson College is a member of the Southern Inter-Collegiate Athletic Association and the South Carolina Inter-Collegiate Association and engages in inter-collegiate baseball, football, track, tennis, basket ball, has three literary societies, four student publications, a cadet band, a course of lyceum lectures and entertainments, etc., etc.

Scholarships and Examinations.

The College maintains 168 four year scholarships in the Agricultural and Textile Courses, and 51 in the One Year Agricultural Course (October 1st to June 1st.) Each scholarship is worth $100 and free tuition.

Scholarship and entrance examinations are held at the county court houses at 9 A. M. July 10. Write for full information in regard to the scholarships open to your county next session, and the laws governing their award. It is worth your while to try for one of these scholarships.

Those who are not seeking to enter on scholarships are advised to stand examinations on July 10 rather than wait until they come to College in the fall. Credit will be given for any examination passed at the county seat.

is a flourishing Sunday School and Y. M. C. A.

Financial Support.

The College is founded on a covenant with the agricultural people. Back in the 80's the advocates of Agricultural and Industrial Education promised that if given the tax of 25c per ton on the commercial fertilizers sold in the State, the Trustees would organize not only an efficient system of inspection and analysis to protect the farmers from imposition in the purchase of their main commodity, but with what remained after paying the cost of this protection, would build and operate a College. During the history of the College, the tag tax has averaged $110,247.62 For the past three fiscal years it has averaged $238,958.02. The Legislature of South Carolina makes no appropriation for the support of Clemson College.

In addition to the fertilizer tax, the College receives from the Federal Treasurer $25,000 annually, and a small amount comes from tuition and interest on the Clemson and Landscript Funds. The South Carolina Experiment Station is supported entirely by funds from the U. S. Department of Agriculture, and has no part in the College work.

Courses of Study.

Agriculture, (7 Courses), Chemistry, Mechanical and Electrical Engineering, Civil Engineering, Textile Engineering, Architectural Engineering.

Four-Weeks Course in Agriculture.
Four-Weeks Course in Cotton Grading.
Two-Year Course in Textiles.
One-Year Course in Agriculture.

COST.

The cost for any of the twelve regular four-year courses or the Two-Year Textile course is $133.40 per session. This amount covers uniforms, board, room, heat, light, water, laundry and all fees except tuition. **Tuition is $40.00 additional to those who are able to pay.**

The cost of the One-year Agricultural Course is $117.95. This amount covers the same items as are listed above.

Clemson's Public Service.

Out of the fertilizer tax only about $130,000 is expended upon the College. Nearly $100,000 annually represents the cost of public service rendered to the farmers. This public work includes not only the fertilizer inspection and analysis, but veterinary and entomological inspection, cattle tick and hog cholera eradication. Branch Experiment Stations, scholarships, co-operative experiments, Extension and Demonstration Work, etc. The College writes nearly 85,000 letters every year giving specific information, and sends out nearly half a million bulletins and circulars.

A higher standard for commercial fertilizers is maintained in South Carolina than in any other Southern State. The inspection and analysis carried on by the College insures the attainment of this standard. The farmer, even if he and not the manufacturer pays the tax of 25c per ton, gets value received many times over in the increased value of his fertilizers. In addition, a great Agricultural and Mechanical College has been built up worth over a million and a third dollars, enrolling annually nearly 850 young men, and demanding no appropriations from the State Treasury for its support.

Next Session Opens September 9, 1914.

Write at once to W. M. RIGGS, President

Box P Clemson College, S. C., for Catalog, Scholarship Blanks, etc. If you delay, you may be crowded out.

---

posit her first money and write her first check knows it is not. I remember full well my first experience.

The Girl Who Must Make Her Own Living: Stenography

For the one who would rise to the top of the profession, the first great fundamental is keenness of perception. For this there must be a certain amount of native ability, to be sure, but, far more important, is a sane and sensible method of living. The girl who wants a clear mind must sleep with her windows open, take her daily bath, avoid greasy and indigestible foods, use tea, coffee, and other stimulants with great circumspection, and go to bed early, conserving both eyesight and strength.

Knowledge:—The second requirement is a clear knowledge of the fundamental principles of rhetoric and composition. An intimate acquaintance with Browning, however delightful, is not as necessary to the stenographer as the knowledge of when to use "will" and "shall," "was" and "were," a comma or a semi-colon, "principal" or "principle."

She should be a quick but careful worker, and at all times train herself to greater speed and carefulness in details. So also should she train her powers of concentration; nothing is more irritating to a high-strung, nervous employer than seeming indifference in looking out of the window or observing the clock. No time-server ever yet gave satisfactory service.

She should endeavor to free herself of mannerisms, whether it be tapping her finger, scratching with her pencil, arranging her hair, chewing gum or toying with the edges of the leaves of her note book. These may seem trivial things, but they go far towards making the difference between the $5 and the $50-a-week salary.

Personal Appearance:—Another point to which young people are apt to give small care is the question of dress and deportment. The type of employer who wishes to be charmed is the employer whom the young girl should avoid. She should remember that she is now a business woman, that her dress should be plain, her hair neat, her hands clean and sensible, in bearing she should be quiet and dignified, never laughing or speaking loud, never chewing gum or making a box of candy conspicuous. Neither should she permit young men or girl friends to call her up during office hours. In short, she should remember that she is an intelligent piece of office furniture, and as such, should be efficient and inconspicuous, and that she can achieve this best by modesty and an attempt to sink her personality in that of her employer.

Remuneration

Unless she be unusually bright, her first position will doubtless come through the business college and will pay her from $5 to $10 a week. If she have the requirements of a good stenographer and live up to them, her pay will rapidly advance to $10 a week. If her speed be great, she may become a court stenographer at $150 a month. If

she be faithful and efficient, and find a position as secretary with an appreciative employer, she may obtain $200 a month as secretary. Nowhere is there a position where one's pay is more closely identified with the quality of work given.

The Girl Who Must Earn Her Own Living: Teaching School

The Less Attractive Features to be considered in selecting teaching as a profession are that it is very

trying to the nerves; if the position be in the country districts, she has little choice of boarding place; the teacher frequently has to walk long distances; the school rooms are cold and lonely; she has much planning to do, many papers to correct, much thought to be given to matters indirectly connected with school life; the school may be lacking in all that is attractive, internally and externally; she may have little help from trustees or parents; she has no good library; can teach but a limited number of weeks a year; must teach several different grades, and do them all well.

The country teacher frequently starts in as low as $40 a month, for a limited number of months, but she may rise to school principal, or on up through to county superintendent. There are a few cases in Southern states where the pay is as much as $2,500 a year.

Provide a Convenient Kitchen for the Good Wife

AFTER she began her recent "model kitchen" contest we prevailed on Mrs. Hutt to have some photographs of her own kitchen made, believing they would be interesting to all our women readers. about it is that the cost of properly equipping the kitchen is so very little as compared with the cost of properly equipping the farm. A good range will not cost much—unless you buy it from a traveling agent—

A CONVENIENTLY ARRANGED KITCHEN—MRS. HUTT'S (SEE ARTICLE ON PAGE 14)

One view of her kitchen we are presenting herewith, while another photograph taken to the right of this view is given on page 15. It is easy to see that not many steps are wasted in this kitchen. Part of the range is to be seen on the extreme left, then the sink is right at it, and then right at the sink is the work-table with every needed cooking utensil or convenience handily in its place above or below.

As will be seen from our editorial, "Practical Southern Chivalry" (which we had written before this photograph came in), The Progressive Farmer is just as anxious to get good equipment for Mrs. Farmer and the girls as for Mr. Farmer and the boys. And the fortunate part

and waterworks will cost much less than you probably think; while as for the score of little time and trouble-saving contrivances in this photograph, a few cents apiece will get most of them for your life-comrade and help-meet.

The Progressive Farmer believes in economy, as everybody knows, but we also believe that *there is no truer economy than that which saves the strength, health and happiness of the wife and mother.* See if you can't lighten her work and lighten her heart by making her kitchen a little more convenient.

Make you the kitchen the most convenient, attractive room in your home.

This kitchen will be one that is dear to the heart of stout women; nothing to stoop for, nothing to reach up for, and everything possible near and movable.

Why do I prefer the acetylene system?

1. Because it is the only artificial light that one can ascertain the exact color of fabrics as in daylight, making it the only substitute for daylight.

2. To light it requires no pumping to tanks. You are at no expense for mantles or globes, as the acetylene light is an open light.

3. I deem it the cheapest light on the market, as I have eight lamps, seven indoors and one porch light, and my average light bill is less than $1 per month.

4. It removes all the drudgery of lamp cleaning and filling, so dreaded by our wives and daughters.

5. My wife says she can see to do particular sewing and fancy work better after the lights are lighted.

How It Helps The Farm Woman

This Engine Turns the Washing Machine and Saws the Wood at the Same Time; Also Is of Untold Joy to the Kiddies

First, the gasoline engine pumps water to kitchen and bathroom, saws all stove and house wood, runs the corn sheller, turns the

washing machine. We have used two belts and washed and sawed wood at the same time. It runs the feeder to cut up all corn shocks for feed, and runs a corn and cob crusher. We use a hose to wash off the automobile and buggies, and it would churn, but we have six little children and they take the churning by turns. The engine also turns the rock grinder.

I think the gasoline engine is a great thing. Several years ago a man owed my husband some money. He had waterworks and was going to move away, so I told my husband to let us get his tank and bathtub and put in waterworks. He was anxious to get a car, but I said: "I had lots rather have waterworks than a car" (he has a motorcycle), so he went to getting cedar sills and built a high

tower and got the tank and bathtub, and now I have 60 gallons of hot water all the time, and a cold water pipe in the kitchen also, so all I have to do is just turn on all the cold and hot water I need.

The bath tub has been of untold joy to the kiddies. We've never paid out a cent for repairing waterworks, as my husband put them in himself. Any man could fix his wife running water if he would just know how easy it is.

How to Make a Fly Swatter

Buy some wire fly screening. Cut it in pieces five inches wide and eight and a half inches long. Bind the two sides and one end with black cloth. Next, fold over the two lower corners of the unbound end and secure this into a strong and slender, wooden handle, 10 inches long.

In making this handle your ingenuity will devise everything from soaked cedar with split ends to

combinations of rulers and tacks.

It is the finest thing in the world for swatting flies. There should be a nail in every room, on which is always found one or more of these swatters.

A Dish Drier

At last I have it! A dish washer? No, but the next to it—a dish-drier. Very simple; but I am proud of it for it is my own idea and works like a charm.

To make it I used a 25-pound lard can, in which I drove nail holes just as much as possible all over the bottom and several inches up on the sides, driving the nails from the inside out so that the rough surface would be on the outside.

In washing dishes I use two dish pans, placing the lard can in one of them and washing them in the other. The cups are washed first and turned down in the bottom of the can, then the plates, etc., are turned over on the top of these. As soon as the dishes are all in, a kettle of boiling water is poured into the can and of course runs on through, filling the dish pan. Then holding the handle of the can and sousing it up and down in the water every inch of the dishes is thoroughly washed. Now the can is lifted up and held a second or two until the water drains off, and in a few minutes every dish is as dry as a bone. The can is then taken to a safe and the dishes put away. Only one trip, you see.

I am 13 years old and I will tell how I wash for a family of ten. Mamma has a Greenville washer and wringer. We paid $2 for the washer. It works with a lever. It is so easy to wash that it is almost play. I put in from four to eight pieces at a time; rub five minutes in warm water and soap, take all through in this way twice, then boil and rinse and have as nice clothes as anybody with little labor. When dry I take all the sheets and underwear and press with the wringer. This saves lots of hot work.

I have twin baby brothers one year old, and a great grandpa 100 years old, and he is living with us. He was given a birthday dinner when he was 100, March 27, 1912.

Where Shall the Wedding Be?

Home Wedding
When I arrived I saw the minister standing in the bay window that had been transformed into a bower of beauty by a profusion of mountain laurel. Just as I entered the groom and his best man took their places before him, coming from a side room. In a moment four little girls in white came through the crowd of guests with white ribbons, marking off an aisle for the bride to pass through. As they stood still holding the ribbons, Lohengrin's

Wedding March began on the violin, and the bride came down the stairs on the arm of her father, passed up the aisle and stood before the minister. After the ceremony the bride and groom simply turned and received the congratulations of their friends.

Ice cream and cake were served in the dining room by the bride's young friends. Meanwhile the bride had gone upstairs to change her wedding dress for her going-away gown. As she came down the stairs she stopped and threw her bouquet into the group of girl friends below. The one who caught it really was the next bride as time proved.

They rushed to the carriage to find that the horses had been unhitched and the young men had taken their places. They were hauled to the new home, about a half a mile away, given three cheers and then promptly forgotten, while the young men rushed back with fun and laughter, each to seek the girl of his choice and beg her for another dish of ice cream.

—A Barn Wedding

Father said, "Now, Jeannie, we've lived in this neighborhood too long to split our friends in two and say, 'Some of you come, some stay away.'"

"But, father," protested the girl, "we just can't have everyone. We have no room and the crop has been poor."

The old man said nothing, but next morning announced a scheme that when carried out brought joy to many.

The wedding was at five o'clock in the afternoon on the broad porch, the friends for miles around filling the lawn. The barn was large and almost new. All the lanterns for miles around were borrowed so the barn was beautifully lighted. Old and young danced there—the Virginia Reel and every square dance they could remember. The music was the music that only a fiddle in the hands of one who knew the old tunes could produce. Those who did not care to dance found happiness walking or playing on the lawn or rocking on the porch. They ate bins of doughnuts, barrels of lemonade and bushels of pop-corn balls.

Hints That Will Help the Young Wife

Every man ever married had to be trained by his wife, just as every woman has to be trained by

her husband—unconsciously perhaps but still trained. Sometimes the year or so of adjustment is bad, sometimes not, but remember this, the results depend on your own good sense.

Know your own mind, have your ideas about the home. When your husband wants three kinds of pie for breakfast, or says you ought not to "friz" your front hair, do not say, "All right, dear," nor "You shan't have it so," but laugh and then read up on digestible breakfasts or the power of beauty, and then later have a discussion in which your information makes you sweetly reasonable. Jolly good nature in a wife, coupled with energy and brains will keep almost any man inspired with love for his wife and the feeling that his home is safe in her hands.

Have him sit at the head of his table, if he will, and you sit at the foot. He may not like carving the roast any more than you like serving vegetables and beverages, but he will be thankful in the years to come to be regarded as the dispenser of material blessings. Handing out a few dollars now and then will never win this for him.

Give the Bride-To-Be a Shower

How would a flower shower be—every guest giving a potted fern, palm, geranium, or other plants, with which to take the strangeness from the new home? The young men could join in by making fern boxes, flower stands, etc.

Apron Shower.—An apron shower is pretty. There can be all kinds, from the dainty sewing aprons to the useful blue-checked variety. One friend might ask the bride to go driving while the rest of you gather and paper the dining room with the aprons, tacking them on the wall. She will not be allowed to go into the room until refreshment time.

Miss Indignant.—I agree with you that it was not the lady's place to reprove your hand-holding, but do you not think it a little deserved? The man does not, as a rule, offer public demonstrations of affection to the girl of native dignity.

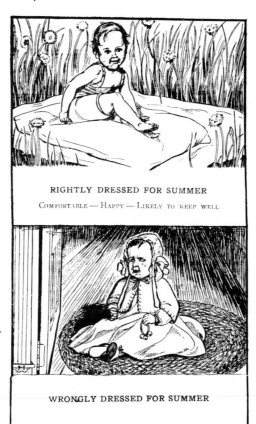

RIGHTLY DRESSED FOR SUMMER

COMFORTABLE — HAPPY — LIKELY TO KEEP WELL

WRONGLY DRESSED FOR SUMMER

"Children are Just Little Imitations of Yourself"

Training children is an absolute walking in darkness so far as I am concerned. It would be an easy enough matter if they remained children, or if one knew the future for which they should be prepared. I have but one gift—writing—yet, I was taught everything but that— French, German, music, painting—everything and anything, and the one thing I really needed, English composition, was almost entirely ignored. That is what I mean about preparing a child for its future, or rather, the impossibility of doing so. It is like putting the little souls and all their belongings on a ship bound for an unknown port.

I am a firm believer in telling the story of life to children as soon as they begin to ask questions. Not all at once, but by degrees, and as they are old enough to understand. The origin of life is the most sacred and beautiful thing in the world and we should pass the story on to our children in all its purity and teach them that they should regard their body and its functions with reverence and love, and not ever speak of it lightly. We mothers on the farm, where the wonder of life in its various forms is ever before us, have exceptional opportunities for telling the story in the best way and I believe it is our sacred duty to do it. A child thus made acquainted with the mystery of his being is safe-guarded to a great extent against the vulgar talk of playmates who may not have been so well taught. All children delight in mystery, and in finding out things they think the grown-ups don't want them to know. Remove this element of mystery by telling them things yourself and you remove the temptation to discuss them with other children.

The greatest foe of country children's teeth is, in my opinion, sweetgum. All the children I recall with defective teeth have been or are great sweetgum chewers. Once a child gave one of my children some of the sticky nuisance, and it required much time to rid the child's teeth of the coating which stuck as tight as pitch. I never got all of the gum off. It had to come off by degrees.

Table Manners

Do not rush into the dining room.

Never lift up a dish in order to remove everything from it. It is better to leave a little.

A knife is never used to carry food to the mouth. It is a divider.

Always keep all your food on your plate, bread, celery etc. Do not spread a whole slice of bread at a time.

Do not play with articles on the table, scrape the knife or fork on the tablecloth, twirl the napkin ring, etc.

Home-made Christmas Gifts for Children

NOTHING is more acceptable, or will stand harder wear than the cloth animals for the younger children. Scraps of material may be utilized, and with good patterns and good clean cotton for stuffing they are not difficult to make. Little sister will love a set of clothes for her dollie, while big sister will appreciate the paper pattern and materials with which to fashion her own outfit.

6943—Doll's Set of Clothes

For both boy and girl dolls. The boy has a Dutch suit with high-waisted trousers, in bloomer or open edge at the knee. The girl has a pretty skirt with the same blouse as the boy.

The pattern is cut in sizes for dolls measuring from 14 to 26 inches in length. Price of pattern, 10 cents.

C. 104—Elephant

This favorite animal figures in most fairy tales. It may be made of gray flannel or felt with a saddle blanket of bright colored velvet. The tusks may be omitted for very small children. The pattern is cut in one size and costs 10 cents.

C 100—Billy 'Possum

This is a favorite animal with little people. It can have the body made of gray or tan felt or flannel. It is not necessary to have the animal in its real colors and if preferred a bright red flannel may be used for the body, with a brown head and paws.

The pattern is in one size only and costs 10 cents.

C 102—Rabbit

Rabbits are both white and gray and there are also some which are white with bright tan patches. The plain colors are easiest to make and white canton flannel or felt and gray felt can be used. If one has the patience to line the ears with pink they will be more natural. The eyes are always amber. The pattern, C 102, is cut in one size and costs 10 cents.

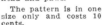

6950—Girl Doll's Set of Clothes

Giving dress, petticoat, drawers, wrapper, pajamas and a hat. These may be made of remnants of material which are at hand, with possibly a new piece of goods for the dress.

The pattern is cut in sizes for dolls measuring from 14 to 26 inches in length. Price of pattern, 10 cents.

Address, Pattern Department, The Progressive Farmer.

Anatomically Educated

"Sonny's" mother stepped out on the porch one day to see if he could be seen playing, and was just in time to discover him running for home with a most terrified expression on his face, caused by a friendly little dog tagging after him. His mother called, "Why are you running from that little dog? He won't hurt you!" To which he replied, with quite an air of disdain, "Mother, don't you suppose that dog knows I'm full of bones?"

THEODORE ROOSEVELT TO THE BOYS OF AMERICA.

OF course what we have a right to expect from every American boy is that he shall turn out to be a good American man. Now, the chances are strong that he won't be much of a man unless he is a good deal of a boy. He must not be a coward or a weakling, a bully, a shirk or a prig. He must work hard and play hard. He must be clean-minded and clean-lived, and able to hold his own under all circumstances and against all comers. It is only on these conditions that he will grow into the kind of a man of whom America can really be proud. In life as in a football game the principle to follow is: Hit the line hard; don't foul and don't shirk, but hit the line hard.

Answer to "boy."

The reason a bird does not fall out of the tree is that the muscles are so arranged that when the bird bends its "knee," the toes close. Therefore, the foot remains firmly clamped around the branch until the bird rises from its sitting posture.

Dandelions Boiled

Gather them before they bloom and become bitter. Cut off the roots, wash well and boil in as little salted water as possible. Drain, season with butter, salt and pepper. Serve with a little vinegar and hard-boiled egg.

The Percolating Coffee Pot

A percolating coffee pot is the greatest, most money-saving article that has been placed in our kitchen recently.

The coffee is not placed in the water, which is placed in the pot, but in a perforated cup fitted at top of pot, connected with the

water below by a tube, thru which the water is forced up, as soon as pot with cold water is placed on a hot stove. The water drips over the coffee, and by the time the water boils, the essence has been drawn from the coffee, and coffee, clear and delicious, such as you never drank made any other way, is ready to serve.

Sun-Preserved Strawberries

Use equal weights of sugar and strawberries. Put the strawberries in the preserving kettle in layers, sprinkling sugar over each layer. The fruit and sugar should not be more than four inches deep. Place the kettle on the stove and heat the fruit and sugar slowly to the boiling point. When it begins to boil skim carefully. Boil 10 minutes, counting from the time the fruit begins to bubble. Pour the cooked fruit into platters, having it about two or three inches deep. Place the platters in a sunny window in an unused room, for three or four days. In doing this be sure to keep protected from flies. In that time the fruit will grow plump and firm and the syrup will thicken almost to a jelly. Put this preserve, cold, into jars or tumblers.

To Cook Sparrows

Cut off the legs and wings at "knee and elbow;" skin beginning at the neck, slit down the spine with a sharp knife. Open out the bird, remove the viscera, wash quickly. Never salt and soak as poor cooks sometimes treat fowl. Brown in butter or dripping from breakfast strip, add water or milk and let simmer with cover on. Season with salt and pepper. These may be broiled and served on toast, seasoned with salt, pepper and butter, or the breasts can be wrapped in a piece of bacon, put in a quick oven and served hot.

Peanut Butter

Roast the nuts, shell and rub in a towel to loosen the brown skin, which must be blown off, dust lightly with salt, grind at once, pack into glasses, cover and keep in a cool place. Some people like to add a little mustard, paprika, red pepper, or cottonseed oil.

Things to Make

When I see a pair of wrens twittering and searching under the eaves, I fix up a tomato can for them. I remember one pair that went to the clothes line and filled, or tried to fill, a shirt sleeve with sticks. I hung a gourd on the line and threw an old sack over it; they built and raised three broods in it.

Bird boxes do not need to be painted; anything will do that is fixed securely. I made several from half-gallon cooking-oil cans by cutting doors in the sides and bending the pieces down for a place for the birds to alight on, taking care that no sharp edge is left to cut their feet. I find it easier to first fasten a box to a short piece of plank; then nail the plank to the tree.

To Make Cockroach Powder

The cockroach is a hard insect to destroy and success usually results only from long careful, persistent treatment with a mixture of 3 parts of flour with 1 part of plaster of Paris. Set this dry mixture in a low flat dish where the roaches can reach it and put a saucer of water beside it. Any roach that eats and drinks at these two dishes will cease to be troublesome.

Ordinary Whitewash

This is made by slaking about 10 pounds of quicklime with 2 gallons of water. The lime is placed in a pail and the water poured over it, after which the pail is covered with an old piece of carpet or cloth and allowed to stand for about an hour. With an insufficient amount of water, the lime is "scorched" and not all converted into hydrate; on the other hand, too much water retards the slaking by lowering the heat.

China Berry Chains

Here is an inexpensive method of making very pretty beads. If pale dyes are used, very dainty effects can be obtained. A silver, gold or glass bead between each china berry adds to the appearance of the string.

Did you ever soak and string allspice with tiny beads of contrasting colors? They make brown, fragrant neck decorations.

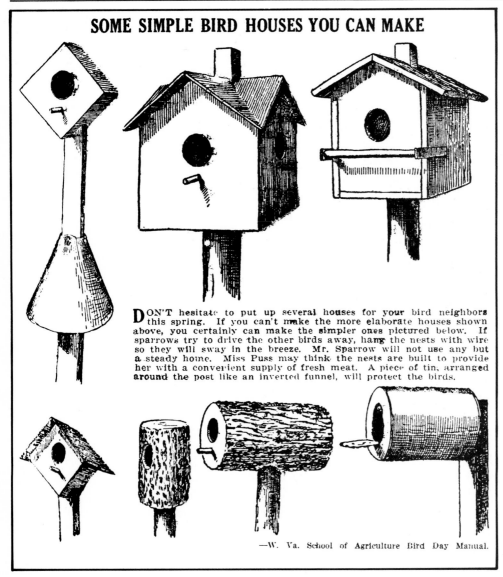

SOME SIMPLE BIRD HOUSES YOU CAN MAKE

DON'T hesitate to put up several houses for your bird neighbors this spring. If you can't make the more elaborate houses shown above, you certainly can make the simpler ones pictured below. If sparrows try to drive the other birds away, hang the nests with wire so they will sway in the breeze. Mr. Sparrow will not use any but a steady home. Miss Puss may think the nests are built to provide her with a convenient supply of fresh meat. A piece of tin, arranged around the post like an inverted funnel, will protect the birds.

—W. Va. School of Agriculture Bird Day Manual.

In the South the china umbrella tree, with its china berries, are grown almost everywhere, so I am writing to tell you how to make beads of the berries. It is best to gather about a gallon at once, as they are troublesome to prepare, and a large number can be pre-pared almost as easily as a small number. Boil them about 15 minutes, to a gallon putting two tablespoons of soda. This softens the pulp, which is to be washed off. Rub and wash about six times. Now dye in boiling water and Paas egg dye, or use cake-coloring. It is rather nice to have beads to match each dress. String on waxed string that you can get from the shoemaker. If strung before they are dry, the hole in the ends will be large enough. If you wait long you will have to use a hat pin to pierce the seeds.

The Old-fashioned Rose Jar

When roses are in full bloom is the time to gather the leaves. There is no need of sacrificing the buds or newly opened roses. Gather them into a shallow box or basket in the twilight of a dry sunshiny day. Spread the petals on papers in any airy apartment, scatter salt over them and toss every one repeatedly until dry and then fill the jar, adding aromatic roots, leaves and blossoms of herbs and many choice flowers that flourish in the summer garden and combine delightfully with the perfume of the roses. Orris root or powder, sweet flag, lavender and thyme; apple and rose geraniums are delicately aromatic and lasting.

The extracts, essential oils, spices, cinnamon bark, sandal wood and heliotrope, carnation or jasmine blooms may be selected. When the jars are filled, it is well to turn the contents up from the bottom, occasionally.

Small jars of this are much appreciated for Christmas and birthday gifts, and, above all, by the loved ones that have gone far from the old home, to whom the lasting odors of the rose jar will bring tender recollections of the joyous days before they closed the garden gate at home.

FIGHTING FOR YOU!

Will You Let Them Starve?

Look at these lines of marching men, stretching away into the distance as far as you can see. Next year there will be thousands—yes, millions—of splendid men like these fighting, suffering untold agonies, dying on the bloody battlefields of Europe. Your sons, your brothers—the flower of America's young manhood—fighting, suffering, dying for YOU. Yes, for you who sit there so calmly in your comfortable home reading these words. Fighting, suffering, dying that you and yours may live in peace and enjoy the liberty that your fathers left you.

Wake Up, Texas! Don't Let Them Starve!

What can you do to help them? What will you do? Raise

Fifty Million Bushels of Wheat in 1918!

Let this be the battle-cry of Texas! Let this be the slogan on every farm! Let this be the song in every throat!

Remember that the Germans are now sinking ships faster than they are being built and that millions of bushels of wheat will be sent to the bottom of the ocean by German submarines. Our soldiers in Europe must be fed. Our allies must be fed. Unless we feed them they will starve. If they starve, their cause is lost, our cause is lost, and Germany wins and rules the world.

As you and yours have lived in peace and prosperity

HELP YOUR COUNTRY NOW IN HER HOUR OF NEED!

Profits in Wheat and Cotton

Some people say that cotton will go to 35c. Perhaps it will. Nobody knows, but it has not been there yet. Wheat has been to $3.00 and it is just as likely to go there again as cotton is to go to 35c. It is anybody's guess what the price of these two staples will be next year, but it is almost a certainty that they will both be so high that there will be a mighty good profit in either of them.

But just bear in mind these three points: 1. These millions of men going to the war mean a much worse labor shortage than we have today, and cotton requires far more labor than wheat. 2. You can raise two crops a year on your wheat land—a légume or forage crop in the summer after your wheat has been harvested. No second crop can be raised with cotton. 3. You can pasture your wheat during the winter and save many dollars that you would otherwise spend for feed.

When they ask whether you are planting more cotton or more wheat, answer

MORE WHEAT!

The Texas Industrial Congress, and
The Texas State Council of Defense

FRANK KELL, Chairman, Food Supply and Conservation Committee

"The War to End War"

The place in its country's destiny that the *Progressive Farmer* had forcast for the South in 1912 was filled in an unexpected way. In 1917, the American South was called upon to feed, not just the nation, but the world. Southern farmers were urged by President Wilson himself "to show their patriotism . . . by resisting the great temptation of the present price of cotton and helping, upon a great scale, to feed the nation and the peoples everywhere who are fighting for their liberties and our own."

The "temptation of the present price of cotton" must have been especially great, since, when the war had begun in Europe three years earlier, many cotton farmers had been panicky that the war would stop Europe's importation. They had sold their cotton for whatever they could get, thereby driving prices even lower. The *Progressive Farmer* had fought this trend. At the same time it had tried to explain the war in Europe to its readers in a humorous and dramatic way using its fictional "Uncle John:"

On the War Situation—1914

"I hearn that they wan't no market fer cotton, so I 'lowed I'd go to Laurel and see the Hicks Mercantile about it, an', by gum, I found they didn't want no cotton shore 'nuff! I went all over town an' ask every feller I seen an' the best any of 'em would do was to offer to loan me

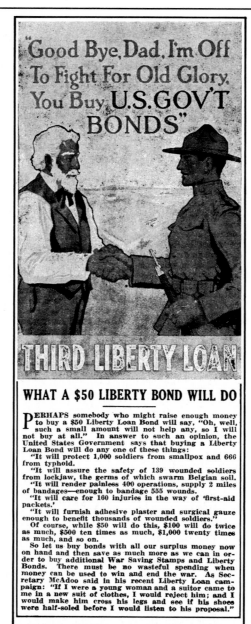

"Good Bye, Dad, I'm Off To Fight For Old Glory, You Buy U.S. GOV'T BONDS"

THIRD LIBERTY LOAN

WHAT A $50 LIBERTY BOND WILL DO

PERHAPS somebody who might raise enough money to buy a $50 Liberty Loan Bond will say, "Oh, well, such a small amount will not help any, so I will not buy at all." In answer to such an opinion, the United States Government says that buying a Liberty Loan Bond will do any one of these things:
  "It will protect 1,000 soldiers from smallpox and 666 from typhoid."
  "It will assure the safety of 139 wounded soldiers from lockjaw, the germs of which swarm Belgian soil."
  "It will render painless 400 operations, supply 2 miles of bandages—enough to bandage 555 wounds."
  "It will care for 160 injuries in the way of 'first-aid packets.'
  "It will furnish adhesive plaster and surgical gauze enough to benefit thousands of wounded soldiers."
  Of course, while $50 will do this, $100 will do twice as much, $500 ten times as much, $1,000 twenty times as much, and so on.
  So let us buy bonds with all our surplus money now on hand and then save as much more as we can in order to buy additional War Saving Stamps and Liberty Bonds. There must be no wasteful spending when money can be used to win and end the war. As Secretary McAdoo said in his recent Liberty Loan campaign: "If I were a young woman and a suitor came to me in a new suit of clothes, I would reject him; and I would make him cross his legs and see if his shoes were half-soled before I would listen to his proposal."

twenty-five dollars a bale on it. Said they didn't want to buy it at all; that Yirrup and Stir-up wuz in a big rucus, an' all the ships was sunk an' the mills shot down, an' that them fool furriners was so busy a shootin' each other that they wuz a payin' mighty little attention to whether they had any clothes or not, any way. . . . it

seems that a feller over there they call the Kayser got to eachin' fur a fight, an' pulled off his coat an' axed the Czar of sumthin'-or-other what he wuz goin' to do about it. Then the Czar didn't say nothin', but started to shuckin' his coat, too. From this the thing started, an' now they say that Ireland an' Jaypan an' Novy Scoshy air into it, with Turkey an' Pee-ru gettin' ready, an' that what they all want ain't cotton, but sumpthin' to eat."

"Sumpthin' to eat" was what Woodrow Wilson and the rest of the nation called upon the South to furnish when the United States entered the "war to end war" in 1917. One of the *Progressive Farmer's* writers, on a trip North, heard

a very remarkable reversion of public opinion as to the South's place in the nation. Over and over for the first time in my life, the question was asked, "What of the South? Will she, with her wonderful climate, be able to feed us? We can manufacture everything but food. The South must furnish that or another winter will see America go hungry." I told them the South could and would raise food in untold quantities . . .

Clarence Dubose of the U.S. Department of Agriculture tried to give a sense of the urgency of the cause:

. . . in his field, far from the fury of battle . . . the American farmer will say whether autocracy or democracy shall rule the world . . . In a sense the war will be won or lost in the fields, gardens, orchards, pastures and hog lots of the American farmer . . .

Sixty year old Southern Americans had been four years old at the beginning of the Civil War. They could remember vividly and describe to their children a very different kind of war—a war bitterly, agonizingly fought in their own gardens and hog lots. How could this far away war in "Yirrup and Stir-up" have meaning enough for them to resist the price they could get for their cotton and plant food instead?

Herbert Hoover, wartime Food Administrator, found a dramatic way to bring the war close to home. Out of his office came "Meatless Tuesday, Wheatless Wednesday and Porkless Saturday," bringing the great far-off war with its demands to plant and conserve daily to every dinner table. (So well did the responsibility to "preach the gospel of the clean plate" become ingrained in our parents and grandparents that we as children felt its weight years later.)

But there remained the problem of a deeper commitment than mere "doing without." To commit their bodies or the bodies of their sons, to commit their life's labor to this far-off war, farmers must believe the lack of such action would have a deep and devastating effect upon their daily lives. That many had difficulty in espousing this cause is shown by the *Progressive Farmer*'s repeated attempts to convey a sense of urgency to its readers. One old man questioned the editor about it: "My son has gone and I should like to know what is to be gained by it?" The editor replied

PRESIDENT WILSON APPEALS TO THE SOUTH TO HELP FEED THE NATION

in an editorial. The war was a "high and holy cause." It was not just a matter of making the seas safe from submarines so that farmers' products could reach European markets. With Woodrow Wilson's plan for a League of Nations, this was a "war to end war." It was "America's gift to the world."

Possibly the pragmatic farmers, immersed in their daily battle for survival, found it hard to join yet another battle, to give another gift. Possibly they found the arguments—tested against their own reality of red clay—wanting. At any rate the United States government was apparently afraid that they lacked enthusiasm, for it requested the *Progressive Farmer*, in March 1918, to print an article. It was written by Herbert Quick of the Federal Farm Loan Board, "in order to give our people a clearer understanding of the issues of the war as they affect our farmers and the duty of farmers to lend their savings to the Government . . ." It said in part:

It is impossible to set the farmers of the United States on fire by means of any sudden spark of rumor . . . but when the farmers do ignite, they burn with a slow hot fire which nothing can put out . . .

This war was at first hard to understand. No armed foe invaded the United States. The night skies were not reddened by the burning barns of America. It seemed to many of us that we were not at war, the thing was so far off, and it came to us in so unfamiliar a guise . . .

The Kaiser began foreclosing his mortgage on our farms when he declared ruthless submarine warfare, and the war is our answer to his bill of foreclosure.

Our contribution is, first, our sons and brothers for the trenches; second, the last pound of food products which we can grow by mobilizing our scanty labor-supply . . . and, third, for War Savings Stamps and Liberty Bonds.

If grandfather gained a "clearer understanding" of his duty and let his savings go, the day was not far off when he would rue it. The Armistice was signed on November 11, 1918. If our grandparents assumed that they could go back to their life as it had been before the war, they were soon to find they were mistaken.

Fats Are Very Precious

Our Armies Use Fats by the Ship-load and Must Have Them to Keep Up the Fight

Save fat—Fats are the most valuable one thing in continuing this war. Our munition factories are bound to have them in large quantities, or their output of explosives is limited; our men are compelled to have them to eat.

Never before in world history did we suffer for fats nor realize their value. Oh, how we have wasted them, little knowing that we were wasteful. Germany is near the breaking point because of lack of them.

Fats supply energy. Without fats people's flesh melts from their bones and they weaken.

The Privilege of Paying Taxes

Women Have Much to Do With Men's Attitude Toward Taxes; That Is, Whether They Shall Be Paid Grudgingly or Gladly

Whenever I hear people complaining of paying taxes I wonder at their lack of gratitude for the gifts that are theirs. The amount of taxes a man pays is nothing more than the estimated measurement of his worldly possessions. With what envy must the man who pays no taxes look upon the man who has something on which to pay them.

War Expedients

In using sugar substitutes, half sugar and half syrup is best, as too much syrup gives a rather hard and gummy result.

Soy bean meal gives a rather nutty flavor if too much is not used.

Letter from a Reader

I am worn to a frazzle with this new un-American slogan, "Eat less." I believe it should be changed into "Raise more and eat all you want to." Raise enough to have plenty and to spare for yourself and for all the world. If we lived in Alaska or Siberia with that deadly destroying cold to fight and only a few months in which to cultivate crops it would be another matter. But here in the South, if we don't raise food enough, starving is actually too good for us.

United States Soldiers Not Allowed to Have Liquor

Parents need have no fear as the boys are more protected than if they were at home. Intoxicating liquors are forbidden to all who are preparing to battle against the Huns. All of you mothers who fear for your boys, read the following prohibition law recently passed.

"Alcoholic liquor, including beer, ale and wine, either alone, or with any other article, shall not, directly or indirectly, be sold, bartered, given, served, or knowingly delivered to any officer or member of the military forces within the United States, their territories or possessions . . ."

Roast Oppossum and Sweet Potatoes

Chill thoroughly after skinning and drawing. Save all the inside fat, let it soak in weak salt water until cooking time, then rinse it well, and partly try it out in the pan before putting in the opossum. Unless he is huge, leave him whole, skewering him flat, and laying him skin side up in the pan. Set in a hot oven and cook until crisply tender, taking care there is no scorching. Roast a dozen good sized sweet potatoes, in ashes if possible; if not, bake them covered in a deep pan. Peel when done and lay, while hot, around the opossum, turning them over and over in the gravy. He should have been lightly salted, when hung up, and fully seasoned with salt, pepper, and a trifle of mustard, when put down to cook. Dish him in a big platter, lay the potatoes, which should be partly browned around him. Add a little boiling water to the pan, shake well around; and pour the gravy over everything. Hot corn bread, strong black coffee, or else sharp cider, and very hot sharp pickles are the things to serve with him.

Plant Fall Potatoes

The Kaiser in his gilded chair
With scowling brow and tousled hair,
   Is swearing at potatoes;
For days and weeks his horrid thot
Has been "I wish they all would rot,
   Old Uncle Sam's potatoes!"

He knows full well, in all his might,
He cannot long keep up the fight,
   If we devour potatoes
And send our wheat to whip the Huns,
And back the men behind the guns,
   With armies of potatoes.

"If all those folks are going to eat
That Irish crop, and save their wheat
   By cramming down potatoes,
They'll lick us quick and sure," quoth he—
That beastly Bill across the sea—
   "Torpedo those potatoes!"

We'll get the best of Kaiser Bill,
If all of us will eat our fill
   Of mealy, plump potatoes;
So let us hasten to the store,
And buy a peck or two, or more,
   Of fall seed potatoes.
      —E. H. M. B., N. C.

The Girl Who Travels

Every year we urge the girl who is going away to school to consider her conduct on the train. No one asks her to be a prude, to sit up in a corner in prim rigidity when she is young, alive and interested in everything and everybody; but this we do ask, that she be sweet, friendly and courteous, but never soft, silly or looking for admiration. There is a certain impersonal air about the right girl which all recognize and respect.

There is scarcely a train on which one can get nowadays but there are many soldiers on it. They are happy, care-free and eager for entertainment. Should a girl not talk just a very little to some clean, manly-looking chap when he is kind enough to carry her suitcase in and out of the train for her? Sad as it seems to say, she should not unless her mother or some responsible older person is her companion. It is a case of the ninety and nine being denied for the sake of the one who would betray the trust.

Dress quietly but neatly. A dark dress with a couple changes of neat collars and cuffs enables one to keep clean. A suit, shirtwaist and quiet hat are always in good taste. Very low necks and thin stockings are abominations.

Talk quietly. Untravelled young persons sometimes think they appear merry and attractive when they giggle and chatter. A thoughtful observance of the most

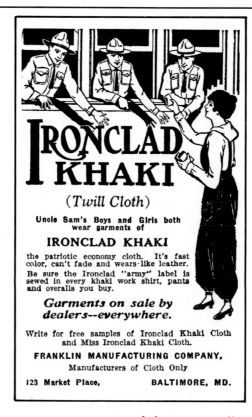

attractive persons of the train will reveal the fact that a real lady reserves her gaiety for less public places.

Reading on the train is bad for eyes but good for morals. A girl provided with some light reading becomes absorbed in it and is not likely to seek entertainment of a more dangerous kind.

Managing Economically

'I'm saving all I can, but I never seem to get anything ahead to buy thrift stamps.' How often we hear this expression from farm women.

Let me tell you of a few ways I have discovered.

Perhaps you have to buy a package of dye to color some winter clothing. If you had intended to color it brown, instead of paying ten cents for a package of dye, get a bucket of walnut hulls or bark and boil till the water is a thick ooze; then strain, put back in kettle, throw in goods, and cover with boiling water and boil (stirring constantly) for half an hour. There is enough for one thrift stamp.

If you have to have postum for breakfast, take a cupful of wheat bran, an egg, two tablespoonsful of molasses, mix, brown carefully in oven, then proceed as you do for postum and you'll not be able to detect the difference.

Page 93. With washing machines, vacuum cleaners and "water systems" appearing in some homes by 1927, women who had been busy previously with chores now had a little time for handwork. Ordering these items "all-stamped" with the pattern made it possible for the unskilled or beginner in "fancy work" to produce a pleasing result without having to create a design herself.

Page 94. In the 20's, advertisements began to emphasize the characteristics (actual or desired) of the potential user more than the characteristics of the product. Clean teeth took a back seat to romance.

Page 95. Throughout the century women wrote to the Progressive Farmer inveighing against other women's slavish devotion to fashion trends. In the 20's many were scandalized by the unseemly skirt length, but others were delighted with the ease of dress and bright colors in vogue at that time.

Page 96. Those of us who have complaints about television will smile at this ad for radio, labelled a "noisy nuisance" in 1925. By the 1930's radio was so much a part of farmers' (and even more of farm women's) lives that a letter contest between the radio and washing machine ended in almost a tie.

All Stamped~You Add the Embroidery

by Leonore Dunnigan

Clever aprons for those who would look attractive about the house

Pillow slips are lovely embroidered in white or pastel shades

Charming dress in sheer voile for the very young

The very latest in a luncheon set with basket pockets to hold the napkins

Edges of runner come hemstitched ready for hand-crochet edge

A vanity set for girl's own room

"...and Jane, dear...Jack just raved about my teeth."

"I just smiled my prettiest smile... and let him rave. I could have said 'Of course I have beautiful teeth... I've used Colgate's all my life'. But I didn't want Jack to think I was a living advertisement for Colgate's tooth paste."

* * * * *

Beautiful teeth glisten gloriously. They compel the admiration of all who see them. And there is health as well as beauty in gleaming teeth, for when they are scrupulously kept clean, germs and poisons of decay can't lurk and breed around them.

Remove Those Causes of Decay

Save yourself the embarrassment so often caused by poor teeth. Fight the germs of tooth decay.

Colgate's will keep your teeth scrupulously clean. It reaches all the hard-to-get-at places between teeth and around the edges of the gums, and so *removes causes* of tooth decay. It is the dependable tooth paste for you to use.

Here are children in Passaic, N. J., using Colgate's to fight tooth decay. Colgate co-operates with thousands of school officials and health authorities in teaching dental hygiene.

The principal ingredients of Colgate's are mild soap and fine chalk, the two things that dental authorities say a safe dental cream should contain. The combined action of these ingredients washes, polishes and protects the delicate enamel of your teeth.

Use Colgate's Regularly

Just remember that beautiful, healthy teeth are more a matter of good care than of good luck. Use Colgate's after meals and at bedtime. It will keep your teeth clean and gloriously attractive.

And you'll like its taste . . . even children love to use it regularly.

Priced right too! Large tube 25c.

Summer Frocks That You Can Make
at Very Little Cost

4188
34-44—14-18
45 cents
Emb. 12820
25 cents

4212
12-17
40 cents

Coat 4258
34-44—14-18
50 cents
Frock 4190
34-50—14-18
35 cents

4248
34-44—14-18
45 cents

4226
34-50
45 cents

4209
34-44—14-18
50 cents

4276
34-44—14-18
50 cents

Ensemble
4250
8-15
45 cents
Mon. 558
50 cents

4181
1-5
35 cents
Free Emb.

4273
2-6
35 cents

3914
34-44
14-18
50 cents

3152
34-44
14-18
45 cents

For Style and Economy Use
PICTORIAL PRINTED PATTERNS

The beautiful fashions that you see illustrated here are only a few of the many styles available to you every month in the Fashion Section of Pictorial Review. And for every style shown, there is a special printed pattern.

Pictorial Printed Patterns are accurate, economical and easy to use.

They are guaranteed as to style and fit. Money will be refunded for pattern and material for any loss, due to defect in the pattern.

These patterns are on sale at leading stores in your trading center—or they may be ordered by mail. Use coupon below for prompt mail service.

She fought radio three years
—now see what she says

SHE is a doctor's wife in a little town in Oklahoma.

"Come right in," she said to the pilgrim who was inquiring about radio. "It's time I made a confession to someone.

"I fought radio for three years. Wouldn't let my husband get a set. Told him it was a noisy nuisance.

"Then one evening I heard a good set at a friend's. We bought one like it the next day— and, oh, what a pleasure it is!

"Don't you realize, you people in the big cities, that this is the only way we have out here of hearing really fine music? Don't you realize that it has increased our interest in life just 100 per cent—that it is making the word *home* mean more than it ever did before?

"My husband comes in from his country rounds with stories of what a blessing radio is to the farm families. Can't you picture what a change this has made?"

The doctor's wife proudly showed her visitor the set that had won such a place in her affections. It was an Atwater Kent Receiver and Radio Speaker.

Yes, women have taken to radio because as home-makers they know it is needed in the home. And they have taken to Atwater Kent Radio because it is beautiful with a beauty that goes deeper than the rich mahogany case, and embraces beauty of design and beauty of workmanship, upon which quality of performance depends.

ATWATER KENT MANUFACTURING CO.
A. Atwater Kent, President

4769 WISSAHICKON AVENUE   PHILADELPHIA, PA.

Send for it!

We will gladly send you a copy of this beautifully illustrated 32-page booklet if you will just write and ask us. In it you will find not only complete specifications and prices of Atwater Kent Receiving Sets, Radio Speakers and other equipment, but an interesting illustrated description of the largest Radio manufacturing plant in the world.

Hear the Atwater Kent Radio Artists every Thursday evening at 9 o'clock (eastern daylight time) through stations—WEAF *New York;* WJAR *Providence;* WEEI *Boston;* WFI *Philadelphia;* WCAE *Pittsburgh;* WGR *Buffalo;* WWJ *Detroit;* WCCO *Minneapolis-St. Paul;* WOC *Davenport;* WSAI *Cincinnati.*

Model 20 Compact—$80

Radio Speakers from $12 to $28

Model 10—$80 (without tubes)

Prices slightly higher from the Rockies west, and in Canada

5th make 10.6%
4th make 10.6%
3rd make 13.9%
2nd make 28.4%
ATWATER KENT 36.5%

The farmer makes his choice

Atwater Kent led all other makes in the answers to the question of the Meredith Publications: "What radio set will you buy?" The chart shows the relative standing of the first five makes.

Atwater Kent also led in answers to the same question asked by the Capper Publications.

Columbia Grafonola

"And, oh, she dances such-a-way"

You'll never need to leave your favorite partner in the middle of a dance. With the Columbia Grafonola you can dance to the last lingering note and step. The Non Set Automatic Stop takes care of that. This exclusive Columbia feature is at its best for dancing. Nothing to move or set or measure. Just start the Grafonola and it plays and stops itself.

The leading stars of the stage make records exclusively for Columbia

Standard Models up to $300
Period Designs up to $2100

COLUMBIA GRAPHOPHONE CO.
New York
Canadian Factory: Toronto

Clarence Rowe

Columbia
Grafonola

The Power That Liberates

The twenties were hard times for our grandparents on the farm, and harder by contrast to the good times of most of the rest of the country. Between 1920 and 1921 farm prices fell 44%. Many bankruptcies and mortgage foreclosures occurred. Throughout the decade, cotton was considered a depressed industry. In 1922 the *Progressive Farmer* reported figures from the Secretary of Agriculture: purchasing power of railroad employees was 51% greater than in 1913 and coal miners' 30% greater, but the purchasing power of the farmer was 25 to 45% *less* than in 1913. The *Progressive Farmer* urged the need for cooperative marketing in order to warehouse surpluses and create pressure to reduce acreage. In 1926 Clarence Poe, its far-seeing editor, wrote an editorial, "Who Should Stay on the Farm?"

In many parts of the South this crop season has started off inauspiciously. Crop prices are low and crop prospects none too good.

Under such conditions it would not be surprising if more than the usual number of farm families are debating the question as to whether they ought to farm next year . . . Or possibly the question is not that of a whole farm family moving, but simply as to whether a son shall leave the old farm and try some other work instead of farming.

The bright lights and apparent comforts of the city must have been especially tantalizing to the young. One mill girl was quoted: "Here ya draws yer own pay enve-lope and gives what ya wants to yer folks, but there ain't no pay envelope [on the farm]."

Americans were out for fun—after the scrimping and sacrifice of the war, which had taught them the ephemeral, almost whimsical, nature of savings and work, and even life. Americans were ready for the reward which seemed to be rightfully theirs—the liberation brought by the harnessing of power. Mass production of automobiles had made them cheap enough for many to buy—at least "on time." (More than ¾ of American cars bought in 1925 were purchased "on time," liberating Americans from the old puritan ethic of work and savings *before* buying.) Washing machines and vacuum cleaners liberated them from constant bondage to dirt and scrubbing. Oil stoves liberated them from hot kitchens and chopping wood. But the greatest change was a whole industry devoted to "fun."

Radio and movies were born to entertain. The moneyed class had always been entertained at concerts and plays. Now radio and movies brought entertainment within the range of most pocketbooks. A great mass of people were thereby liberated to being entertained, not (as formerly) by doing something, but (as the rich had always been) by just sitting there. Radio and movies brought to tightly knit communities ideas, styles, and ways of living from other places and times, liberating those communities somewhat from rigid custom. Radio and movies and advertising brought longings for things that others had, or appeared to have. And not just longings for the things themselves, but for the lives those people in the ads and movies seemed to be living.

Farmers complained that they had to get to bed too early to "sit up of an evening to hear a fine program" on the radio. And farmers, being more dependent on their land and their neighbors than on trends and styles, could turn their backs on these new "radio" ideas for awhile. But plainly, they could not keep the young people from responding to them, as we see from a comment in 1926 by Mrs. Hutt, the *Progressive Farmer's* women's editor: "The ambition of many a youth is to have a silk shirt to puff out in the breezes when he speeds to the town movies in his daddy's new flivver." If they took the *Progressive Farmer*, farm families could learn, especially from the ads, about new styles and new ways of living, conveniences and even "scandalous" behavior that could be tried. Ads for toothpaste showed how important brushing was to romance. Ads for the phonograph showed handsome young people dancing, an activity which was regarded dubiously by many and with downright horror by some. And even the coffee ads changed from picturing a sweet old lady, to a girl wearing a low-necked dress and a rakish smile, to a sure-enough vamp.

Advertisements in the *Progressive Farmer* had been getting bigger and prettier with fewer words and more pictures. There were full-page ads—even an occasional double-

"LISTENING IN"

The rapid development of the radiophone has made it possible for people living in rural communities to hear daily important crop and market news, and also concerts of various kinds. Nearly all of the state agricultural extension divisions are installing broadcasting stations so that market news and weather conditions, etc., can be sent out to the county agents every day. Farmers having a receiving set can "listen in" on the news. The receiving sets cost anywhere from $25 to over $200.

page spread. In the early 20's the *Progressive Farmer* ran several full-page ads for advertising itself, the new and growing art that

materially reduces selling costs by increasing the demand for and distribution of the products of hundreds of thousands of factories. Indeed many of the things we count today as necessities or simple luxuries could not be made and sold at their reasonable prices except as advertising has created a broad market for them, making millions of sales at little prices and little profits.

In 1922 color advertising bloomed in the *Progressive Farmer*. The effect, set against the black and white ads, which had not been considered drab until color's arrival, was startling. We can imagine Grandmother leafing through her *Progressive Farmer* of September 23, 1922, wondering what advice on skirt length or dish

The Power That Liberates / Introduction 99

washing it might have for her. We can see her coming suddenly upon a full-page ad for soap in glossy but delicate color: elves and butterflies would transport her to fairyland if she used this particular soap. This picture must have seemed, not like a request to buy soap, but like a gift from soap. (In fact, this particular ad did describe a promotional gift she could get just by listing which of that company's products she used. She didn't even need to send wrappers.) We can imagine Grandmother running her hand over the smooth page, perhaps cutting it out and hanging it on the wall. Color had been liberated and brought beauty. The *Progressive Farmer* was sensible of its good fortune. A woman's page editorial stressed that

it is a compliment to the farm women of America that the most exclusive advertisers are now presenting their most beautiful advertising copy in farm papers. They have never done so before. I hope our farm women will show their appreciation of the compliment these discriminating advertisers pay us by asking for prices, folders, and further information.

In 1920, Warren Harding was elected president of the United States after a campaign promising a return to "normalcy." But if "normalcy" meant life as it had been before the war, only enhanced by modern conveniences, the decade following the "Great War" proved

THE 40TH DOOR

WITH ALLENE RAY

(*From the Novel by Mary Hastings Bradley*)

In Ten Weekly Chapters

Her hiding place was the tomb of an ancient king!

Hamid Bey, the cruel and sensual Turk, to whom she had been given as bride by the man she thought to be her father, had relentlessly followed her American rescuer and her to the ancient tomb where the explorers had just made a big discovery. The soldiers were at the door. Hastily the young American swathed her in the wrappings of a mummy, and laid her in the sarcophagus.

What happened?

See this fine and exciting story brought to life on the screen, with a superb cast which includes Bruce Gordon, Frank Lackteen, Anna May Wong and many others whom you know.

There will be a theatre near you which will show it. We will be glad to send you FREE, a set of eight pictures from the play.

Pathe Exchange, Inc.,
35 W. 45th St., New York.
Please send me the set of eight pictures from "The Fortieth Door," free. The motion picture theatre I attend is

Theatre................. Town...........
My name is...........................
Address ....

Pathéserial

that such a life was no longer possible. The conveniences themselves were not just life-made-easier (lights without lamp chimneys to clean, water without the long hard walk, carriages without a horse to feed.) The conveniences were an assault on and liberation from the rigid unity of the former life, the cohesive community with its values of hard work and saving.

There were other liberations. In 1920 the power of the United States Constitution in the 18th (Prohibition) Amendment had, presumably, liberated men from the possibility of destroying themselves and their families with drink. The 19th (Woman Suffrage) Amendment had liberated women from the status of "imbeciles and criminals" and men from the entire burden of government with its consequent tyrannies. And perhaps it was all these liberations coming together that liberated an entirely new age category.

The *Progressive Farmer* recognized it by instituting its first regular column with a box around the heading: "Twixt Twelve and Twenty." "Teenage" was being liberated from the strictures of being either child or adult—of being either totally dependent and subject to adult whims like a child or totally independent and held responsible for all acts like an adult. More and longer education had become the continuing ideal of American parents for their children. "One needs more education to get along in this life today than formerly . . ," wrote one girl. "The problems of today are different and we need more education to solve them." Young people were staying in school with their peers, without adult responsibility, longer than ever before. For centuries, children had been simply children (to be guided or ordered about according to the will of the parent) until they married, or left home, at which time they became adults. In 1912 Father had been urged to give his daughter a cow (a symbol of adulthood?) before she married, so that she wouldn't be getting married just to get her cow. A mere ten years later, Daughter cared little for cows, whatever they might symbolize. She was off for a ride in the flivver. A non-age, a limbo age, which had increasingly its own styles and mores and was influenced more by its peers than its elders (who, after all, had never been there) was appearing.

The mood of a large part of the country—wild spending and no thought for the morrow—must have just suited the new age category—the romantic teenagers whose older brothers and friends were returning (or perhaps not) from a brutal war during which millions of men in trenches had been lost to gain a few miles of territory. After such disillusioning experiences, youngsters could easily turn (with the rest of the country) from the values of hard work which they had been taught, to hedonism. What is perhaps more surprising is that apparently many of their elders, themselves demoralized by war and increasingly cut loose from the strong bonds of community by the automobile and mass communication, were ready to follow their lead. No wonder Mother and Grandmother were at a loss to advise this new breed of child. How could they know how short skirts could be and still be

"nice," how close boys and girls could get and still be "nice," what kind and time of an automobile ride should be "nice?" Mother and Grandmother had never even dreamed of any of these things in their youth. How could they judge to what degree their children should do them? Luckily, the *Progressive Farmer*, in 1929, gave the teenagers their own advice column with editor, Catherine Lee.

All these liberations came more slowly to the farm. The farm depression allowed neither the money to indulge in all these leisure-bringing conveniences nor the wild abandon that came with a new sense of the purposelessness of life with all previous restraints and world-views overthrown. And even as power did begin to liberate farm families from the worst of the toil and loneliness, from one thing it could never liberate them completely. The farmer could never be completely freed from the land. So perhaps his inevitable ties to it and its eternal cycles gave him a ballast, a purpose, when others might view life as random and purposeless. Clarence Poe urged the boy who loved the farm to stay:

The soothing music of God's winds in the pine trees about country homes on starlit nights carries a peace with it never found in the clamorous jazz of the city dance halls where pleasure-mad young men and women forget that "flaming youth" means burnt out old age . . .

The farm, he said, was still the best place for the "creative impulse" to be exercised, for people to live in neither poverty nor wealth, and for work itself to be "a singing with the hand."

Do Girls Like Starlight or Daylight Boys?

"What is a flapper?" It is the modern and rather joking name applied to the girl who is, as Longfellow describes it,

Standing with reluctant feet,
Where the brook and river meet,
Woman and childhood fleet!

She is a little different from the old-fashioned girl in that her hair is bobbed, she wears sensible, broad-toed, low-heeled shoes, dresses that do not encumber, stays that do not devitalize, vesture that does not baffle. She looks the world squarely in the face, laughs heartily, plays the game honestly and with it, has lost none of her infinite patience with detail and the capacity to love, sorrow and console. She is the embodiment of the best of the past and just enough of its mistakes to keep her human. God bless our clear-eyed, big-hearted flappers, the mothers of tomorrow, the source of power that lies behind all human destinies. Let us love them for their virtues, not berate them for their confusion of sex and soul; and then just as surely as morning rises into noon so will the transient vagaries of the flapper merge into the mature understanding of the woman.

Why?

When one asks herself why Mary Bell Smith wears her skirts so short, her necks so low, her petticoats so thin; why she allows James Henry Jones to touch her; why she chews gum and wears most unbecoming wads of horsehair over each ear covered by a thin shell of her own hair, one gasps for the answer. To talk about the pendulum having swung too far, about the war's reaction and such generalities may be true but it does not give us something definite to grasp, some stick as it were, with which to tighten the slackened strands of social relationships.

Suppose you were the King of Cannibal Isles who could devour all who refused to obey you in your effort to bring the world back to a sane view of life. Where would you begin?

You would begin by coming down so hard on having one standard of morals for boys and another for girls, that it would soon be a thing of the past. The girl has rightly or wrongly given herself the liberty accorded her brother. The fact that she does not avail herself of the license is due to her sense and backbone.

Being a young woman of 21 who has had experience in petting parties, I feel that I know who should bear the blame.

When a girl reaches the age of 17 she feels ancient if she has no beau. She has the feeling that youth is quickly slipping away from her and that if she does not do something to become popular she will soon find herself an old maid.

So she begins to overdress, to stand an extra hour before the mirror, posing and admiring her many coquettish expressions with which she means to vamp admirers. She learns to apply a triple coat of orange rouge—also the lipstick. She gives her moonbeam stockings an extra roll lower and steps out to find fun and popularity.

In my flapper stage the young men with whom I associated were older than I and their pretty compliments completely turned my head. I felt happy and secure in what I thought was their most profound admiration, until my flapper

ways grew old and my once ardent lovers turned their attention to more sensible girls or to younger flappers who were just embarking. And now I am without the friendship of the finer men I might be enjoying without going in for petting parties.

A few days ago a letter came from a man who deplored the lack of delicacy of feeling between young men and women that permitted them to wear such immodest costumes as are worn at some bathing beaches. At the same time came a wail from the mother of a girl of ten or twelve years of age about the difficulty she had in maintaining her daughter in that sweetness and dignity which is its own defense.

Here is a part of the mother's letter: "When my little girl goes to the village some kindly but unthinking old man says, 'Who is your sweetheart?' or 'How is your sweetheart today?' I do not want my girl to think of boys as anything but playmates for years to come, and she would not if some older people would use more judgment.

"Then my daughter went to a children's party, and the disgusting kissing and hugging games it is impossible for me to describe. If my girl has been encouraged by older people to kiss any young man, clean-mouthed or otherwise, at this age, why should she be censured by those same people a few years hence for doing the very same things she is now being induced to do in these, the years in which her character is crystallizing? We parents should think well before we permit any boy to kiss or lay familiar hands on our daughters."

Do Girls Best Like Starlight or Daylight Boys?

I like a boy who takes me on starlight rides for that is the boy who has worked all day the same as I have and now spends his leisure generously taking me in the starlight to church meetings, to call on friends, to social gatherings, to lectures in town or to the movies. If he can't behave in the dark, I don't want him in the light.

Well, Well, From a Farm Boy, Too

From my own masculine standpoint, the girl preparing for marriage rather than for self-support attracts me. A self-supporting girl makes me think of a school teacher, no joy, or a nurse.

Honestly, I do not think that the average high school girl should think of either marriage or self-support. Rather she should look upon the world in jovial mood; have a good time while in school, be a typical flapper, even paint and bob her hair if she desires.

I believe a girl would come nearer getting married to the right kind of man if she got out and supported herself than if she sat up preparing herself for marriage and waiting for the wind to blow her some sort of a man.

F. Scott Fitzgerald, the famous author, in a recent interview in New York City, said:

"The Southern girl is easily the most attractive type in America. No matter how poor a Southern girl may be and many of them are very poor, she keeps up her social activities. In New York, when a girl's family loses its money, she drops out of the running. This is not true in the South.

"Can you imagine a New York girl having a good time at a party when she knows that she is not so well or so expensively dressed as the other girls?

"Now, in the South, the girls, because of their tradition of before-the-war culture and their sense of old-world courtesy, know how to enjoy themselves despite financial embarrassment.

"A Southern girl will slip into a simple muslin or organdie frock, go to a dance, entertain men on a rickety old porch, have a thoroughly good time, and make no attempt to conceal her poverty."

Nobody's Business
By Gee McGee

My First Love Affair

I was coming 17 when love first shot its arrow into my gizzard. I had seen my then future wife but twice, but I knew then and there that I would die if I did not marry her at once.

As for me, I was not a thing of beauty, nor a joy forever; I was not acquainted with store-bought clothes. I had a jeans coat and a pair of jeans britches, and a pretty little striped calico shirt. I wore a No. 8 shoe on my right foot, but it took a No. 9 for my left. I was then slightly pigeon-toed, and was somewhat stooped from plowing a fast mule.

As to her, she was a bunch of dewdrops, a plate of sunshine, a vase of lilies, and her lips looked like rose buds, and her stockings of tan radiated real beauty, and displayed real art, but then it took an accident or a calamity to see above a girl's ankles. I fell for her hard. She was buxom, and wore No. 7 shoes but, feet never stood in anybody's way then when love was knocking at the door.

Well, she told me I could come to see her on Saturday night. I was so happy I thought I'd die. It seemed three weeks from Friday afternoon till Saturday night. I begun to doll up about 3 p.m. I first made a trip to the creek. I washed all over with lye soap. My skin shone like a moonbeam, and my whole body was red but clean.

Up to that time I had never been introduced to underwear. In fact, none of our family was ever burdened with any excess of clothes. So I got a pair of sister's old black stockings and cut the feet out of them and put them on. I blacked my shoes with soot and shined them with tallow. I got my daddy's razor and scraped my face good, but did not dull it any as my beard was soft and tender, all three of them.

I then got some lard and plastered my hair to my head so tight I had to pry it loose next morning with a case knife. I found a little bit of lily white and I rubbed that on my cheeks with a little red calico rag. Man, that pinkness brought out undiscovered beauty. My britches struck me about 4 inches above my brogans. My coat fitted me so tight I looked like a bologna sausage.

My next job was getting out of the house without any of my brothers or sisters seeing me. I had never tried to dress up before, and if they had seen me life would not have been worth a six-pence.

I began to get excited about that time. I tried to think what I would say to my sweetheart. I walked a while and then ran a while, and I studied up several nice things to say—like this: I am so glad to see you, you are so pretty, I am glad I met you. I seen you yesterday but you never seen me—ansoforth.

But on I went, I got there. I walked up the steps. The thermometer was below freezing, but I was above melting. Never sweated so in my life. My mouth was dry, my breath was short, my tongue

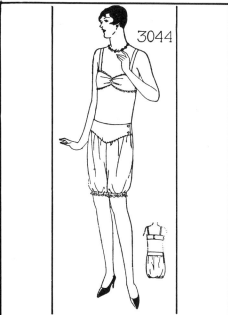

In this day of short skirts and automobiles every woman should wear bloomers. They are modest and comfortable. This style has a shaped yoke which adds to one's slender appearance. A firm brassiere is a good foundation for a good fitting dress and graceful outline.

was glued to my throat, my stomach hurt, and my shoes began to pinch my toes.

The old man come to the door. I said, "Is she here?" He said, "H— no, brat—do your maw know where you air tonight? Daughter's gone to a party if you happen to be looking for her." Slam went the door. I went home with a broken-heart, and never have had any use for that man or that woman since.

If a young man should come to call on me for the first time about the first thing I would notice would be how he was traveling. The car to win my admiration

need not be expensive, but I would want to see how it was kept. If it is in a neat, clean condition that shows a careful driver; if shabbily kept and all covered with mud that shows recklessness.

"When a boy caller is going home, is it right to accompany him to the gate?" Honey child, you did not tell me whether that gate is 10 feet or half a mile from your front door. Whether or not it is right is not a matter of rule or etiquette but plain common sense. Should the moon be glorious, the hour early, the gate but a few steps from the porch, and mother and father on the veranda, there is no reason in the world why you should not be a little informal by sauntering to the gate with him.

The limit of your immediate home is the house, however, and your duties as hostess cease there. This with the fact that a real gentleman leaves you safe in your home and something might happen to you on the way back from the gate makes it better for you to say "Good night" within the house or on the porch. As for you, you do not want to let him think you are hanging on to him until the last second, and, as for him, it saves him the embarrassment of wondering if he should not see you back to your door.

It must be wonderful to be a girl born in this generation. She has freedoms and opportunities that were never thought of a generation ago. Today she is brought from babyhood to womanhood through development instead of repression. Why, when I was a little girl the motto was, "Children should be seen and not heard," or "Better bear the yoke in your youth," or "Spare the rod and spoil the child." Finer far is the motto of today, the advice of the bird mother to her fledgling, "Learn to fly with your own wings, my little one."

The generation of yesterday, as a whole, craved happiness but made few plans for getting it. The generation of today lives happiness and makes plans for keeping it. Isn't that so?

Consider the clothes we wore, for example: Layer upon layer of lawn, steel jacketed corsets to cramp, voluminous skirts to impede, trailing frills to stir and catch the dust, collars that bound, hats that soared aloft and required skull tight hair dressing to anchor them. As for shoes, the toes were compressed while we tipped and tilted on tall funny heels.

"I am looking for a wife," says a correspondent, "and I am not looking for one who wears high heels and thin silk stockings." Then he adds, "especially on country roads on a blustery winter day." So far, so good, but here are quotations from two girl's letters. The first says: "I want to have a good time but the boys like to take out girls who dress like picture freaks

A NEW STUNT—A DISHWASHING CONTEST FOR FLAPPERS

"Fine!" said the managing editor (a man), "if we could only get all the flappers entered into a daily contest of that kind." "Fine!" said Mrs. Hutt (a woman who has washed more than a few), "if we could only get all the dirty dishes entered in a contest of that kind daily."

and act as though they were made to be handled. Even my brother says, 'You're a fine chum and lots of fun, sis, but when I go out for fun I want a girl who dresses like a dream and don't have to get home until the show is over.'" The next letter is from a girl who says: "Father always said 'Learn to cook,

girls. Learn to be useful,' or 'Now buy a coat that is plain and sensible.' He came home with a stepmother for me about a month ago. She is dainty and giggling and knows nothing about work. She says pa told her he wanted her for his wife and not his servant."

Now, how can one give advice in the face of circumstances like these? I'll tell you. Suppose we give the Farm Women's Page to the boys one month to tell what they want and to the girls another month and let them answer for themselves.

I want my husband to have good manners, be free from the use of tobacco, intoxicating liquors or slang. He must eat anything, not snore or grit teeth while sleeping. He must be early to rise, full of life and have a stately carriage of his body, a quick springy step, brown eyes, dark brown hair, medium complexion and a good education.

The qualities I wish my future husband to possess are the following: (1) A Yankee, (2) good health, (3) able financially to travel, (4) a teetotaler, (5) snoreless, (6) quarrelless, (7) bathe all over daily, (8) high school education, (9) not fond of kissing and hugging, (10) thoroughly wash his hair twice a week.

OKLAHOMA'S HEALTHIEST FARM BOY AND GIRL

My husband must not be handsome. I am afraid some pretty little blonde stenographer might captivate him in his sleep, and then I would be left a wailing widow.

His Girl's Dumbdora

"Does your sweet mama know anything about automobiles?"
"I should say not. She asked me last night if I cooled the engine by stripping the gears."

Girls are more attractive to boys because of powder, paint, perfume, high heels, and permanent waves.

Some girls may have attractive features but have some blemish which can be easily hidden by powder, skillfully put on. If a girl hasn't any color in her cheeks a tint of rouge is the thing; it brings out the color of her eyes and hair. Lipstick put on carefully is attractive too. If one has beautiful white teeth the red lips make them appear even whiter. If one hasn't the most beautiful curves in her lips she may change them slightly with lipstick without marring her facial appearance. This is an age of color so let girls blossom forth in their brightest hour—but not too "brightest."

Perfume used sparingly is good but too much isn't pleasant to anyone.

High heels help the general appearance of a girl. They appear to make her feel well-groomed too. (Of course in choosing a wife a chap thinks common sense and health are better than high heels.)

Take a Kodak to the Fair

With a Kodak along you'll make pictures for fun and a practical record of whatever interests you—cattle, horses, hogs, machinery—pictures full of pointers to apply when you're back on home acres.

Autographic Kodaks $6.50 up—at your dealer's

Eastman Kodak Co., Rochester, N. Y.

Permanent waves are beautiful if they are well kept. If the hair is arranged attractively the waves add more beauty.

Even if a girl hasn't God-given beauty she has no excuse for not being attractive nowadays.

Out of Uncle Sam's family of more than 100,000,000 he has been giving about 4,000,000 of them some extra training during the war. The large majority of them are young men, the pick of their families. They were selected from all walks of life, labor, agriculture, merchandising, banking, manufacturing and so on. The war is over now and the home-coming is in progress.

There is Farmer Sammie, Teacher Sammie, Banker Sammie,

Merchant Sammie, Lawyer, Doctor, Laborer, Cook and Bottle Washer Sammie. When they arrive home the distinction will begin.

How about Farmer Sammie in the army who has worked all his life for a bare board and clothes? He has been drawing his $30 to $50 per month and better board, clothes and comforts than he was accustomed to. His Uncle Sam has taught him he was a joint heir with banker, lawyer, merchant and mechanic, and equal to them in every respect. He has taught "Farmer Sammie" what sanitary, comfortable living is; what a bathtub, theatre, hotel and good "eats" are, with salary enough to enjoy a taste of them. He has been given scientific training in business, mechanics and many other callings of life. His vision has been broadened. He had likely never been further from home than the county or state fair. Now he has seen some of his own country and likely, France, England, Italy, or Belgium. He has learned something of the world and the people.

When "Farmer Sammie" returns home, will he be satisfied with his former job? Does anyone believe that men who fought as they did at Chateau Thierry and Argonne Forest and absolutely refused to be taught how to retreat, will longer accept a bare supply of victuals and clothes, and none of the comforts of life?

Under present conditions of pricing and distribution of the products he produces, the "cut over" swamps on poor sandy hills of the South, or the arid sections of the West, even as a gift, if

compelled to make it his home, will have very little attraction for "Farmer Sammie." The cause that has been driving the pick of our farm boys from the farm for 50 years, that of having no voice in the price of their products, no profits, no comforts, and scant necessities of life, will have to be corrected before "stay on the farm" or "back to the farm" will be heard.

"Are kisses really unhealthy?" comes in a letter from a maiden in Tennessee. Bless your heart, dear, how can one answer truly at this distance. Go to the dentist and have him make your teeth perfect, go to the doctor and let him assure you that no contagious germ dwells in you, gargle your throat, then kiss the baby—if that is whom you are desirous of kissing. No harm can come of it, especially if you kiss baby on that sweet little place, beloved of mothers the world over, the back of the neck.

I want my daughter to marry a farmer. I'll tell you why.

First, her father, grandfather, and ancestry for generations back were farmers. While none of them have been very wealthy, none have been poor.

There is a certainty that goes along with steadiness of purpose in the occupation itself. That quality of being indisputably established appeals to me.

They Must Decide Themselves— Do I want my son to be a farmer? This is a question which I have been trying to solve since I held my first born to my heart. Do I want this boy to be a farmer? This child with his father's honest eyes, his father's firm mouth, do I want him to travel the same path, the same rugged, beautiful, struggling life his forefathers have traveled for generations? Since then other sons have come to us, both beautiful promising lads. Do I want them to struggle with the problems of yesterday's and today's farmer? Do I want them to lead the average, hard, open, clean life of a farmer with the average recompense?

The boy who is not liked by the well-meaning girl is the one who will call for her after dusk to carry her for a spin in his flivver and then keep her out until a very late hour of the night.—R.L.H.

Can a Girl be Safe in a Short Dress?

For many moons now our men have been seriously concerned about the length of the skirts of the woman-folk. It and the price of cotton are equal rivals as subjects of conversation where men gather together. Appeal after appeal has come to us to give space to that subject, to urge longer skirts, to write smashing attacks upon those that are short.

"Short dresses are not safe," we said to ourselves. Then we

Attractive Frocks for Summer Wear

2399—Two-Material Dress for Spring Wear. Cut in sizes 16 years, 36, 38, 40 and 42 inches bust measure. The 36-inch size requires 1⅜ yards 36-inch figured material with 1½ yards 36-inch plain material. The short sleeves are finished with turn-back cuffs.

2466—Sports Frock with Front Fulness. The pattern comes in sizes 16 years, 36, 38, 40, 42 and 44 inches bust measure. Size 36 requires 3 yards 40-inch material with ⅞ yard 36-inch contrasting. Can be made with long tight-fitting sleeves or short.

2505—Attractive Design for Sports. The pattern is obtainable in sizes 16 years, 36, 38, 40, 42 and 44 inches bust measure. The 36-inch size requires 2 yards 52-inch bordered material with ⅜ yard 27-inch contrasting and 4¾ yards of ribbon for trimming and tie.

2468—Dress with Gathered Flounce Popular. The pattern comes in sizes 16 years, 36, 38, 40 and 42 inches bust measure. For the 36-inch size you will need 4⅛ yards 36-inch material. Even the amateur sewer could complete a frock like this in an afternoon.

2496—Design with Front Panel. The pattern comes in sizes 36, 38, 40, 42, 44 and 46 inches bust measure. The 36-inch size requires only 2⅝ yards of 40-inch material with ⅜ yard 44-inch material for contrasting. Dress can also be made with long tight-fitting sleeves.

Price of each pattern, 20 cents. Two patterns ordered at one time, 30 cents; stamps or coin (coin preferred). Write your name and address plainly on your order sheet, being sure to state number and size of pattern wanted.

Our new fashion book contains hundreds of styles—styles for morning, afternoon, and evening wear during the summer. It contains embroidery designs and nine picture dressmaking lessons. Send 15 cents now for your copy. Address Pattern Department, The Progressive Farmer.

watched women climb into cars and teach calves to drink from buckets. We discarded that reason.

"Short skirts are not healthful," we said. One day it was very dry at the community fair and, my, how those long skirts did stir up the germ laden dust to be breathed by the just and unjust. The difference between these and the short-skirted girls was as the difference in dust raised by the automobiles and bicycles. The next day it rained. The long skirts were wet and sodden. Many of the women

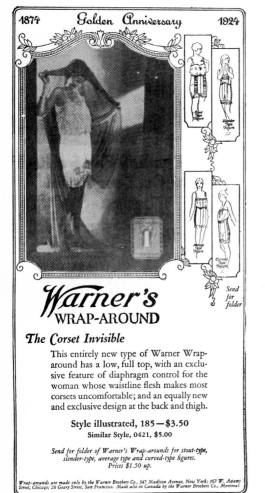

Warner's WRAP-AROUND

The Corset Invisible

This entirely new type of Warner Wrap-around has a low, full top, with an exclusive feature of diaphragm control for the woman whose waistline flesh makes most corsets uncomfortable; and an equally new and exclusive design at the back and thigh.

Style illustrated, 185—$3.50
Similar Style, 0421, $5.00

Send for folder of Warner's Wrap-arounds for stout-type, slender-type, average type and curved-type figures. Prices $1.50 up.

Wrap-arounds are made only by the Warner Brothers Co., 347 Madison Avenue, New York; 367 W. Adams Street, Chicago; 28 Geary Street, San Francisco. Made also in Canada by the Warner Brothers Co., Montreal.

sat in them an hour listening to the lectures. Many a cold was the result surely. The abbreviated skirts caught no more water than a man's trousers. We checked off the healthful idea.

Argument there was that the men must deem long skirts more convenient. We watched baby-laden women climb stairs, we saw skirts catch on buggy steps, snags, and weeds. "Nay, nay," we said, "Let us seek further."

"Women have too much to do. Long skirts are more easily cared for," but one ironing day, one Monday brushing of Sunday's clothes convinced us otherwise.

"Moral grounds? Could it be that?" Now we had the solution. A setback came when a grayhaired old lady said, "Have the mothers, who always stand first in finding and removing stumbling blocks from the pathway of their sons and daughters, have they protested?" "No," we answered. "Not once." Were we not correct in assuming that the length of woman's skirts had in no wise upset the morals of any community?

"Modesty might be the consideration." We pondered on that too, but since modesty did not seem to be a strong point of menfolk at bathing beach, in fields, or elsewhere that it clashed with convenience, we still questioned.

"Now we have it. It is beauty," said a fleeting idea. We gazed around us and decided that a beautiful thing indeed is the low heeled sensible shoe so much in vogue and the well-stockinged ankle.

"Girls," I said in despair to a high school class, "Why do you wear short dresses?" "They are so

comfortable," was the reply. "Why do some people wear them too short?" "They have no sense," said one girl. "They can't see themselves," said another. "Wisdom is justified of her children," I quoted, for here was the reason and the solution.

"Are brassieres fashionable?" They certainly are. Few well-dressed women go without them.

Should Women Wear Corsets?

Should a woman who is really not stout, but who is a little plump, wear corsets? My sister tells me I should but I think I look all right without them.

I am afraid, my lady, that you are the one to decide that. The trouble is that too many women refuse to study their own outlines in the mirror. The wearing or the not wearing of a corset is, after all, one that should not be determined by fashion or fancy but by common sense. Too often the woman puts on her most flattering dress, stands in front of a mirror and takes a pleased look at herself. What she should do is see herself as she goes hustling down the street past a shiny store window that acts as a mirror. The corsets of today are not the instruments of torture they were when women looked like hourglasses. They are girdles, cleverly designed to mold and support the figure rather than restrict it. I suggest that you get a flexible, topless corset with brassieres that reach below the waist.

A girl wants to go visiting in the city for two weeks and wishes to know what to get with the least money possible. Enough underwear to save troubling the hostess with your laundry, a dark silk petticoat, a good sensible long coat, and if possible a pretty fur piece. This can be worn sometimes without the coat.

One good wool, and one silk or finer dress will be found useful. If the friend entertains, a pretty light dress will be needed.

The Sweetest Story Ever Told

"Tell me, do you love me? Whisper softly, sweetly, as of old,—
Tell me that you love me, for that's the sweetest story ever told"

© 1919, G.-D. Co.

NATIONALLY PRICED

Three models, all playable by hand or by roll, sold at the same prices to everybody everywhere in the U. S. freight and war tax paid. Price branded in the back of each instrument at the factory.

White House Model $675
Country Seat Model 585
Suburban Model 495

Gulbransen Trade Mark

YOU need think of nothing but the song and the joy of singing it—if you have a Gulbransen Player-Piano.

The Gulbransen is so Easy to Play. It seems to understand. It responds to your wishes. It helps you tell your story—sympathetically and without effort.

The words to be sung each moment are always before your eyes as the roll unwinds—printed on the roll. You cannot "lose the place." No notes to read; no fingering to practice. The Gulbransen does all that for you—and makes no mistakes.

The pedals act so gently that a tiny baby once played the Gulbransen (as shown in the picture at the left) and gave us the idea for our trade mark.

You have never tried a player that is so responsive to the lightest pedal touch. Or one from which you can get such delicacy of expression.

If you would love to sing without the drudgery of playing, go in and try a Gulbransen at our dealer's store.

You'll know him because he shows the Baby at the Pedals in his window and newspaper advertising. Or, write us for his address and our catalog.

These love songs and thousands more are ready for you in player-rolls. Our dealer has them:

A Little Love, a Little Kiss	Dearie
Somewhere a Voice Is Calling	Sweet Adeline
The Sunshine of Your Smile	A Perfect Day
When You Look in the Heart	Sweetheart
of a Rose	The Rosary
I'm Sorry I Made You Cry	Till We Meet Again
Love's Old Sweet Song	I Love You Truly
The Sweetest Story Ever Told	

GULBRANSEN-DICKINSON CO.
819 North Sawyer Avenue, Chicago

GULBRANSEN
(Pronounced Gul-BRAN-sen)
Player-Piano

Talking Machines and Moving Pictures

Some people play well, have fine voices, and are artists in other lines, but there are many homes deprived of artists, especially in the musical line. Where no natural talent for music exists, there it is that the Victrola, Edison or other good talking machine comes in and plays a most important part in the social life of a home or even community.

Listen with me to an opera: One catches the largeness and high range of Galli-Curci; the richness of McCormack gifted with a voice of superb beauty; the ever popular Gluck.

How many of us in rural districts, or even small towns have the opportunity of hearing the wizard of music, Jascha Heiftez? Then there is our own popular Geraldine Farrar, so dear to the heart of the American public. All this has a lasting and wonderful influence in the home.

Moving pictures as an institution are not bad. On the other hand, if proper pictures are shown, they can be of great service and help in continuing the development of the human race. It is up to parents, on the farm as well as in the city, to use their influence in securing pictures that are inspiring, uplifting, informing, and amusing without being vulgar.

There is need of a law compelling film censorship, but in the

meantime parents can do a great deal to prevent the showing of bad pictures. Moving picture concerns are going to put out films that will make money. So long as we continue to go to see them without discrimination, they will continue to produce pictures which, to say the least, are in no way helpful to those who see them. As soon as we begin to select the gold and reject the dross, profit and loss will tell the producer more emphatically than anything else just what kind of entertainment people want.

Some of the Recent Motion Pictures

Don Q, Son of Zorro.—In this picture Douglas Fairbanks is a young Californian in Spain, and his remarkable dexterity with a whip leads him into many adventures. Mary Astor is the lovely Spanish girl into whose garden he falls. The action moves rapidly and the story is full of romance, thrills, hairbreadth escapes, amusing situations and beautiful backgrounds. "Don Q" is likely to be one of the most popular of the 1925 motion pictures.

The Gold Rush.—Here Charlie Chaplin is a tramp in the Klondike. He becomes snowbound in a cabin with a lunatic, falls in love with a girl of the dance hall, and is blown by a blizzard on top of a lost mine which makes him a millionaire. This is not as side-splittingly funny as one or two other Chaplin pictures have been, but it is an excellent comedy.

Lights of Old Broadway.—Marion Davies is the Irish heroine in this picture, which shows New York in the period when electricity was supplanting gas for street lighting. It is not quite up to the standard of her former picture, "Little Old New York," but it is an interesting picture and well worth seeing.

Graustark.—Norma Talmage plays the part of the lovely Princess Yetive who falls in love with an American. For anyone who likes a story of this romantic type, it is a beautiful and satisfying picture.

Old Clothes.—This is a sequel of Jackie Coogan's former picture,

"The Ragman," and is much like it. Jackie plays Cupid in a love story which has nothing unusual about it, but his own performance is as delightful as ever.

The Freshman.—Harold Lloyd goes to college in this picture, in which he plays the part of a boy who wants to be the most popular student in school. There are not as many laughs in this as there were in "Girl Shy" or "A Sailor-Made Man" perhaps, but the football game at the end is one of the funniest scenes in which this popular comedian has ever appeared.

The Desert Flower.—Colleen Moore is shown living in a boxcar on the desert, wearing an original costume of gunnysacking decorated with bottle tops. She gets into some amusing situations and finally achieves her pet ambitions—to have a handsome husband and ride in a private car. All the family will enjoy Colleen in this picture.

Dancing is so popular that we cannot ignore it, much as we might care to. It has come to us from Bible times, but has been frowned upon by the Church, rightly so, probably. The more it was frowned upon, the more the respectable ignored it and the more the reckless embraced it. If, therefore, the young people of any neighborhood insist upon dancing, the best course would seem to be to have it under the protection of the school, mens' and womens' neighborhood clubs or the homes. Every effort should be made to ex-

clude the dancing where partners are held in a close position, and every effort made to substitute dances such as the quadrille, the Virginia Reel and the minuet, in which the older people can join. It is the fun, the action, the music that young people like. Where parents attend, the danger of the drive home is largely eliminated.

Tell them the truth,— tell them everything!

He had decided to leave her—to save her the pain his confession would cause. Yet she begged him to stay—begged him to tell everyone the truth! It meant poverty, failure, disgrace perhaps, yet she was willing to share these trials with him!

The truth! What had he done? What terrible deed menaced the world of ease and luxury his daring had won for him? And why was she ready to sacrifice her name, her future—everything?

And why—but you must read for yourself this great love story by Juliet Wilbor Tompkins. Everyone will read "The Glory" for it is the latest novel by America's most popular woman writer. They will buy it next winter at the bookstores. But it is to appear *first* in McCall's Magazine, and you can read this wonderful full-length

$1.50 Novel for

This special 25-cent subscription gives you four big issues of McCall's, including "The Glory" complete, also 16 other absorbing stories, scores of articles, all the latest fashions, hundreds of beautiful pictures, housekeeping secrets, etc.

25¢

(35c. In Canada)

"Folk Dances"—the old time games or sports, exercises in costume to music, the girls and boys in alternate groups have no dangers. They bring the neighborhood together and are one of the best forms of physical training we have. Persons of all ages can indulge in them, and a Victrola can furnish the music.

Moving pictures have come to stay. Let us then, patronize the clean, wholesome films and refuse to countenance those that teach treachery, bloodshed, faithlessness and irrevence. If one accidentally sees an objectionable film, let her speak to the manager on her way out of the house, but ask that he let her know when he secured one with a good moral and good scenery. When he does, be liberal with your praise.

I want to say that if this thing of dancing is half as bad as we have been told that it is, causing, as Billy Sunday and other noted authorities say, the falling of three-fourths of the girls who go astray, and that it is embraced so much by the reckless, isn't it a pretty good thing to let *entirely alone?* Why would we embrace such a thing and throw around it the sacred influence of the home if it leads to all those bad things we are so often told of by those in a position to know? Isn't it a dangerous thing to fool with at all?

We are told further by this writer that it is the fun, action, and music that attracts the young people. Granting that this is true, and probably it is, couldn't the same thing be said of the drinking of wine and many another harmful indulgence, first taken as a simple and harmless thing, later to become a curse? It is the tendency of any thing that we should regard, it seems to me, and what it *eventually leads to.* If it is wrong for a young man to embrace a young woman in the parlor alone, would it not be just as much so to the tunes of music in the dance hall? Man is of a dual nature and all know that the natural or animal has every advantage over the spiritual, and when we do those things that fire the lower order of thinking, we are on dangerous ground and encouraging the animal instead of crucifying the desires of the flesh and keeping it in subjection . . . A Father

Housework to Radio Music

Not the least of things interesting and electrical is the radio set so frequently found in the modern house. This wonderful invention enables the listener-in, even on the lonely plantation, to hear the music, lectures, and news broadcasted from various stations. The housewife who can tune in will get information and enjoyment, will learn the latest market reports and prices on food products and will be able to set all the clocks right by adjusting them each evening to standard time as given via radio. And as a sickroom visitor or one to amuse the children when they are confined to bed, radio is a real pal.

One may also lessen the fatigue and monotony of many tasks by

doing them to the tune of radio music. Dishwashing does not seem drudgery and goes much faster accompanied by sprightly jazz, while brushing up the living room, is more fun if done to a gay two-step. Beating cake, making beds, and other housework duties involving rythmic motion are performed more quickly and with more enjoyment with music's aid.

"Please give us a reason for playing tennis. Sister and I love it but mother declares we can get all the exercise we need in housework." Doubtless your mother is right; especially if she needs your help. There are a few things mother forgets though and one is that housework has not the inspiration of tennis. Who ever shouted and laughed and opened up unused cells in her lungs when she wiped a dish as she has when she has side-swiped a ball? Tennis brings people in touch with others who are young in years or heart; it takes them into the great outdoors, it makes the blood run faster.

When country people get more tennis and other games that make them laugh and that develop good sportsmanship, then will women do the dishwashing with more vim, have more strength for the endless round of duties and know more intimately the good in their neighbors. Anything that brings young people together in broad daylight in wholesome sport is good.

I'll Be Anything, But I Won't Be a Drudge

Several months ago I had a serious disappointment, one that concerned the heart of contentment in our farm homes. It was the month that we had the letters about improved methods of doing the family washing. Can you believe that out of almost 700 letters received only five told of really efficient equipment for the work, only 32 were partly supplied with improved equipment and, as far as one could tell by the letters, 592 depended on woman muscle power to haul the water, fill tubs, place an outdoor iron pot and do 50 other things that could and should be done by machinery. Let us hope

NO COUNTRY HOME COMFORTS AND CONVENIENCES
—The News Letter, Department of Agriculture.

this month's letters on home conveniences will show more advance.

Raise the Standard

Our vacuum cleaner is a great boon and we have a big oil stove which helps greatly.

How can we expect a high degree of happiness or a high standard in our homes while some Southern farmers permit their wives to stand and wait on them and eat after they have finished.

There are women who chop cotton until dinner time, go in and get dinner and chop again. It is uncivilized. Surely some one needs to be put on the witness stand.

Make the automobile do the pumping. Jack up the hind wheel of the car and connect it by a belt with a jack on the pump or the wheel of the washing machine. Then start your car. Watching results while you do something else is easier than doing the work yourself.

We do our washing ourselves, with a machine. But in cold weather we found it very disagreeable to get up so early. Finally we hit upon this plan: My husband turns the machine and wringer during the evening, we put the clothes through the hot rinsing water, then in the morning there is only the blueing, starching and hanging out to do, and we get up only a few minutes earlier than usual. Besides my husband gets his night's rest after the washing and is fresh for the day's business.

Being Modern

Being modern does not depend on the years one has lived, nor does an enjoyment of living," declared Mrs. Alice T. Pitchford, 86-

PA HELPS WITH THE WASH

year-old mother of Mrs. G. E. Wheales of Rocky Mount, N.C., after her first airplane ride. Mrs. Pitchford climbed into the plane without assistance and after the ride she said: "It was just fine and

I wouldn't have missed it for anything. There is one thing about being up in the air, " she added, "and that is that up there you don't hear any political arguments."

———

I read in the paper about an elderly woman who was having her first visit to Washington. She had never seen a tall building nor street cars before. Traffic towers and the Washington Monument were marvels to her, and when she went up in an elevator she knew it was not running. Great was her astonishment when she got out and found that she had been going up all the time. That woman got her thrills all at once. That's the way life is sometimes. After we've gone along the road of life with everything somber, suddenly sunshine bursts upon us and a dozen adventures crowd upon us, making up for lost time. As Stevenson said, "Life is so full of a number of things, I'm sure we should all be as happy as kings."

Why Every Woman Should Vote

The basic reason for the ballot is the right of the majority of the people to rule. Men who cannot vote are not free men. Therefore woman is not free, because we deny her a voice in the basic principles of liberty though she may be a citizen of "The land of the free and the home of the brave."

I believe in woman suffrage because I believe that women should have every right that men have. Moreover, states that have woman suffrage have found it to be good and none of them have ever reversed the law, though some of them could have done so without the women's consent.

When our wives, mothers and sisters vote, saloons and white slave traffic disappear. Take women out of the church and you have nothing left. Take women out of anything, and you have taken the life, love and beauty out of it.

And as election day is the greatest day we have to make real progress toward a higher, better world in which humanity may live, we cannot on this great day do our duty without the assistance of our good women.

I wish to say in regard to the objection we often hear that woman will lose her exalted position if she stoops to vote, that that exalted position which she enjoys is breaking her back slaving over a wash tub. And the sooner she gets away from this exalted position the better for women and all the rest of the world.

To us is credited the assertion that we want to be equal to men. It isn't true; never once have we doubted our equality.

Thank Heaven for Tennessee

In September, twenty-seven million or more women will cast their first votes at the primaries for the next President of the United States unless some court decision sets it aside temporarily. In November they will vote at the elections. It is the end of seventy years of insistence on the part of the women of the nation to have a say concerning the laws under which we are all governed and the spending of the taxes of which we pay our share.

Thirty-five states had ratified suffrage and thirty-six were necessary. The eyes of the world were on North Carolina as the thirty-sixth state but fear of the loss of a few votes back home made the Old North State lose the honor.

Two days later Tennessee considered the question. The vote was taken and it stood 48 to 48. Then there rose to his feet on the floor of the house of representatives Mr. E. B. Turner, the youngest member of the house. The floor and the galleries were hushed for a moment and all faces were turned to where he stood. In a quiet voice Mr. Turner announced, "I wish to vote 'aye' on the question."

And thus did we women cease to be classed with idiots, imbeciles and criminals, as dependents of the state and became citizens entitled to vote on the same basis as men as is our right and responsibility. It enfranchises the other half of the people of a country that once declared it believed that "taxation without representation is unjust." It is a victory won by no individual or group but by all those women and men since the time of the Revolution who have protested against the humiliation of disfranchisement and have proclaimed the equality of men and women.

We are told that woman's place is at home in spite of the fact that 8,000,000 women are forced to leave home in quest of bread. The home does not stop at the threshold. All outdoors is her home, just as long as she must prepare her child to live there. Women's refining influence, goodness, love, spirituality and sweetness purge a community of it rottenness and keep clean the hearth. Her glorious mission in a community is that which

Christ placed in her hands to fight the devil and all his works. It is just as necessary for a woman to go to the polling booth as it is to go to church.

"My idea of dressing well is having sensible shoes, no run-over heels, simple pretty wash dresses

Miss Zula Hight
KITTRELL, N. C.

Who Earned a Pure Bred Registered Poland-China Pig in just Seven Days

Miss Hight earned her Poland-China pig in just seven days. On February 21st we received the first order on her pig club, and on the morning of February 28th, we received an order for 28 subscriptions, which completed her club.

WHAT SHE DID IN SEVEN DAYS
You can do in just a few days, if you will just make up your mind to do so, and go at it with a determination. Right in your community there are hundreds of new and renewal subscriptions to be had, if you will just go after them.

TO OWN A PURE-BRED PIG
Will be a mark of distinction for you in your community and will start you on the road to prosperity. It will mean the laying of the foundation for a comfortable income for you all through life, and last but not least when old age overtakes you.
Write today for full particulars and supplies.

Pig Club Department, The Progressive Farmer.
Rush me full instructions and supplies. I want to earn a pure-bred registered pig.

Name...

Postoffice...

Route..................... State.....................
Raleigh, N. C. Birmingham, Ala. Memphis, Tenn. Dallas, Texas.
Address your nearest office.

for the house and simple but well made clothes of good material for festive occasions. Once when little Betty and I were dressed in pretty blue and white calico dresses she said, 'Mother, you and I are just as beautiful as God makes the blue and white sky,' and turning to my husband who was near, she said, 'Don't you fink so, Daddy?' He caught her to him and said,

'Child, there never was a sky as beautiful as you and Mother!'"

Business Trains for Marriage

The truth has been borne in on my mind by seven years of business life that it will pay all girls to earn their own living for at least four to five years before they marry.

During my business career, I have seen men with their coats off, spiritually as well as physically. I know when the veneer knocks off just how many men are mean, stingy, and high tempered. I know other men who are kind and tender as well as honorable and honest. When I choose a man for a husband I feel I am not as apt to be fooled in him.

Page 121. The Progressive Farmer began to use full color covers with its September, 1932, issue. This impressionistic cover of December, 1932, shows what must have been a familiar scene at Christmastime, the home folks welcoming back the "prodigals" who had left the farm.

Page 122. One of the greatest advantages proclaimed for children growing up on the farm was the possibility of learning in the most natural circumstances how new life is created, nourished and cherished, how it passes on life again and eventually returns to the enfolding earth. Children could see themselves as having a place in this great natural cycle.

The Progressive Farmer
and Farm Woman

Kentucky-Tennessee
Edition

REG'D U.S
PATENT OFFICE

Vol. 45. No. 4. Two years, $1

SATURDAY, JANUARY 25, 1930

I believe any girl who has held down a good position for three years will learn how to give the soft answer that turns away wrath, how to stop the snappy comeback that trembles on her tongue, and how to refrain from reminding a man of the mistakes he has made.

A Personal Question

A lady entered an English railway station and said she wanted a ticket for London. The pale-looking clerk asked, "Single?"

"It's none of your business," she replied. "I might have been married a dozen times if I'd felt like providin' for some poor, shiftless wreck of a man like you."

Page 123. The glow of sunset on the home farm is punctuated by electric light brought in by the high wires. Before rural electrification, celebrated by this 1934 cover of the Progressive Farmer, *a farmer wanting electricity had to buy his own generating plant.*

Page 124. Another much-proclaimed advantage of farm life for children was the responsibility required of them. They could progress from small tasks to larger and more difficult ones. They could know that their particular job was needed and, even when very young, that they had an important place in the family enterprise.

—Courtesy Pathe Pictures, Inc.

THINKING OF MATRIMONY BUT WONDERING WHERE THE MONEY'S COMING FROM
Charles Ray, who is Pathe's "Dynamite Smith," returns to his interpretations of the plain people, in a scene from an old film, "The Egg-Crate Wallop."

Beauty Aids

"What is the correct way to take a shower bath? We have one installed but I do not like it." If you are well and vigorous, the best plan is to turn on the water for one minute then step out and dry yourself vigorously with a crash towel. These are rough enough to stimulate but not chafe the skin. Shower baths are not meant for cleanliness and therefore no soap is used with them, except, perhaps, in summer when men are in from the fields. A cleansing bath is at about 100 degrees temperature and calls for soap.

Has your hair become dry and lifeless on account of exposure to the hot sun or much sea bathing? An excellent preparation to restore the lustre is composed of two drachms of castor oil and six ounces of cologne water.

A few drops of this dressing are poured into the palm of the hand. A soft, spotlessly clean hairbrush is gently rotated on the palm so that the dressing may be evenly distributed on the bristles. Now you are ready to apply it to the hair, which should have received a previous brushing with stiffer bristles. The dressing is gently spread over the hair and later a soft silk handerchief is used to give the final polish.

"How can I get rid of freckles?" Try lemon or cucumber juice.

"Please tell me how to make the hair on my head thick." We have given many methods on this page. If all have failed, rub the scalp gently each night with the tips of the fingers dipped in a very little vaseline. Wash, using mild white soap, every two weeks. Keep brushes clean. Continue treatment for a year.

Gum chewing is ruinous to beauty of mouth and to a refined appearance.

Jealousy or other violent emotions will make wrinkles, bring gray hair and alter an otherwise lovely face.

If the lips are dry use cold cream, or, what is better, a lipstick, which contains an oil and camphor. The expression can be controlled more or less. One can keep the corners from sagging by thinking a happy or amusing thought, can prevent flabbiness by holding them tight, or avoid a hard, firm line by controlling the nervous tension that induces it. Young people can prevent the circles at the side of the mouth from forming, in large measure, by simple massage.

The well groomed woman's trusted aid for centuries has been the beauty mask. It is used for keeping the skin clear and removing fine wrinkles. The clay, the oatmeal and the egg packs are used most frequently.

First clean the face well with a cleansing cream, wipe off the excess, wash with warm water and a mild soap, dry well and apply a skin food with a gently upward rotary motion; wipe clean, put on a little witch hazel or toilet water. The pores are now free of dirt and closed.

Beat two egg whites slightly and apply to the face with a soft brush; when dry put on the beaten yolk of the egg and let dry. Leave on half an hour.

If the skin is sensitive use cold cream to soften the egg but if not use warm (not hot) water. Pat the skin dry; apply face powder. Actresses use this every night for about 10 nights and then about once in two weeks thereafter.

Fotching Up the Boy

My household directions for "fotching up the boy" have been short and swift. As I think of them they follow:

By my plan of keeping clean inside just as you would keep clean outside—without comment and simply as a matter of course.

By not hounding him into a corner by too many unnecessary questions.

By never admitting in his presence that a boy is capable of underhanded doing.

By suggesting to him that if he ever felt any superiority to any human being that he go upstairs and take a bath and get over it.

By intimating that no one is ever offended by refined language and decent manners.

By maintaining a great respect for any reserve he may have attained.

By respecting him as an individual.

By realizing that he has his own leadings, intuitions, tastes, and preferences, and that he may be an older, more inspired soul than I am.

A GOOD THING

By praising him very often.

By leaping upon him and changing conditions on the minute when he slumped.

By everlastingly sharing with him the great universal joke.

By understanding when he was bored by Milton's "Comus" and by being thrilled when he chose to read it.

By loving him when he came from the boiler works covered with soot and by continuing my affection when he was in fresh linen.

By accepting at home all the courtesies I wished to have him distribute abroad.

By running along with him in the study of the stars, the garden politics, the daily news, industrial and social affairs, cookery, and everything from boilers to trench mortar.

By my faith in him.—His Mother.

Glad He's a Boy!

There isn't anything in the world that beats the fun of being a boy! The worst trouble I have is that there is only one of me, and there is pleasure enough in reach to supply half a dozen like me. I could enjoy going to school 365 days in the year. I could spend as much time in the library reading things I want to read. I feel as if I could beat Huckleberry Finn hunting and trapping all winter and fishing all summer. I delight in working on the farm every pleasant day.

As it is, I am going to produce some things which will make some

THE KELLY KIDS AND THEIR GOOD TIMES ON THE FARM

In connection with our recent prize offer for Southern farm photographs, the judges found three pictures of so nearly equal merit that the $25 was equally divided among them.

One of the prize-winning pictures was this double-jointed photograph of "The Kelly Kids and Their Good Times on the Farm." The seven youngsters are full-fledged members of The Progressive Farmer Family, their parents, Mr. and Mrs. C. B. Kelly, having been friends and readers of The Progres- *sive Farmer for many years. The ages of the youngsters range from twelve years to sixteen months.*

With this healthy, happy, hustling group of seven Kelly kids to back up her faith, Mrs. Kelly has decided that it is no mistake to follow Mrs. Hutt's advice on the care and rearing of children, as she has been following it in The Progressive Farmer all the years these youngsters have been growing up. Don't you think this is a pretty fine family?

of the old, experienced farmers open their eyes and keep up with my lessons besides. I would not swap living on the farm, with my books (even if I do sweat over them), my dog (though Papa claims he is worthless), my bicycle (even if it does go cranky sometimes), my traps and fishing tackle (which are often lost), my watch (which does run part of the time), and my future (which my school missus says is doubtful unless she is very strict), for the presidency and the White House.

I want to make a plea for the wee girl, for she will be a wee girl but once, dear mothers, and she is the sweetest, dearest thing on earth. Do not scold and nag her; do not, for pity's sake, spank her; and never for one moment let her think that your love has waned. Keep her neat, mother. Make her plenty of plain, neat underwear and dark, serviceable dresses and bathe her little body and change her clothes every day. Do not give her a soiled, limp bonnet and then scold her because you catch her bareheaded in the sun. Make her several bonnets—pink, blue, buff, or darker ones if she prefers them and then give her a clean one nearly every day. Make her pretty little nighties. She will love them so, and her dreams will be the sweeter if she cuddles down happily on going to sleep.

Clothes are for Girls

How are you dressing that girl? I am led to ask from one I just saw. From the way she bulges I know she had on a heavy union suit, then there are drawers of close woven white stuff, the kind that is so hard to wash, a skirt of dark flannelette underneath one of white, a dress tight in the waist, tight in the neck, tight in the cuffs, but dark and serviceable surely? I doubt it, for her mother is always tired and always complaining of the washing.

The Power That Liberates / Fotching Up the Boy   129

They certainly have more sense about dressing children now. My child the same age has on three garments, a low neck, elbow sleeve, knee length union suit of medium weight cotton, a dress hanging loose from the shoulders and bloomers to match. She also has on socks instead of the greenish black stockings worn by the other child, necessitating supporters. This other child has a cold continually. For cold days my girl has a good all-wool sweater.

I have a pet crow two years old, and of all the mischievous things, this crow takes the cake. We had to cut his wing to keep him from pulling the whole roof off the house, and had to make a cage to keep him out of the house and hen nests. When he gets in a hen's nest, he never stops when he has eaten enough eggs, but breaks all he can find. If he can slip in the house, he gets on the table, eats everything he can find, and eats all the cream and clabber he wants. Mamma declares then she will kill him, but he has some amusing tricks.

A Saturday-Night Boy

"You dirty boy, you," said the teacher.
"Why don't you wash your face? I can see what you had for breakfast this morning.
"What is it?"
"Eggs!"
"Wrong. That was yesterday."

Put Your Boys and Girls in Club Work This Year

HERE is an Alabama pig club girl who, according to the Alabama Extension Service, recently sold the eight-months-old pig shown with her for $86.40. The pig weighed 540 pounds and sold for 16 cents per pound. This pig came pretty near establishing a world's record for weight and rate of gain.

Similar records are being made in corn club work, in poultry club work, in the baby beef clubs, and in domestic science work. Boys and girls are learning new ways of doing things; scientific knowledge of feeds and feeding, of soils and fertilizers, of plant nutrition, of foods and cooking,—and all this is opening up to the minds of club members a new world of thought and study. And a wonderful field it is, too. In the old days, farm boys "slopped" the hogs; today the pig club boy gives them a balanced ration. A few years ago we "plowed" corn; today the club boy cultivates his corn, being careful to save the root system as much as possible while doing it. The club girl is learning about the various kinds of human foods, how they should be prepared and served, and how they should be balanced to promote human health and well being.

Progressive Farmer readers should encourage their boys and girls to enlist in some form of club work activity this season. Not only is the information gained of real value to the members, but the association with others engaged in similar work and the friendly rivalry are worth much to the future farm men and women.

These clubs, in fact, are stepping stones to a better Southern agriculture. In just a few years, the farm boys and girls of today will be the farm men and women of the South. What *kind* of men and women they shall be—whether alert, well-informed, progressive, or the reverse, is largely in the hands of their parents. Put your boys and girls in club work, and you will be helping them to become better farm men and farm women and better citizens.

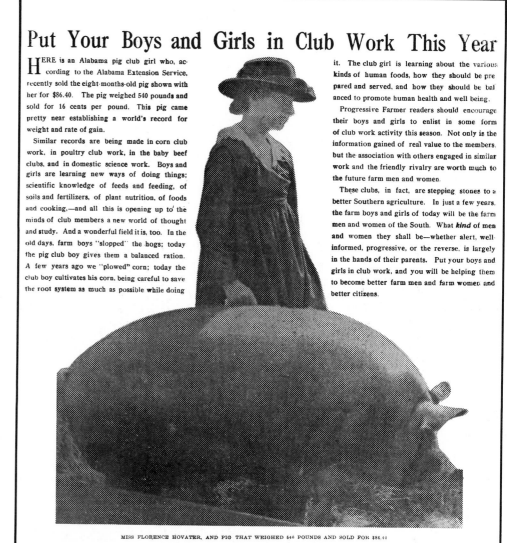

MISS FLORENCE HOVATER, AND PIG THAT WEIGHED 540 POUNDS AND SOLD FOR $86.40

Demand a New Deal for Your Girl's Education

While visiting a school I overheard this dialogue between an unimaginative teacher and a small boy who was helping to remove some cobwebs from a cabinet in the classroom.

"Spider-webs are very beautiful, aren't they, Miss Andrews?"
"Hold the pan higher."
"All spiders aren't bad spiders; some spiders are good spiders, aren't they, Miss Andrews?"
"Watch what you are doing."

"I know a story about a spider. Miss Holmes told a story to her class about Robert Bruce and the spider—"

"When?" severely. The child hung his head. "If you loiter at her door again, I'll keep you in." A sullen look appeared on his face and the work was continued in silence. After he had left the room she turned to me and said: "That boy gets sulky spells. Oh, he likes nature work and stories, but I never could tell a story."

Upon my suggestion that stories stimulate the imagination, she held up her hands and with a look of horror declared: "Imagination! You don't have to stimulate children's imagination. The trouble is they have too much!"

We women should demand—I didn't say ask or beg or coax or plead or tease, I said demand—a new deal for our girls' education. It's been a matter of books long enough; now we must make it a matter of preparation for living. Drudgery for women there always has been—always will be—but it's time to make it an intelligent drudgery and also do away with all that is useless, and much of it is. We should work and plan together until each county would have its farm life school, where every girl in the county could have at least six months and as much more as

possible in learning all the new and easy and economical ways of working, for there are now about as many labor-saving devices for women's work as for men—the great difference being that women don't use them because they can't get them. And with the cooking should go practical lessons in sewing, nursing, sanitation, gardening, poultry raising, laundry, the thousand and one things that a busy wife and mother is called on to do at one time or another.

Then I would wind up the graduating classes by a week's lectures to both boys and girls on the actual cash value of the work done in the home by the wife and mother—what it would cost the man in money if he had to pay some other woman to come in and cook and sew and wash and iron, and tend to his children and milk and scrub, not to mention nursing him if he were sick, and work fifteen hours a day doing it. Put it all down in cash on the blackboard

and not let a boy graduate till he knew it by heart. Maybe then he wouldn't think that all the labor-saving devices should go to the barn and none to the kitchen. My! but I see so many tired faces among the women!

Just for Fun

(School teacher to boys): "Now, all who desire to go to heaven when they die, stand up!"

Little Johnny remained seated.

Teacher: "Why Johnny! Don't you want to go there too?"

Johnny: "Yes, ma'am, but not if that bunch is going.

Don't Forget Me!

Behold, Me, the Baby, potential Salvation!
Your Soldier in embryo, Hope of your Nation.
I am your citizen, your Statesman, your Power.
I am the Bud. Your Future—the Flower.
Guard me and care for me, cherish my soul,
Triumphant, unhindered, I must march to my goal.
A sound mind, a sound body, good health to me give,
Love me and guide me, teach me to live.
This your Reward—I'll lead you, Victorious.
Strength shall be yours, mighty and glorious!
Guard me and care for me, show me the way.
Do not forget me, I will repay.
For I am the Baby, potential Salvation.
Your strength and your Future.
Hope of the Nation!

Every Woman A Gardener

If you want a foreshadowing of Paradise, come to Bramlette at five o'clock in the morning, and we'll make coffee and steal the family cream and go out on the porch and drink four cups of coffee apiece and listen to the birds—redbirds and mocking birds and hermit thrushes; and look at the purple flags—thousands of them too—and every blade of grass dew-spangled—and pinks and boxwood and honeysuckle all perfuming the air—and if we talk it will be only of happy and beautiful things and pleasant people.

More and more I find I depend on my blooming shrubs; there is so much more of them. Take the lilac in bloom: you have anywhere from six to eight feet of purple fragrance and beauty, while in a flower you have about two feet. And a lilac is good for a life-time. Wasn't it Oliver Wendell Holmes who said that if Satan tempted him it would be with the perfume of the lilac for it was the most exquisite and irresistible thing in the world?

I wish you could see my view of the railroad tracks and ugly factories—and I say "mine" advisedly, for I made it mine.

I hated it for six months—mourning and grumbling that I should have to carry that burden of ugliness all my beauty-loving days. One fine morning it dawned on me that many well-meaning people dragged through life with burdens because they hadn't initiative enough to lay them down. While the world is so full of beautiful green growing things a view can be changed. When my mind had once grasped that fact, I went to work. First I set out a row of tall-growing evergreens, because I wanted a winter outlook as well as a summer one. In between and in front of the evergreens, I set out judas trees, dogwood, service berries, fringe trees, holly, cherry and all sorts of small blooming shrubs. They are planted close together and with no more regularity—except the row of evergreens—than trees grow in a forest. Indeed, a forest growth was my model, and that side of the lawn is now an abiding delight all the year, while in the spring it is a bit of Paradise with trees and shrubs a dozen different shades of green and the white blossoms of service and dogwood and the exquisite pink of a judas tree, and mocking birds singing and swinging in the treetops.

Mistakes Some Women Make with the Soil

They stir the earth in the flower pots just after watering.

They do not break the crust in the garden as soon as the ground is workable after each rain, to prevent the escape of moisture.

They put sour-land plants from swamps in soil suited to upland plants and vice-versa.

They do not imitate nature in watering the ground when it is shady. They put potted plants in

A PROPERLY HANDLED GARDEN BRINGS BOTH PLEASURE AND PROFIT

soil from which a previous plant has extracted the nourishment.

They sprinkle a little each day when they should water well, let dry and then water well again. This permits necessary air to get to the roots.

They think they can get best results by preparing the garden when ready to plant the seeds. It should be manured and deeply plowed or spaded when the crop is taken off.

They use the same spot of earth for the same type of crop year after year.

They plant the family orchard on freshly cleared ground. It should be planted to peas for a year before the trees are put in.

Every woman is a potential gardener whether she realizes it or not. In the final analysis, I suppose it's just the proof of atavism or reversal of type—noble sounding words that mean only that you like to do what your grandmother did. And the reason she liked gardens was given long ago by Lord Bacon, that "wisest, brightest, meanest of mankind" who yet wrote of gardens in such an altogether delightful way that, so far from condemning him for accepting bribes to make laws instead of interpreting them as they should be, one feels like giving him more bribes, as a slight token of regard for writing his matchless essay on gardens. Don't you remember its quaint beginning—"God Almighty first planted a garden and indeed it is the purest of human pleasures?"

The mimosas are in bloom. If you want to go to the Tropics and can't, the next best thing is to get

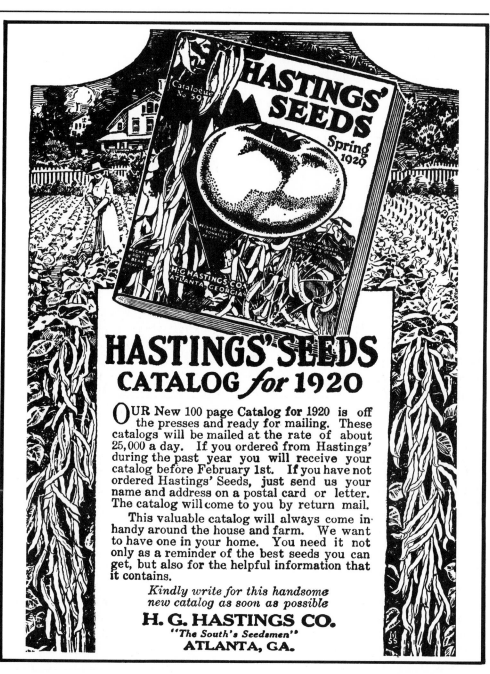

a bowl of Japanese plums, a wet towel (the plums are squshy!) and go sit under a mimosa in full bloom and watch the humming birds and eat plums. You can

imagine they are mangos and still have the best of it for mangos taste like peaches flavored with sweetened turpentine. Do you remember Wordsworth's beautiful poem about the daffodils—how years after he speaks of seeing them with "that inward eye which is the bliss of solitude." I always recall these lines when the mimosa blooms, for it brings back Trinidad and the humming birds and giant ferns and nutmeg trees and the deep blue water and flying fish of the Carribean Sea and all that realm of dreams, the Spanish Main. Mrs. Lindsay Patterson.

Down close by the garden wall I planted thyme, parsley, sage, anise and sweet marjoram. This year I intend to plant other old-fashioned, sweet-scented herbs, and especially those which French cooks use in the making of their delicious and appetizing soups. Near my garden is a running brook in which grow quantities of mint. This we used in iced-tea and in garnishing the pretty watermelon cocktails which we often served at our dinners. On the banks of this brook I planted water cress. One day, I remember that our dinner consisted of nine different vegetables. With the products from my garden, corn, old field peas, Irish potatoes, the luscious Porto Rico yams, cantaloupes and muskmelons grown by my husband in an adjoining field—not only was our own table supplied with vegetables all summer, but we gave to our neighbors, canned quantities and had many turnips left to feed to stock and pigs. In my fall garden I had cucumbers, French endive, mustard, squash, okra, tomatoes, beans and rutabagas.

1. Do not allow flowers to die on the plants. Just as soon as the blooms begin to fade, cut them off.

2. Give each plant plenty of room, whether it is in a box or pot or in the open. Nothing is to be gained by crowding too much.

3. Those who would protect the flowers and shrubbery from harmful insects and diseases should keep on hand a spray pump or dust gun and spray or dust material to combat them.

4. Dahlia stalks are easily broken. Keep them well tied to the stakes.

5. When dahlia blooms are removed from the stalk, cut back severely. This will cause them to branch near the ground.

6. Keep the flower vase full of water, as flowers will keep much better when most of the stem is in water than if only an inch or two of it is covered.

7. That portion of the flower stem that is to be put under the water should have the leaves removed. To leave them on is to materially lessen the life of the flowers.

8. Gather flowers in the morning, as they contain more water at this time and will last longer than if gathered in the middle of the day or in the afternoon.

9. Cut off a bit of the stem of the flowers in vases every day or two. The ends of the stems become clogged and decayed. Therefore, to keep the flowers from dying, this should be done.

10. Always, cut flowers with as long stems as possible, as a long-stemmed flower is far more beautiful than a short-stemmed one. Then, too, such flowers will usually last much longer.

The lettuce birds are prettiest of all, and they seem to stay together always. I remember once going up to a big sunflower in full bloom and frightening off a flock of the yellow lettuce birds, so much like the yellow sunflower blooms I hadn't noticed the birds at all until they flew up in the air. My eyes nearly popped out of my head with utter amazement, for my first thought was a miracle had happened, and the flowers had grown wings and started to use them. When you spend your life watching growing things as I do, nothing is too wonderful to happen.

If you think it's silly to feel that way, stop work fifteen minutes and try to understand how a tiny brown seed, so tiny you can scarcely see it, holds in its compass, not only life but color: one of bloom, another of stem, another of leaf and another of root; then form: one of flower, another of leaf, another of stem, another of root; flower, leaf, stem and root, each performing a separate office absolutely essential to the well-being of the plant, each doing its work in order to support its life, more unerringly than you and I do to support our life. And if you think a vine has no mind of its own, try to curl it the wrong way; you can't do it.

The Stomach Lies Close to the Soul

From an old Southern plantation whose name stood for all that was excellent in kitchen and pantry came a recipe for curing meat that has proved invaluable to us and to many others, for the last fifty or sixty years.

I have never eaten a Westphalian ham, so cannot speak of that, but our hams cured by this recipe are better than the Smithfield hams it has been my good fortune to taste.

4 quarts of salt
4 pounds of sugar
3 ounces of saltpeter

This quantity is sufficient for 100 pounds of meat. Mix thoroughly together, breaking up all lumps. When the meat is cold rub in two-thirds of this mixture, and pack meat in tight cask or tub. The next day take out and rub in remaining third of mixture. Return meat to cask, putting pieces that had been on bottom on top, that is, reversing order in which they were.

One week after, remove meat and reverse it.

One week later remove meat and reverse again, having poured pickle from bottom of cask into some vessel in which it can be boiled. After boiling it, skim carefully, and when cold, pour it over meat.

Let it stand another week, then remove from cask, wash it thoroughly in warm water, wiping it as dry as possible and hang up for continued drying. In two weeks, instead of the old method

MAKING THE CAKE ACCORDING TO THE BOOK

of smoking, I apply some good liquid smoke. The smoke I use necessitates several applications. At the end of this process the hams and strips are bagged.

This strip is as delightfully flavored as that put up by first-class meat houses. As a precaution we use our large hams first. A first class grocery house in a nearby city

offered a prize for the best home-cured hams, to be cut in their store, and one cured by this recipe won the prize.

Rabbit Recipes

The rabbit should be fresh and the body free from unpleasant odor. If young, the paws and ears will be soft; if old, they will be stiff.

Skin the rabbit, remove the entrails and wipe well inside and out with a damp cloth. Split it down the back, and, unless it is to be broiled, divide each half into four pieces.

Panned Rabbit—One rabbit, 2 eggs, salt and pepper, 1 tablespoon chopped parsley, a little grated nutmeg, one-fourth cup fine bread crumbs.

Divide the rabbit at the joints and stew until tender. Butter a pan and lay the pieces over the bottom. Beat the eggs, mix with the other ingredients and spread over the rabbit. Set in a hot oven and bake until brown.

Barbecued Rabbit—Leave whole, skewer flat, grease all over, lay on rack in pan, and roast in hot oven, basting every five mintues with hot salt water. When crisp take up and serve with a sauce of melted butter mixed with equal quantity of strong vinegar, boiling hot, made hot with red and black pepper, minced cucumber pickle, and a bare dash of onion juice. This is as near an approach to a real barbecue, which is cooked over live coals in the bottom of a trench, as a civilized kitchen can supply.

Suggested Menus

Breakfast.—Oranges peeled and cut in slices, oatmeal molds, milk and sugar; breakfast strip, scrambled eggs, grits warmed over in milk. Muffins. Cocoa.

Dinner.—Stewed chicken, gravy, rice, scalloped tomatoes, beet and English pea salad with lettuce, light bread, cold cup custards with preserved strawberries and cream.

Supper.—Curd cheese mixed with salt, pepper and cream, light bread. Peach jam, sand cookies, milk.

Breakfast.—Fresh or canned berries; cream of wheat, cream; salt pork with milk gravy, canned sweet potatoes, browned corn muffins, coffee.

Dinner.—Boiled ham hot, whole hominy, kale; lettuce and snap bean salad, French dressing; bread pudding with raisins, hot lemon sauce, tea.

Supper.—King's toast, biscuit, butter. Prune whip, fruit juice.

The President at His Meals

Housewives will be interested in knowing what the President eats, and to know on what Mrs. Harding feeds him to make him so healthy. The President has an excellent appetite. A typical menu

"NO NOBLER TASK SHALL I EVER ASK, THAN TO LIVE AND LOVE AS I TOIL"

HORACE, THE FARMER LAD—How to Tell the Age of a Turkey

By Pat Gordon

for the day follows: For breakfast he has a half of a grapefruit, bacon and eggs, the bacon cooked to a golden brown, buttered toast, and coffee, followed by waffles, such as Mrs. Harding has made famous. His luncheon is a substantial meal, usually including a meat and two or three vegetables, but the dinner is the principal meal. It is complete from soup to nuts. He enjoys his meals and mixes with them a full amount of laughter and light-heartedness.

Make Lard This Winter

Farmers' wives all know that leaf fat makes the highest class lard. Fat taken from the back, the ham, and the shoulders also yields satisfactory lard. Gut fat, on the other hand, makes a product that is strong-smelling and off-color, so this fat should never be mixed with that obtained from the other parts of the body.

To make satisfactory lard that will keep well, the following suggestions should be observed:

1. All scraps of lean meat should be removed, as lean strips are almost sure to cling to the cooking vessel and get scorched, giving an unpleasant odor to the lard.

2. The fat should be cut into small blocks or strips, from one to one and one-half inches square, as nearly equal in size as possible, so they will "try out" in about the same time.

3. A clean vessel should now be filled about three-fourths full of fat and a quart of water poured in. The small amount of water is used to prevent the fat from burning when the heat is first applied.

4. The kettle should be kept over a moderate fire until the cracklings are brown and light enough to float: it is necessary to stir frequently else the fat will burn.

5. When done remove from fire, allow it to cool slightly, and then strain through a muslin cloth into a suitable vessel, a large earthen jar probably being the most suitable.

6. To whiten the product and develop smoothness or "grain," it should be stirred constantly while cooling.

7. When solidified, cover the vessel carefully and place in a clean, cool, darkened place.

A Step-Saving Farmhouse

Two letters from farmers' wives lie on my desk:— ". . . I have lived in man-planned houses all my life, and I am acquainted with every inconvenience that the mind of man could conceive. The kitchen, dining room, and living room were usually in a row,—in one house, it was 48 feet from the front door to the kitchen sink; I literally had to walk miles every day while doing my housework."

". . . I wouldn't have a basement laundry unless I were twins, or at least had a sister with me on wash-days. Otherwise, I would have to dash madly up the steep cellar stairs every 10 minutes or so, to answer the telephone, look after the cooking, see whether baby was in mischief, and so on!"

Well, now let's see whether a man can plan a farmhouse that will really save all this wearisome waste of steps.

We'll begin with the kitchen. The sink must set under a window, to get every bit of light and breeze. At right and left, we will make built-in cupboards, within arm's length; then Mrs. Farmer can put in dishes and utensils, or take out foodstuffs, with scarcely a step. We'll make cupboards large enough to hold all the groceries and other supplies.

The kitchen table is on casters; Mrs. Farmer can trundle it over to the sink, or back to the stove, as she pleases. My wife says this saves her a lot of steps.

By the way, there is space for oil-stove as well as range, in the kitchen; no need of putting the oil-stove out on the porch, or down in the basement, as so many farm women are forced to do.

I have left off the dining room. "We never use it, except on Sundays!" writes a farm woman. But on the screened porch I have put a breakfast nook, table and benches: this will make a delightfully cool and comfortable place to serve a meal, in summer time. It is only two or three steps from the kitchen range whereas a dining-room table is usually a dozen or more.

As a matter of fact, this breakfast nook can be used nearly all the year; the screened porch is equipped with movable glass sash, to be put in when winter comes.

This screened porch has two stationary wash-tubs on it; so that the woman who isn't "twins" may do her washing here, and not have to "dash madly up the steep cellar stairs every 10 minutes or so." The water, of course, must be cut off from inside the house, on cold nights; but in the day-time the

heat from the kitchen stove will keep the porch warm enough.

The men-folk—especially the extra farm hands—will wash up at the laundry tubs, when coming in from work.

This saves the kitchen sink; every farm woman hates to have a lot of men crowding into her kitchen and messing things up.

The two first-story bedrooms cut out a very great many steps. There is space for two more bedrooms if desired, in the attic; but they will not be needed on the smaller farms.

Builders and architects who don't know much about farm life, usually put the bathroom upstairs; but, as every farmer's wife knows,

Waterfy Your Home With the Leader

Putting in a water system to supply your home and your stock deserves careful consideration. A mistake is serious and expensive. A convenience that doesn't work right, that has to be tinkered with, is an *inconvenience*.

Don't run any risk. Be safe, sure, certain. Install the

Leader

Home Water Systems—Leaders in fame as well as in name.

We know all systems, but we sell the Leader because it has been proven best by years of test. It will last a life time. It is the only home water system where the tanks and pumps are manufactured, and the whole system completed and tested as a unit in one factory. Since 1903 the Leader has given satisfaction.

If you don't know the local Leader dealer, write us

THE MOTOR COMPANY
Winston-Salem, N. C.
UNIVERSAL MOTORS COMPANY
Atlanta, Ga.
AUTOMOTIVE ELECTRO COMPANY
Richmond, Va.

Established 1903 **Leader** Tanks, Pumps and Power Equipment

that's all wrong! "I want the bathroom close to the kitchen so I can supervise the children's baths, or bathe the baby, and still keep an eye on the cooking," wrote a farmer's wife to me, the other day. "And, of course, the downstairs toilet, close at hand is a great comfort and step-saver to me, personally."

There is another very good reason for the first-story bath. Many farmers cannot afford to put in a complete water system; but they can afford a bathtub, with drainpipe. Sometimes a pump is set up at one end of the tub, to supply cold water. However, hot water (and sometimes cold water, too) must be carried from the kitchen stove. An upstairs bathroom would scarcely ever be used, under such conditions.

This house is supposed to be built of cement block, stuccoed, but, of course, any other materials might be used instead.

The cost of this house? A mighty difficult question to answer! Building costs depend entirely on the local prices of labor and material, and these prices vary greatly in different places. However, I think $3,500 would be a fair average, though, of course, in your particular locality, this estimate may be too high or too low.

Now, I wonder if I have succeeded in planning a real step-saving farmhouse. What do you think Mrs. Farmer?

We have lights in every room and one on the back porch also,

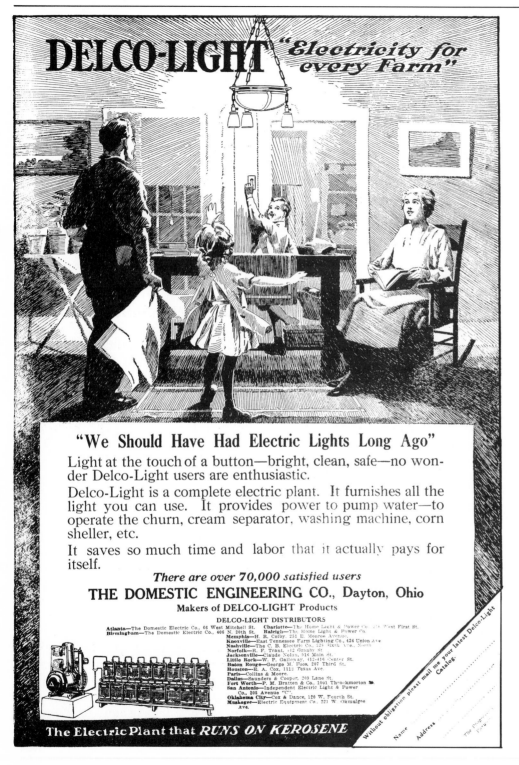

which lights up all the back way, the lot, smokehouse, wood pile, back yard, etc. This is a great comfort on cold winter nights. No more cleaning and lighting of lamps, no more lights to be kept burning at night for the baby; just reach over your head and turn on and off the light as needed. With a large fireplace in the living room and nice light over head, we are prepared to read and study with some satisfaction this winter.

Complete Water System for $250

After living twenty years in the city, we decided to build in the country. We felt that we could not afford to install running water at building time, but I also felt that I could not live without the water, so I put my wits to work.

I called on all the best plumbing shops in the city for prices. I found that the most expensive part of the plumbing is the plumber, so I decided to do my own work.

I bought all porcelain fixtures for the bathroom and kitchen sink, and a 30-gallon tank for hot water. Fortunately I had a nice range with hot water back. I bought a gasoline engine, 1½ horsepower, with pump and jack together. I found a 300-gallon metal tank at the junk yard. It was a rejected gasoline tank, but all right for water. This I bought for $10.

I had all pipes cut to fit, and asked the plumber about anything I did not understand.

The 4-inch sewer pipe runs 150 feet from the dwelling (on the opposite side from the well) and

Quite So, Isn't It?

empties into a small stream. Each joint of pipe was sealed with cement.

With the aid of my brother, who was handy with tools, we installed a water system that gives perfect satisfaction after two years use.

Do not wear your clothes two weeks to save washing but change twice or more a week. Little-soiled clothes will almost boil clean while very dirty ones require much elbow grease. Also change towels several times a week and they will wash easier, last longer and look better.

Turns Tadpole Pond Into a Lighting System
(First Prize Letter.)

Husband and I own a very fertile little farm of 140 acres. However, after providing all the equipment necessary for the convenience and operation of our farm, I never could get him to feel like buying a lighting system. I would try to console myself by thinking how Abraham Lincoln studied by pine knot illumination. Yet, possibly by having been reared in a "middlesized" town, I could not help feeling that my children in this age of the world, should have better light than Abe.

Through our farm runs a small creek and at the lower end of the farm is a small lake or pond covering about two acres. I had watched my husband turn the banks of this creek from a willow thicket to a producing pecan orchard. But just how to make the pond produce seemed to baffle him.

Observing this pond literally abounded with tadpoles, I determined to turn it into a duck field. After ordering eggs I hatched something more than 200 little ducklings, which at the age of two weeks, I took to the tadpole pond.

In less than two weeks, to my dismay, I discovered the pond was infested with mud turtles and that the ravages of their appetites had reduced my flock to less than 100 ducklings. Armed with a rifle I soon "troubled the waters" of our pond till their presence was negligible. I built a small pen and a house on the bank for my ducklings and it was interesting to watch them devour the tadpoles and to note the development from ducklings to full grown ducks.

The next year with the absence of the mud turtles and with the aid of my past experience I easily grew more than 600 ducks with which I purchased my long hoped for lighting system for our home. And I am still converting those worthless tadpoles into fine ducks, from which I reap much money, besides most delicious dishes for our table. Today I would rather part with our car than the lighting system I produced from my husband's tadpoles.

By All Means, Furniture That's Useful

The first consideration in buying furniture is usefulness and suitability to the purpose for which it is wanted. A chair is meant to sit on. This may seem an unnecessary statement, but from the chairs seen in many houses, it would seem that this is frequently forgotten. Now, if a chair is meant to sit on it must have strength to hold us. The chair must be solidly built and with a broad enough seat to accommodate the body. The legs must be staunch, but need not be heavy as piano legs, as are some of the so-called mission type. Next, a chair must be comfortable, so we demand a back that curves comfortably to the spine and has no strange protruberances that stick into us. The chair legs must be the right length for the different types of chairs. A good sewing chair is low, a dining chair the right height for the table at which it is used, and an easy chair is made in proportion to its depth, for the deeper the seat the lower the legs may be.

Having selected a chair suited to the purpose for which we wish it, strong and well-made of substantial material and of comfortable proportions, we naturally think of whether it is beautiful or not. All ornaments should seem to be a part of the furniture itself, not an afterthought after the piece was finished. Simple carving of wood where it is a refinement of the

Reclaim the House As Well as the Land

While you're reclaiming and improving the land don't neglect the house. One is as important as the other. Reclaim the plastered walls and ceilings. They show the first signs of deterioration. They are sure to crack and just as sure to fall.

Cover them up with Beaver Board. You can easily do the work yourself. You can reclaim waste spaces about the house. New houses and additions take the same treatment because Beaver Board can be nailed to new studding as well as to old walls.

Beaver Board is built up into large flawless panels from fibres of white spruce. Your nearest lumber yard will deliver it or you can take it out on your next trip.

Just look for the Beaver Board trademark plainly *printed on the back* of every panel. Send for our new book "Beaver Board and Its Uses." Ask about Beavertone—our new velvety paint for Beaver Board.

THE BEAVER BOARD COMPANIES
Administration Offices, Buffalo, N. Y.; Thorold, Ont., Canada; London, Eng.
Offices in principal cities of the United States and abroad
Distributors and dealers everywhere

basic lines of the chair is good, a quantity of machine made scrolls and knobs which jut and drip from sides and back of the chair like lace from a collar are bad. Better a perfectly plain chair.

Select Pictures with Care

It is very important that no pictures which are not suitable be hung in the home.

The pictures in the parlor must be selected with care. I once visited in a home where a beautiful "sweetheart" picture hung in the parlor. The mother, daughter and son-in-law were in the room when I remarked about the beauty of the picture.

"Yes," said the son-in-law, "every time I came to see—— before we were married, I saw that picture as soon as I came in the parlor, and it seemed like a dare to me. It made me think about hugging and kissing too."

I resolved right then that pictures of that kind were not the kind of pictures for my parlor, no matter how beautiful they might be. Especial care should then be used in the selection of pictures for the rooms where the young folks entertain their company, for no mother wants the furnishings of her home to lead her children into temptation.

Get brilliant colors; don't be afraid of them. If you are, spend a few weeks looking at sunsets and flower gardens until you grasp the joy to be derived from just color—

nothing else but pure, beautiful, soul-stirring color—and make yourself comprehend that what is so lovely out of doors is equally lovely within. So if there is an all white groundwork for the combination hall-parlor, library and all around living room—decide upon your favorite color. If it's blue, a blue and white room is as unusual as it is beautiful. Stick to solid colors for the rugs if you can possibly afford them, for they give the best effect unless one can afford Chinese rugs which are far and away the most beautiful of all floor coverings. It is not at all necessary to have expensive chairs and tables for the hall. The porch chairs and settees come in splendid shapes and all sizes and the home artist can paint them white, making her own cushions and coverings of cretonne. If she can paint flowers or even conventional designs, she is most fortunate, for the new flower furniture is lovely and not at all difficult to do. On the white chairs and tables and settees, paint favorite flowers or scattered bunches of all sorts of flowers and in that case make the cushions of a solid color to match rug.

A fixed bathtub in the house is a benefit to every member of the household and especially to the children, because it encourages habits of cleanliness. Who does not look with more favor on a bath when warm soft water can be readily run into an attractive white-lined tub, than when the only accommodations are a cold portable tub which must be brought from the cellar and hard

water carried from the well and heated in the wash boiler, carried outside and emptied after used, and all utensils cleaned, dried, and put away, five unnecessary operations? All that should be needed is simply to clean the bathtub after using and take care of the towels.

Hot Rocks to Warm Up Hands and Feet

For warming up cold hands and feet, a nice smooth hot rock is just as good as a hot water bag, and has the added advantage of never wearing out.

Grandmother has quite an assortment of rocks,—little, big, long, round, flat ones. On bitter cold days the warmth of the heater does not comfortably reach the far window where the light shines best. But with a big hot rock under her feet, a flat little hot rock in her lap handy to cold fingers, and the littlest hot rock slung in a bag over the rheumatic shoulder, grandmother manages to keep quite snug.

On a long cold drive a hot rock at your feet and another in your lap or pocket will go far towards making things comfortable. If your hands and feet can just be kept warm, the rest of the body seems to take care of itself.

At bed time a warm rock slipped between the sheets is fine for taking off the chill. Rocks retain the heat a remarkably long time. Washable bags of denim made with a draw string at the top are kept to slip over the hot rocks used in

the house. When used in the buggy or car the rock wrapped in a neat paper package and tied with a string is as inconspicuous as any other parcel.

Grandmother's Quilts Becoming Popular Again

Old and Young Alike Searching Out the Most Famous Patterns
By Mrs. W. N. Hutt

At no time in American history has there been displayed a more ardent love for old houses, old furniture, old songs, and old quilts. In every state in our dear country this spirit is being felt. The wealthy are preserving rare old homes, and restoring them to original appearances. You and I are looking about among kin and even more remotely for choice chairs and tables of olden days. The radio has helped to revive the rhythm and feeling of the good old songs. And in city and country the love for old quilts has claimed the attention of old and young folks alike.

In my home town, the missionary societies of many churches have grasped the idea of quilting for funds and their treasuries have never been so well filled. A good pattern is chosen at each meeting, and the members each piece or applique one or more blocks ready for the next session, when the joining and quilting are completed. They have orders waiting, and their fame is far-reaching. This might be a suggestion for the home woman who wishes to earn a little this winter.

Christmas Work for Long Evenings

An attractive magazine rack may be made by covering an old rack with cretonne or any other decorative material. Simply cut the fabric into pieces of the right size, allowing a half inch for turning under on all edges, and glue it to the rack with best quality liquid glue.

Where an old rack is not available, an inexpensive new one of unfinished wood may be used or the rack may be made by hand from an old packing box or from discarded pieces of lumber.

A dainty and useful set of shoe-trees will make a charming gift for Christmas, birthday, anniversaries or for the departing guest. Jade colored ribbon is wound about the metal part of an inexpensive foundation and fastened into place with glue. Glue is also used to attach a ribbon covering to the wooden part of the tree and to bind it with gold braid. An interesting and original touch is given with the tiny rosettes of rose satin ribbon centered with a few yellow flower stamens.

Now that fans are being carried all the year round they make acceptable gifts and are surprisingly inexpensive if made at home. A fan was made by gluing satin ribbon to a purchased wooden stick foundation. Decorative flower motifs cut from figured satin were attached to the satin with liquid glue.

1930–1940

The Poverty of Plenty

The Poverty of Plenty

The thin bound volumes of the *Progressive Farmer* for the 1930's denote lean times. By the time the Depression came to the rest of the country, the farmer had had ten years of it and might even have taken some comfort in others being in the same boat. But it was small comfort surely as mortgage foreclosures continued apace. And even though he was used to it, the Depression was probably more confusing to Grandfather than to city people: he could see the plenty in his fields, yet it seemed only to deepen his poverty.

In the ancient profession of farming, the farmer had, as far as he knew, two adversaries: one was Nature, the noble adversary; the second was himself. If Nature smiled, the harvest would be bountiful, particularly if the farmer had worked hard. A bountiful harvest meant good times. But a farm depression contradicted this theory. The farmer had worked hard, and the harvest was indeed bountiful but then came the paradox: he had produced too much. The fact of many large harvests had created an over-supply, which reduced the price of his goods. His answer (seemingly logical enough) was to work harder and produce more. But this brought prices down even further. For there was another adversary of which Grandfather was only dimly aware: the poverty of the people who constituted his market. The poverty of others became a third adversary, hard to

understand and perhaps as hard to control as Nature herself.

When the European people, impoverished by war and war debts, could not buy American goods, American farmers were in trouble. When many Americans, after the stock market crash, could not buy the farmers' goods, the farmers were in more trouble. The paradox of plenty was compounded by the fact that those who were not buying the farmers' goods were not refraining from buying because of satiety. Rather, they were ragged and hungry and needed the farmers' goods desperately. How could there be too much of something that so many people were without? How could proud American farmers be bound in any way to the poor people of Europe?

Like it or not, understand it or not, they were. American farmers were being forced to see their lives and labor in a larger context. Early American farmers had had to take into account their land, their families and their neighbors. Now the world had shrunk. Now Alabama cotton growers had to consider Texas cotton growers. Now American cotton growers had to consider the shivering masses of the world who had no money to buy their cotton.

What could be done? For years the *Progressive Farmer* had been urging farmers to organize in order to control acreage and have some control over the market. In previous years of crop surpluses, campaigns to reduce acreage voluntarily had resulted in up to 15% reduction. But now a 15% reduction would not be enough; drastic measures were required. Many cotton states enacted their own man-

datory acreage reduction laws, but a few did not. Those states that did not reduce their acreage would reap the benefits of the higher prices produced by the other states' reductions. Surely a national program was the only way. By the time of Franklin Roosevelt's inauguration as President in 1933, farmers, according to the *Progressive Farmer*, were three out of four in favor of acreage reduction. But in those days the inauguration ceremony was still held in March, and March would be too late for acreage reduction to help in that year. Yet something had to be done before the harvest again flooded the market. Farmers were asked to "plow up" a portion of their already flourishing crops.

A farmer being asked to plow up already growing crops must have felt somewhat as a doctor would feel upon being asked to kill his patients. The *Progressive Farmer* explained.

The farmer has given up the liberty to produce as much of certain surplus crops as he pleases on his own land, for the benefit of himself and the nation as a whole. The desires or wishes of the members of any group or community are never so nearly the same . . . that they can prosper and live happily without each member being compelled to surrender some of his liberty of action for the good of others. The "liberty" to feed and clothe oneself and one's dependents and have some money to spend as he pleases is of far greater value than the liberty to "plant what he pleases on his own land," and by so doing deprive himself, his family, and his neighbors of a fair reward for their labor and a decent living.

Apparently most farmers were ready for the step. Something was being done at last.

The acreage reduction program got under way in 1934. For the next several years there were struggles to achieve a fair allotment of acreage. But one side effect of the government stipends for acreage reduction had perhaps not been imagined. By 1935 almost half the farmers in the South were tenant farmers. While tenant farmers could not have quite the same attachment to the land as owners could, they could still live on the land. If they had a good relationship with the owner, they could still love the land on which they lived and improve it and their dwellings. But money payments for acreage reduction brought a new factor. Although in theory these payments were supposed to be shared with tenants, in practice it was often more expedient to reduce acreage by letting the tenants go who had worked those acres, and investing the money in farm machinery. Tenants complained of being "tractored off" the land. Payments for acreage reduction had the effect, in many cases, of making a farm more efficient, but like the large efficient factories, less human. The *Progressive Farmer* editors worried about farm labor becoming like factory labor, with each person doing a small portion of the job and never seeing or feeling the satisfaction of a total creation.

The Poverty of Plenty / Introduction   147

The small and known world of the early 20th century was impinged upon—clutched at by hands of people far away, people in other states and even other lands whose lives might be unimaginable to our grandparents. Hadn't the assassination of some archduke nobody had ever heard of involved them vitally, tragically in the "Great War?" Wasn't the poverty of far away people ruining their own standard of living? Like it or not, Grandmother and Grandfather needed to know what was going on in the rest of the world. It almost seems as if Radio sprang from this need. Radio, of course, had been around for some years, but now sets were cheaper, easier to use, reception was better and programming more varied. Even in the depths of the Depression, sale of radios did not falter. The whole country could laugh (an activity President Hoover (1929–1933) had recommended as a cure for Depression) at Jack Benny and Charlie McCarthy and hear Lowell Thomas on the news. Farm families loved their radios. A letter contest on whether they would prefer, if necessary, to give up their washing machines or their radios was almost a tie.

Radio brought news of the world to the young people as well, though it may have been a different kind of news they sought. Radio showed them how others their age were living. Its influence was apparently recognized and feared by some families. One youngster complained bitterly in a letter: "My father won't let me listen to the radio when he is at home, and when he is not he keeps it locked up." As well he might. To fathers who wanted to keep the old authoritarian form of family management, radio and movies were a genuine threat. Beset by troubles on all sides, some parents may have felt that they needed the unquestioning faith and unquestioning willingness to work of all family members more than ever before. But even if the radio was locked up, the journey to town was no longer hard enough to keep adolescents from finding out what their peers were doing. Adolescents who were made to work long hours without recreation on the assumption that work was good for their souls and the family finances and kept them out of trouble tended to head for town at the earliest opportunity. This is shown by a letter contest the

Page 149. This color plate and the one on page 124, both painted by artist Anton Cucchi in idyllic colors, may indicate a need to escape the drab Depression days of the 1930's and retreat into the continuing beauty of nature.

Page 150. A budding romance promotes cigarettes—or vice versa. The Progressive Farmer kept a tight rein on its advertisers, rejecting anything it considered improper. A reader once wrote to complain that a girl in one ad was too young to be smoking. The editors replied that they had carefully scrutinized that particular ad and decided that the girl was in her 20's.

— it was ever thus

they Satisfy

Chesterfields are milder and
they certainly do taste better

LA SALLE

BUICK

CHEVROLET

OLDSMOBILE

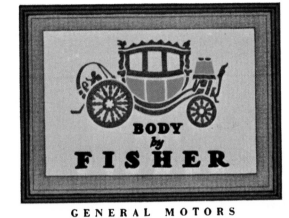

GENERAL MOTORS

PONTIAC

MARQUETTE

VIKING

CADILLAC

OAKLAND

BODY BY FISHER
on these cars - and these cars _only_

The Progressive Farmer

AND SOUTHERN RURALIST

Progressive Farmer held for teenagers in 1937. The subject was "Things I Wish My Parents Wouldn't Do," but it seemed to reveal deeper wounds than expected:

My father is very domineering. I am in my late twenties and have never had a date, because he expects me to conduct my 'company keeping' the same as he did 45 years ago.

I am a boy of 16 in what was once a family of ten but which now consists of only four because my father wishes to rear his children into as near perfection as possible.

I am a girl of 18 and ever since I can remember, Father has been so hard on us we almost feel like running away . . . My sister ran away two years ago and got married.

Dad never gives us any spending money for anything. If we get our crop worked we get out and work for our neighbor and get money for our haircuts. He has made

---

Page 151. From the early days of Henry Ford's Model T, auto makers had, in a generation, branched out to a wide variety of models, as this 1930 ad shows.

Page 152. Valentine's Day, 1941: this may have been the last time, for four years, that the day could be concerned solely with the tremulous sweetness of Cupid without wondering in what circumstances the far-away beloved in the Armed Forces might be found.

---

farm life so hard that one of my brothers and my sister have gone to town and are working for very small salaries.

The *Progressive Farmer* kept up with the changing times. Woman's page editor Sallie Hill wrote:

The patriarchal form of family government is no longer in force. The wise father of today does not attempt to make all the decisions for the family. As the head of the family he organizes a cooperative family group in which all members contribute their share of ideas as well as work.

A "Specialist in Child Training and Parent Education" suggested to the farmer:

The good business man who is raising pigs for market writes for bulletins, or even buys books and actually studies them, so that he may have the latest information on the subject . . . Is he so interested in being a competent parent? . . . Does he go at this important job as intelligently and with as much thought and effort as he puts into raising pigs?

In the *Progressive Farmer* of the thirties, "child development" could be discovered. There was "an increasing interest in parental education." Books were recommended so that parents could understand "the intricate and complex workings of the child's mind at various stages."

Those of us who believe we have weathered every fad of advice on the upbringing of children may smile grimly. But in the thirties, "child development" represented a real departure from the old way of thinking about children. Whereas

children had generally been considered to be owned by the parents, now it seemed that a child owned itself; that a child had certain defined needs, beyond clothing and nosewiping and even kindness, at certain definite stages in its small life. Almost like a plant, a child had an inexorable way of growing that was its own. It could either be stymied (to its detriment) at these stages, or it could be allowed to unfold and eventually to flower. To parents who were not wedded to the old ways, this new way of thinking may have been a godsend, for our parents and grandparents had seen the failure of the old work ethic and the old morality of self-denial explode into "flaming youth." What values then could they teach? They could not even be confident of what values would be necessary in their children's future lives. They could no longer assume that in twenty years grown-ups would be doing the same things that they and their parents had done. They could not assume that adults of the future would live the kinds of lives for which their teaching could prepare them.

The new philosophy of child rearing had the advantage that it did not predict an end result—except possibly a "well-adjusted" person. It did not predict the characteristics that would be required in the new world in which the children would live. Rather, it dealt pragmatically with process. And it was scientific.

Raising the Living Standard

Many millions of dollars will be paid to the cotton farmers of the Southern States in the next few weeks for taking out of production a part of their cotton acreage.

What an opportunity such money brings! To some it will seem miraculous, just as if it had been picked up out of the field where it had been lost. It is true that such good fortune is in a measure a surprise but it is a very pleasant surprise for the money has been earned many times over. The important thing to consider now is, what will the farmer do with this money and with the land which he releases from cotton?

The farmer always talks over with his wife his plans for farming operations. That gives the farm woman of the South an unusual opportunity to help this year because the question as to what to do with the acres that were originally planted in cotton and then taken out of production is an important one. One thing the depression has taught us is to be more nearly selfsustaining. If such acres are planted in feed or food crops the farm woman will need to help plan to save such crops for use next winter. Or it may be that this is exactly the right time to plant such land in soil building crops. Now is the time to work out a better balanced farm system and the woman can help no less than the farmer.

"*Time* for Me *to Lend a Hand*"

Grandmother never waited! When a neighbor's wife was having a baby and the doctor couldn't get there, grandmother put on her bonnet and shawl!

Mother never waited! When the neighbor's house burned down in the night mother opened her door. She said, "Come right in."

The instinct to help is **in your blood.** It has never turned a worthy man or woman down!

A few valleys away may be folks who need your helping hand now. Maybe right in your own town. They're sturdy Americans like you. They want work, but there is no work for them. They don't want charity. But my, how they'll bless you for a mite of help!

Won't you take a look at your fruit and vegetables? Couldn't you spare a few jars? They might help feed families who have no food. Have you any warm clothes that you've put away for "sometime"? They might keep poorer folks warm right **now!** Is there an extra side of bacon or a ham in your smokehouse? It would be a royal gift to mothers who haven't **any.**

Tell your local welfare or unemployment relief organization what you have that you can spare. By giving generously you will have your share in a great common achievement. America is marshaling her forces to deal a death blow to depression. She is setting an example to the world. She is laying the firm foundation for better days for all.

THE PRESIDENT'S ORGANIZATION
ON UNEMPLOYMENT RELIEF

WALTER S. GIFFORD,
Director

COMMITTEE ON MOBILIZATION
OF RELIEF RESOURCES

OWEN D. YOUNG,
Chairman

The President's Organization on Unemployment Relief is non-political and non-sectarian. Its purpose is to aid local welfare and relief agencies everywhere to provide for local needs. All facilities for the nation-wide program, including this advertisement, have been furnished to the Committee without cost.

One of the most important tasks we now have is to see to it that what is gained by cash cotton rentals this summer is not spent this fall and winter for the things which the farm itself ought to produce. There should be no let-up in the live-at-home activities just because cotton money is in sight.

When the actual cash is in hand what will it go for? Women spend or direct the spending of a very large proportion of the wealth of the world. Perhaps this is just as it should be. There is no doubt in my mind that the farm woman of the South will direct the spending of most of the cotton rental money, and my hope is that most of this money will go toward raising the standard of living of the farm family.

Until installment buying became popular many Southern farmers would not borrow money for any purpose. There is a lot to be said in favor of such a plan but it has many disadvantages also. Now with installment buying we have rather acquired a habit of being in debt.

In the past twenty years people's ideas about borrowing money have completely changed. Instead of scrimping as we once did, now the family often borrows money to make an investment in a new home or to educate the children or to meet some emergency. The family uses its credit.

Frocks for Little Girls

TWEED in blue tones with touches of red for the skirt and suspenders and crepe de Chine for the blouse were the materials used for this popular school dress (6984). Red checked gingham with batiste for the blouse would also make a smart combination, and the same is true of jersey or flannel for the skirt and pongee for the blouse. The pattern is cut in four sizes: 6, 8, 10, and 12 years.

6816. Everyone loves to make dainty frocks for tiny girls, and when the design is as simple as this one there is added pleasure. Batiste, dimity, and crepe de Chine are materials suggested. Tiny tucks trim the front across the shoulders, and plait fullness is added at the underarm seams. Short puff sleeves complete the frock. The pattern is cut in four sizes: 6 months, 1, 2, and 3 years.

6985. Cotton print was used for this smart school frock with its panel and front and flared skirt portions. Gingham, linen, and wool crepe are other materials that might be used. The sleeves may be made wrist length or short. Designed for four sizes: 4, 6, 8, and 10 years.

6989. One could have a lot of fun playing in a frock like this, which has bloomers to match, or the five-year-old would enjoy wearing it to kindergarten. Plaits afford plenty of fullness below the yoke, and the sleeves may made long or short. The bloomers are in regulation style with elastic run casings at the top and at the leg edges. The pattern is cut in four sizes: 2, 3, 4, and 5 years.

Order patterns from Pattern Department, The Progressive Farmer and Southern Ruralist, 713 Glenn St., S.W., Atlanta, Ga. Price 15 cents. For other designs, send for our new Fall and Winter Book of Fashions. Price 15 cents.

In small towns it is still possible occasionally to borrow comparatively small sums of money on character and earning power without material security. Where one has lived in a small community for a long number of years, one's reputation is pretty well known.

The Little Folks

If children are to develop a feeling of security, self-reliance, and a courage to meet life with its keen competition, they must have a place to call their own and equipment that can be used with success. The child's play materials are his tools. They are the materials which he uses to educate himself. Let's give him a room of his own or at least a sunny nook in the living room in order that he may have an opportunity to experiment, think, and plan. Provide some low shelves for his toys, blocks, and books. Certainly he deserves a low chair, either a straight chair or a rocker, in which he may sit comfortably with his feet on the floor and his back supported. In addition to the chair, it is desirable to provide a low table suited in size to the child's chair. This table may be used for the meals if he does not eat with the family and at other times for drawing, painting, or other play activities. The table and chair may be painted an attractive bright color that will harmonize with the color scheme of the room and will be easily cleaned.

A bedroom and a bed of his own should be provided if possible.

It is important, therefore, in choosing the child's clothing to keep in mind his need for social and emotional security as well as his need for physical growth. In order to contribute to his sense of personal and social well being, each garment should be suitable to his age and sex and be sufficiently like those of his friends so that he is not contrasted unfavorably or too favorably with the group.

If styles are such that garments bind or pull, harmful effects as round shoulders, varicose veins, flat feet, or a nervous disposition are apt to result. Clothes so made that a child can learn early to dress himself will save many hours for the mother. Make it a point in planning clothes to see the dresses in smart shops, in fashion books, and on well dressed children.

Although human nature has changed very little in the past 1,000 years, our understanding of the behavior of people at all ages has been greatly furthered. Particularly in childhood have we made the most strides in laying bare why we behave as we do, and what can be done to change constructively our ways of thinking, feeling, and doing.

We now realize that the only way in which each child is alike is that he is different in every way. Therefore he must be studied as a unique individual in order that his training may be tailor-cut to meet his specific needs.

It is more important to know why a child does a thing than what he does. This applies to the

Clothes Affect Behavior

Dr. Lee Vincent of the Merrill-Palmer School says: "For years I've been increasingly convinced that there is more connection between behavior problems and clothing than most people would dream possible. Many cases of shyness are due to the fact that children are dressed conspicuously—dainty wash suits for boys who should be wearing wool socks and corduroys or tweed, ruffly dresses on adolescent girls who need simplicity, childish clothes for the boy or girl who is no longer a baby. With young children clothing can facilitate or retard the process of learning in an astonishing manner."

● *Have we ever considered the importance of clothing in character formation? "Simple straightforward clothes help to form similar character habits," Miss Taylor tells us. Cotton even for the best dress is the most satisfactory fabric. Materials should be pre-shrunk and each garment suitable to the child's age and sex.*

interpretation of child strengths as well as weaknesses. If we do not know the causes of behavior, how can we hope rationally to direct and control it?

Regard behavior as a symptom. It is merely an expression of the child seeking to gain satisfaction. The mainspring to human behavior is the emotional-instinctive part of the personality. Our wishes, longings, desires, cravings, specific interests, and ambitions demand more or less realization in terms of performance satisfactions. If reasonable satisfaction is not obtained in socially approved ways, human nature is such that the individual seeks it in undesirable activities. The wise parent and teacher will prevent this.

The most important single factor influencing child behavior is adult example. If parental example is not what it should be, we should not be disappointed when child attitude and action reflect unfortunate "grown-up" patterns. Parental disharmony and lack of unified policy of child management are frequent sources of maladjusted children in the family. First put your own house in order before attempting to correct child misbehavior.

Do not scold, bribe, coax, threaten, or make promises you cannot or do not expect to keep. Be consistent and reasonable in your demands and expectations of child performance. Remember that every child primarily wants social approval, success, love, prestige, and a feeling of security and belonging to the group. But his nature and needs must be adequately understood in the light of his level of development.

Children are not small editions of adults. To be understood we must learn to put ourselves in their shoes—see through their eyes and feel through their hearts.

Young Folks' Problems

Catherine Lee Gives Advice and Answers Questions

Dear Boys and Girls:—
When a youngster of 15 or 16 writes me and complains of a broken heart, I know that there's a girl or boy who isn't playing enough games. Maybe a tennis racquet doesn't seem to you a good instrument for mending breaking hearts, but take my advice and try it and see. Sports are a fine help to real romance but they're death to sickly sentimentality. And, my, what a splendid chance they give you to know each other as you are. The silliest, most selfish little chit may manage to fool some boy into thinking her worth while if he only sees her sitting on a porch or drinking sodas at the drug store, but let him watch her lose her temper over a game and he'll know what she really is. The same is true of boys. The youth without a brain in his head may get by on a "slick line" at a party but it's the

To be a social success, always enter into the spirit of the group you're with. This gay group is enjoying Mardi Gras.

dependable, manly type who shows up well when you're out swimming or fishing with him.

Dear R. R.: How can I refuse gifts from a boy whom I don't even care to speak to? I have shown in every way I know that I don't want his attentions.—E. G.

Return his gifts with a very short note saying simply that you cannot accept gifts from young men unless they are your close friends. Then if he insists upon sending, just hope it's candy next time so you can eat it and say nothing!

Dear R. R.: At a dance, when a boy whom I don't like asks me to dance, what can I tell him?— F. A.

The only way you can refuse is to leave the floor for some reason. You might say that you are tired and must rest a minute or that you want to powder your nose. In that case, of course you can't dance with anyone else either, no matter how charming he is. After a proper lapse of time, you may return to the dance floor and dance with anyone you like. This is merely a way to get out of the situation temporarily and of course cannot help out permanently.

Dances

Some of the points in this article may seem unimportant, but I am trying to put myself in the places of the boys and girls who read our paper, and answer questions I might have asked at their age.

The invitation, be it formal or informal, should be out at least a week in advance (two or three weeks in advance is better for formal affairs) and should be answered promptly. For some small, private (home) dances, the invitation may be telephoned.

If the invitation is formal, then the dress must be also. That means evening dresses for the girls and tuxedo or "full dress" for the boys. If the invitation is telephoned, the girls might ask the hostess what she plans to wear. The boys can ask the "beau" of the hostess what will be appropriate for them. For informal dances we wear our "Sunday" dresses—an afternoon dress of chiffon or silk, and I hear that organdy will be used this winter for evening parties. The boys wear the sack or business suit.

Dressing or coat rooms are provided—one for the girls and one for the boys. These are often on the same floor. If so, the boys wait in the hall for the girls, and then the couples go to speak to the "receiving line" or to the host and hostess. If the dressing rooms are on different floors (the one for the girls is usually upstairs), then the boys wait at the foot of the stairs where the girls meet them to go to speak to the hosts.

In the dressing room don't monopolize the mirrors and other conveniences. While many strangers can take care of themselves, some feel ill at ease. Look out for the comfort of these.

A man always dances the first and last dances and the waltzes with the girl he has brought to the dance. (The orchestra leader usually announces the numbers of the dances.) A man must dance at least once with his hostess, and the host must try to dance at least once with every girl present.

There are two types of dances: (1) program or card and (2) "break" dances. The latter is customary in the South. When a boy "breaks" on a couple, he taps the man on the shoulder and says, "May I break?" The man releases his partner to the newcomer and "breaks" on another couple in the same way.

A boy taking an out-of-town girl (a stranger) to a dance introduces as many men to her as he can before the dance starts. It is courteous for these to "break" on her. During the intervals between

dances her escort brings more of his friends and introduces them. A boy taking a girl who is not a stranger dances with her as often as her popularity will allow. The orchestra leader usually announces "no break" dances, and a man dances the first of these with the girl he brought. A girl may give away some "no breaks" after the first one. Customs vary, so find out what is done in your community.

Although they both may have suffered trampled feet, a man always thanks a girl for a dance and she murmurs, "I enjoyed it, too." Or if she prefers not to tell the "white social lie," she may bow and smile graciously when he thanks her.

Girls, don't be afraid to excuse yourselves to go to the dressing room to repair damages. Remember the advice of the old colored woman, "Make yourself beautiful and skase."

Be sure to thank your host. Usage varies as to this, but the old-fashioned custom of saying "Goodnight" is still good form.

What do you think about a girl past 20 years of age who has never been allowed to keep company yet? I am very much discouraged because I can't keep company with boys.

A. I don't blame you for feeling discouraged. Can't you have a real heart to heart talk with your father and mother and point out to them that you are now old enough to go with boys? They possibly don't realize that you are grown—mothers and fathers find it hard to believe. Tell them you are unhappy and lonely about it, and that when you do finally begin keeping company you will feel awkward and "green" which will put you at a distinct disadvantage. If, however, they are sincerely opposed to it, you must obey them as long as you remain under their roof.

Miss Double X: Don't remove your hat in a restaurant even though you are tired. Your coat and gloves are removed. The coat may be put on a rack or let fall over the back of your chair. The gloves should be held in the lap.

Can you tell me some way to keep a boy from kissing me without being rude? I want boys to like me but I don't want them kissing me. If I try to stop them in a mild way they don't believe I mean it, and if I get rough with them they usually act awfully insulted.

In doubt

Laugh at them. Fighting back is the surest way of urging them on, for their masterfulness demands that they subdue you. But to be laughed at! Don't be scornful, but amused, as though you found them quite ridiculous. I don't guarantee they will like it, but it will hold them in check.

Boorishness at the Table

Bad table manners have wrecked many a romance. To wit, *Disgusted Annie:* "One day my boy friend took dinner with us. All was pleasant enough until he helped his plate and piled so much on it until everyone noticed it. He took two biscuits and two sausages at a time, as though there wouldn't be enough. And he talked with his mouth full—told about their chickens dying with the sorehead. He had no manners whatsoever. I was disgusted and bored almost to tears. After that evening my love had grown cold."

Why Don't You Speak for Yourself?

It was evidently all a woman's idea to begin with—that man must do the proposing. I say so because a great proportion of the hundreds of letters from women said "No" to my question of whether a woman shall propose. The men, on the other hand, were practically unanimous in saying, "Yes, let her!" Only about a dozen men in all held out for their rights. And wouldn't you think women would champion their own cause? In the words of a correspondent, Miss D. R. from South Carolina: "Women have beaten against the doors of stores, offices, factories and even the Cabinet until they have broken down the barriers and gotten in. Now for the thing they most want and benefit most from—the right to propose—they haven't even put up a scrap!"

But there are women who have pioneered in the cause, and it surprised me to know how many happy marriages have resulted from proposals by women; several men and women, too, stated frankly that they had missed their life partner because he was too timid to speak, and she was too diffident to mention the subject herself.

Women are so much more married than men that it is extremely important for them to get the man they want.

I am a mother 45 years old, and I appreciate what my mother taught me, but I believe a modern day kiss and squeeze are no more harmful than an indecent look was 30 years ago. It is just more fun to be outspoken and say what you think than to chase the devil 'round the stump.' The midnight parties have the same point of view that the noonday chats in the shade of the old apple tree did in the days of yore.

What the Book of Charms Told

There's nothing better for dry skin than mutton tallow. That's what grandmother used for keeping her complexion lovely all winter. If you don't like the odor of plain mutton tallow, run down to the dairy and borrow some Jersey cream—the original frosty morning cold cream! Warm it a bit and smooth it on your face. City girls would be thrilled to have the famous cream facials recommended by Cleopatra herself!

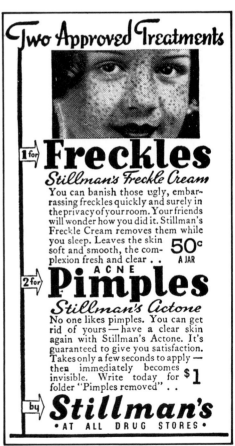

When that magnolia-petal skin of her Young Miss became the slightest bit tanned or freckled despite caution about wearing veils and sunbonnets, Mammy lost no time. For severe cases she used the "horse-radish poultice." Sometimes lemon or strawberry or milkweed juice or buttermilk brought back the fair smoothness. But Young Miss liked best this "delicious concoction." "To one and one-half ounces of cucumber juice (made by grating cucumbers and pressing through a strainer and heating for a few minutes) add one-half ounce of Tincture of Benzoin, one ounce of cologne, and five ounces of elderflower water. Bottle and keep in a cool place."

Does Your Hair Go A-Sparking?

Tonight when your room is dark, run your rubber comb quickly through your hair several times—and watch the sparks fly! They probably won't if your hair is too oily, but if it is too dry, you'll think you're running a lighting plant, provided the weather is crisp and cold.

Cleanliness, massage, and the "hundred strokes of the brush" extolled by our "bandbox" grandmothers make the best recipe for hair beauty.

Reducing

"Motoring is surely a great thing. I used to be fat and sluggish before the motoring craze, but now I'm spry and energetic."

"I didn't know you motored."

"I don't. I dodge."

Quite the Newest Thing

When you see "Gone With the Wind"—the moving picture just released and based on Margaret Mitchell's famous novel with its Southern setting—you will get three hours and 40 minutes of delightful entertainment. Yes, and more—you will get some conceptions of the trend in spring fashions.

The South of about the period of the sixties—not Paris—will be reflected in our 1940 wardrobes. Get out the family album and study your grandmother's pictures about the Civil War period for a real conception of new spring fashions, so surely is the moving picture influencing the mode.

Headline News

Parasols instead of a hat to match your sport dress.

Sunbonnets with ruffles around them or with snoods of fishnet crochet for beach and other wear. One type is made of pique like a skull cap and has a shirred snood which can be reversed and used for a visor.

Important to our Southern housewives is the news that cotton materials are obtainable in permanent finish, sanforized—guaranteed not to shrink out of shape, and fit—color fast, and crease resistant.

Dear R.R.: We've had quite a discussion as to when and where it is correct to wear slacks. Will you settle the question for us? A.T.

Slacks are generally reserved for strictly sports wear such as picnics, hikes, horseback riding, and camps. Wherever you wear them, however, fit them "slack" as the name implies and don't be guilty of wearing "tights" instead. Remember that many cheap materials shrink alarmingly when washed, so whether you buy or make your slacks, either buy sanforized-shrunk material or allow for shrinkage.

WHAT LENGTH SKIRT?

IT ALL depends on the style. In evening wear, dresses are quite long, often to the ankle. But where the style dips in the back, the front hem may be considerably higher.

Afternoon dresses are from three to six inches below the knee, depending on the type of frock, whereas sports dresses are but slightly longer than last year.

In this important detail, as well as many others, it would be best for you to follow an authoritative guide. We recommend our new Spring Fashion Magazine which shows the different types of styles, the new lines and length, as well as the new fabrics.

A Peep "Below the Hem-Line"

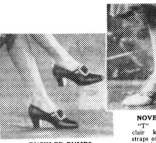

NOVEL STRAPPING
"T" strap of beige clair kid, intertwining straps of delicately darker opalescent kid.

BUCKLED PUMPS
A black mat kid with cut steel buckle is very smart for dress wear.

The Sport Influence Combined in Trio Below

If you desire style that savors of the sport influence, combined with cool comfort, you will realize your wishes in such models as shown below. Clever patterns—leathers in the new alluring shades of beige, brown, and white. Featuring the coming season's popular novelty, woven leather, punched effects, and watersnake. Such styles are suitable with simple daytime dresses for spring and summer.

Dear R.R.: Would it be all right to wear tennis shoes at camp with slacks or shorts? D.M.

A great many girls wear tennis shoes, but I prefer sturdy oxfords because your feet need this support. Never wear high heels with sports clothes if you want to have fun.

STORING AND WRAP-
PING THE BREAD FOR
MARKET

LOAVES READY FOR
THE OVEN. UNIFORM
PANS PERMIT EVEN
BROWNING OF THE
BREAD ON ALL SIDES.

store. Since then we have been making bread four days a week. We have taken on a second store now. That is as far as we have gone yet, but one never knows where a small thing like a dozen rolls will lead.

I long since stopped making rolls and now bake only the loaves. My loaf weighs 1½ pounds and sells for 15 cents. I wrap it in a regular plain white paper and tie with a green cord.

We have enclosed the back porch and are making it as convenient as possible for the bread making, but we still need more space.

How much more do we expect to grow in this? I do not know. I do know that while others have talked depression, we have talked and thought bread.

Beating the Depression With Bread

We live on a farm six miles from Jackson, Mississippi. Early in 1931 I went to see the home demonstration agent about joining the club and selling on the curb market. I made nine dozen homemade rolls to sell on opening day. A customer asked me if I ever made loaves. I had not, but I resolved to try the loaves. The loaves were fine and found even readier sale than the rolls.

I began with the equipment I had on hand, a small mixing bowl and two loaf pans. Soon I bought a large mixing bowl, and four more pans, enough to fill my coal stove oven. I baked twice a week for market. Soon I outgrew my one

little oven and got another stove with two ovens, increasing the number of pans to 54 to fill the ovens.

Mixing soon became laborious, so I bought a large size bread mixer. However, to some extent, we still knead the dough by hand. By the last of August the demand was more than I could supply, working by myself. My best efforts could only turn out 78 loaves. My husband was much interested in my success and in helping the business to grow, so he was glad to learn to help with the kneading. Gradually he has kneaded more and more and now he does it all. I do the mixing, making the loaves and baking.

With that arrangement we could make more than enough to supply the market. September 16 we began selling to a chain grocery

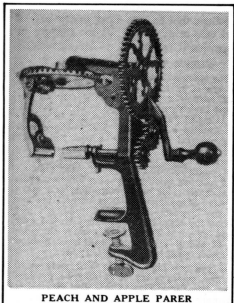

PEACH AND APPLE PARER
There's much waste in paring an apple or a peach by hand. Here's a machine that holds the fruit firmly on two prongs, and when you turn the crank, causing the wheels to turn around, a little blade pares it smoothly.

Ice cream is no longer looked upon as a confection or a luxury. It has a definitely established place in the dairy industry, and in the food habits of all our people. Ice cream is generally regarded as a wholesome and nourishing food, and an essential in the American diet.

Venison Stew

Prepare venison by cutting into inch cubes. Fry out bacon which has been cut into small pieces. Dust venison with flour and brown in bacon fat. Add one tablespoon flour to the fat and then one pint of water, stirring until it begins to thicken. Season with pepper, salt, onion, and four tablespoons of vinegar. Cover and simmer for one hour. Add one grated lemon rind and one teaspoon of meat sauce or chili powder. Cook for about 30 minutes, or until tender.

Random Bits of Static

During the summer most of us do very little radioing, due partly perhaps to the fact that reception is likely to be erratic, and partly because it's too hot to sit around inside (and of course we're all too considerate of our neighbors, if we have close ones, to turn the speaker up so loud that everyone within a half-mile must listen, silly nilly!). But with September, old programs are renewed, new ones—either with new talent or with old favorite performers—are inaugurated, and all of us perk up our

ears and reach for the tuning dial.

September saw the return of Will Rogers to his old Sunday evening program. Will's first speech of this series was broadcast from London. He and Mrs. Rogers and their two sons have been on a jaunt of several weeks through the Orient and across Europe, and in his London broadcast Will gave some impressions of the countries they visited.

I, for one, have missed Eddie Cantor and have been looking forward to his return to the radio. I understand that he isn't coming back to his former sponsor nor, indeed, to the NBC network. But he will be heard, if present plans materialize, over the CBS. I've recently read Eddie's own story of his life, *My Life Is in Your Hands*, and it made me appreciate the banjo-eyed comedian more than ever. I was about six years late reading the book—I believe it was published in 1928—but if you get a chance to read it (and haven't already) I believe you'd enjoy it.

Did you miss those perennial favorites, Amos 'n Andy? Their three-months' vacation ended on September 17. Amos (Freeman Gosden) took his family to Alaska, while Andy (Charles Correll) and Mrs. Correll went to Europe. It was the famous pair's first separation in ten years. The Frank Buck feature will be continued daily, as well as Amos 'n Andy.

I enjoy my radio the first thing when I get up in the morning and the last thing before I retire at night. I can get something I enjoy hearing whenever I have time to listen. The radio is a wonderful invention. When there is going to be a special program I invite my neighbors. I would be lost without it.

I am 61 and our children are all away. It is a satisfaction to know my wife has the radio to keep her from feeling lonely during the day. We enjoy it more than anything except our children.
J. H. W., Alabama.

Everyone knows the feeling when a dearly loved member of the family is away. This is exactly the way you feel when the radio is out of order.

The radio today is like the bards in olden times; countless numbers of people gather in groups to hear their favorite songs or programs.

The Kraft Music Hall is my favorite radio program because I am a hillbilly and can thoroughly appreciate and understand that fellow Bob Burns. I don't believe Bing Crosby can be beaten as a crooner, and I like to listen to a fellow who cannot read music but has the ability to sing as he does.

I love the call, "Farm and Home Hour," and "It's a g-r-a-n-d day here in Chicago." I know this program comes into our home for our special benefit. We depend on it to bring the best in music, most instructive and noteworthy infor-

● Deanna Durbin and Eddie Cantor are a high spot of the week.

mation, and snappy farm briefs. It brings farm activities and national meetings into our home and we enjoy them next best to being there. This program seems to say, "We pledge allegiance to the farms and to the soil on which they stand, one people indivisible, with peace and plenty for all."

Golf for Farm Sons and Fathers

Have you ever been a farmer boy who couldn't get away for the weekly baseball game on a July Saturday afternoon?

Or a farm father who has felt that "boys never think about anything but ball and it's too far to go to Bethel and there's another two hours plowing down in that bottom corn anyway?" That's why I'm proposing a pasture golf course. Honestly, I'm not joking.

The idle rich and city business men have claimed golf for their very own long enough. There's every challenge to skill and keen muscular coordination and good judgment to be found in other games. Any of the family, male or female, can play it. It's cheaper than baseball.

Golf is a game that can be played all year round and as long as one lives.

And it'll give the farm the best cow pasture it ever had. Yes, sir!

We built a 1,975 yard, nine-hole course on a 20-acre pasture for a cash expense of $2.90. Mowing weeds and tall grass helped both the course and the pasture.

To make the course harder we took advantage of a small stream, the "old swimmin' hole" fed by a spring, a tenant house, a thick clump of pines, and a swamp.

We used sand on our greens and No. 3 tomato and quart paint cans for cups. Greens may be made by scraping off weeds and grass and leveling up the soil you have,

though heavy clays would be rather unsatisfactory alone. For wiring greens against stock we used a single strand of telephone wire.

Two or three clubs can be bought for what a good baseball glove costs, and two can play with one set of clubs. I heard of one boy who began playing with a knotted sassafras stick.

Movies Worth Seeing

Snow White and the Seven Dwarfs.—A Walt Disney cartoon presentation of the familiar fairy tale. Everybody's praising it. Nobody should miss it. Young and old alike find it delightful. The outstanding film of the year.

The Littlest Rebel.—A charming picture, with Shirley Temple as the little daughter of a Confederate officer whom she gets into danger and then out again.

The Singing Home

Who has not fallen under the spell cast by happy songs around a cheerful fireside? And who does not thrill to soft melodies floating out upon the stillness of a summer dusk? Memories of these are tender and lasting and play an important part in the strengthening and sweetening of home ties.

Fortunate indeed is the family that possesses a 'singing' mother, but lacking this, there is usually someone with enough talent to act as leader. If there is a musical instrument for background, so much the better, but if not, great pleasure may still be had in unaccom-

panied group singing. In my own family we often join some radio voice in familiar numbers.

The South is noted for a rich heritage of folk songs and spirituals—a heritage too often neglected in these days of 'popular' music. Into these have been woven the joys, sorrows, and even the illustrious history of our people. No better advantage can be taken of the recreational and spiritual benefits of music than will be found in a renewed allegiance of these 'heart' songs and a definite planning for their use in our homes.

Like most farm people we had spent Saturday in town, and returned home late in the afternoon. The car was put into the garage and the gear left in reverse. The selfstarter being out of commission, we had been using the crank.

After supper we decided to go to see a neighbor. My dad and brother went out to crank the car, not knowing the gear was in reverse. When they cranked, the car shot out of the garage, across the road into a cotton field of about 10 acres, ready for picking. It went on across our cotton field into our neighbor's cotton field, running in a semicircle back across our field. The fun came watching Daddy chase the car like a dog after a rabbit. When he got near enough to catch the car, it hit a turnrow, going in another direction. Daddy finally managed to jump on the running board and stop the car just before it went down a 40-foot embankment.

"Fine Features Make Fine Cars!"

. . . and only Chevrolet for '40 brings you all these fine features at Chevrolet's low prices and with Chevrolet's low cost for gas, oil and upkeep. . . . That's why

"CHEVROLET'S FIRST AGAIN"

Eye it · · Try it · · Buy it!

NEW EXCLUSIVE VACUUM-POWER SHIFT

On all models at no extra cost. Only Chevrolet has this marvelous steering wheel Vacuum-Power Shift, pioneered by Chevrolet and supplying 80% of the shifting effort, now made even more attractive in appearance and even more efficient in action.

"THE RIDE ROYAL"

Chevrolet's famous Perfected Knee-Action Riding System*—plus many other advanced features—brings you ride results never before known.

NEW FULL-VISION BODIES BY FISHER

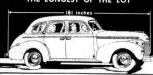

With full 3-passenger front seat and wider rear compartment—with 1¾ inches wider windshield and more vision all around—bigger, more beautiful, more comfortable bodies in every way. De luxe equipment, at no extra cost, on all models includes dual windshield wipers, dual matched horns, electrically lighted rear luggage compartment, and many other comfort and convenience items.

"THE LONGEST OF THE LOT"

181 inches

The Master 85 Sport Sedan, $740

From front of grille to rear of body (181 inches) Chevrolet for 1940 is the longest of all lowest-priced cars!

SUPER-SILENT VALVE-IN-HEAD ENGINE

The master motor of the low-price field—bringing you an unequaled combination of power, performance and economy.

NEW SEALED BEAM HEADLIGHTS
WITH SEPARATE PARKING LIGHTS

The newest, safest and most scientific road-lighting system ever designed for any motor car. Giving full light without glare.

PERFECTED HYDRAULIC BRAKES

Today, as always, the last word in dependability, in ease of operation and in positive safety for you and your family.

Nowhere Else— Features Like These!

NEW "ROYAL CLIPPER" STYLING • ALL-SILENT SYNCRO-MESH TRANSMISSION • LARGER TIPTOE-MATIC CLUTCH • IMPROVED SHOCKPROOF STEERING* • NEW CRYSTAL-CLEAR SAFETY PLATE GLASS • NEW SAFE-T-LOCK HOOD • RIGHT-SIDE SERVICE

Chevrolet has more than 175 important modern features

*On Special De Luxe and Master De Luxe Series
CHEVROLET MOTOR DIVISION, General Motors Sales Corporation, DETROIT, MICHIGAN

85-H.P. VALVE-IN-HEAD SIX

$659

AND UP, *at Flint, Michigan. Transportation based on rail rates, state and local taxes (if any), optional equipment and accessories—extra. Prices subject to change without notice. Bumper guards—extra on Master 85 Series.

Home Crafts

A Modern Sampler

The old-fashioned cross stitch sampler of grandmother's day is popular with the modern needlewoman. Rather heavy linen is generally used for the foundation and the stitches are worked with colored embroidery threads through a canvas sold especially for this purpose. The whole design may be done in black or gay colors may be mingled to give a charming effect.

Anyone who can do simple cross stitch work can easily copy the sampler illustrated directly from the picture. Each little black block represents one stitch. The finished size will depend upon the canvas selected, but it is best to use a rather coarse mesh so that the stitches need not be too small for easy working. Canvas having eight squares to the inch will result in a sampler about twice as large as the picture.

When finished, such a sampler may be framed and used as a delightfully quaint decoration in living room or bedroom or it may form the center of a cushion cover.

Baskets made of native materials—pine needles, honeysuckle vine, willow, and shucks—are a source of income to many women of Mississippi as well as a pleasant kind of handiwork.

Pine needles, though first used in baskets, have other uses. Hearth brooms, whisk brooms, and hat brushes sell well in the Gulf Coast gift shops.

Proper curing of the needles is the first step in making beautiful baskets, trays, brooms, etc. The articles are usually made of brown pine needles. The longleaf needles should be gathered during the winter, as they cure a prettier shade than those gathered in the summer. It is better to break off the branches and tie them with the tops up the way they grew, so that the needles can spread out and the sun can get to all parts of them. They must be watched and turned to cure evenly. If there is too much rain, they will mildew, but a little rain with the sunshine helps to make them a rich brown color. It takes from six weeks to two months to cure them properly. About November beautiful needles can be found on the ground under the large trees, but they must be gathered soon after they fall or they will mildew. They can be kept in a dark closed place for several months to retain the green color, but they will fade after they are made up and exposed to the light. Articles made from the brown needles and brown raffia with a touch of bright color sell better than anything else.

When produced for sale, baskets are usually treated with a thin coat of colorless varnish or shellac to stiffen the article and give it a more shiny surface. However, the true basket artist scorns the use of such a medium, but polishes each pine needle to a high degree and sews the roll in with a firm hand. This same artist proudly reminds you of the aroma of the pine, not found in the highly varnished type.

A beautiful Christmas tree can be produced by the use of ordinary materials to be found in any neighborhood. The children and their mothers must do the work, but the

tree will be enjoyed all the more because of that very fact.

Make a collection of suitable materials. Save all pieces of cord, colored wrapping papers, scraps of wall paper and crepe paper, pieces of tinfoil and cellophane, and bits of gaily flowered cloth. With these materials, crayons, and paste, wonders can be wrought, especially if you mothers will add your own enthusiasm and a 10-cent can of aluminum paint.

If you live where red haws grow, they can be strung for chains. Peanuts alternated with cranberries make attractive chains. Nothing is prettier than popcorn chains, but they need not be snowy white. The popcorn chain can be dipped in dyes to secure new effects. If pieces of bright colored crepe paper are soaked in water, a very satisfactory dye is produced.

Beautiful ornaments can be made of pine cones, silvered with aluminum paint and supplied with strings for hanging. Black walnuts can be finished in the same way. Another attractive one is made by tying a walnut or small apple tightly in the middle of a square of cellophane, which has been lined with another square of brilliantly colored paper.

Other ornaments in various shapes and colors are made from colored paper or from flowered wall paper.

1941–1945
For the Duration

We'll walk barefoot in America if necessary
TO SAVE RUBBER ··· TO WIN THIS WAR

For the Duration

Since 1918 Clarence Poe had been warning his readers at regular intervals to beware of another war. The world's only hope, Poe kept urging, lay in world organization for peace. In April 1942 he reprinted an article he had first published in November 1931 entitled "The Danger of War Threatens All Boys Born Between 1911 and 1927."

To some Americans at the end of the 1930's, Hitler's rasping voice coming over the short-wave set and his diminutive mustache were as ridiculous as Charlie Chaplin's movie made them. Others felt a chill as, over the short wave set, the crowd roared back: "Heil Hitler!"

As preparation for war began in America—manufacturing of war supplies, first for our allies and then for us—the numbing Depression began to ease. Increasingly huge infusions of federal spending (for war production) into the economy created the jobs that some of Roosevelt's New Dealers had predicted they would in Depression days. For most Americans, unless they fought or had loved ones in the armed forces, the "duration" meant jobs and money for the first time in a decade, and rationing.

For farmers, the duration had a somewhat different meaning. Most farmers in 1942 had the most prosperous year in memory with farm prices the highest they had been in a *generation*. The farm problem now was labor, or lack of it. Suddenly farm boys were drafted.

Others went to $4-a-day jobs in the war industry. Even women were taking war jobs. Children were taken out of school to pick cotton which was needed for uniforms, tents, harnesses for parachutes, etc. And if the labor shortage were not difficult enough, mechanical helpers were also in short supply. As one farmer wrote:

There's a war raging. I can't get needed equipment. So we lengthen the day, do chores earlier, do chores later, stretch it out to 15 hours. Even the roustabout harvest hands have upped and offed as war plant "mechanics" at $1.50 an hour. Wife and I, just two, promised to raise 20 acres of marketable peanuts, 12 acres of cotton.

I must join a local group, help each neighbor dig peanuts, so I can get them and their machinery. When at last we get to my patch, I find the worms hit them two weeks back when I was helping my neighbors. Then comes rain and holds two weeks. My late cotton crop (best I had) is ruined. Man says, "Below strict low; 14 cents. Take it or leave it."

Can't argue; got to sell; got to buy fertilizer, get back home, tend to hogs, chickens, cows, mules, mend pump rod if I can get the part.

Disgusted, I sit a minute, pick up a farm paper, and here is some committee appealing to farmers to do something or other in their "spare time." Great Caesar's ghost!

But the dream of the land followed the soldier boys to far-off countries. Some brought it in their bones:

I am in the Army. Now that spring is here it doesn't seem natural, because I am away from the growing crops . . .

To others it was new but no less poignant: "Thousands of us dream only of a secure place on our own land now," one soldier wrote. But he had had no farm experience. He asked, "Is this a dream, an obsession, or can I make it real, and how?"

He Is My Son

Next to food, our boys in the service hunger for news from home. And the only way they get that news is in the letters they get from home. Some towns have one person who writes every single boy from that town every so often just to be sure he is getting his share of the home town news.

A loud-mouthed man was talking in a Pullman smoker. "Son," he said, flicking a fat finger toward a newly-made second lieutenant, "do you know what you're wearing that pretty suit and fighting for? I'll tell you. To save the face of F.D.R. To pull some more British chestnuts out of the fire. Imperialism. International bankers: that's what it's all about."

A friend who was along told me that the reply of the twenty-two-year-old kid was magnificent. He answered quietly: "No. I'm fighting for the right of men like you to say what you want to say in public, without being shot, or having someone knock your head off like I feel the urge to do right now."

A dead silence. Then someone laughed. The fat man got out of there, glaring and mumbling.

NOW . . . Let 'em Have It!

Food for Freedom . . . Now it's Food for Victory

Food from American farms is gaining on every front. Our boys are getting good food — all they can eat. Shipments to our allies are steadily going up . . . Germany's meat ration has again been cut down!

AMERICA'S great Food for Victory program is now a living reality. With the first treacherous bomb at Pearl Harbor American farmers united in angry determination to beat the production goals they set last fall.

We have new goals now and to reach them will call for the greatest production in the history of American agriculture. But reach them we *must* and reach them we will! For the United States is not only the arsenal, but also the food store, for the United Nations. Britain is cutting down her rations to release supplies for the Far East. Russia's "scorched earth" retreat last fall destroyed vast food crops. Hungry refugees by the thousands must be fed.

Our shipments of foods are swiftly increasing. Two months ago we delivered our *millionth ton* of food to Britain. By mid-year more than a *billion dollars'* worth will have been delivered to her alone — not counting Russia or China.

What next year's needs will be, no one knows now, but everything depends upon the American farmer. If he fails, our fighting forces and the men in our factories and shipyards will fail, along with millions of fighters and workers in other countries allied with us.

But America is determined they shall not fail. Food is vital as bullets and the Food for Victory effort insures an ever increasing production as the American farmer's contribution to complete victory and lasting peace.

YOUR FARM CAN HELP
★ UNITED STATES DEPARTMENT OF AGRICULTURE ★

Women Join the *"Field Artillery"*
as International Harvester Dealers
Teach Power Farming to an Army of "TRACTORETTES"

and maybe some ham on the side! Nuts! I'll be island-happy if I get to thinking of it. Island-happy means nutty. The first symptom of it is you start buying coconuts. R.E.S., Chief Petty Officer, Seabees.

I am a widow with four boys in service and four children under fourteen. I never have time to feel sorry for myself. By 7:30 I have cleaned house and leave for work, returning at 5 p.m. Then I lead my gang to the field and we plow and hoe as long as we can see. I make supper; the kids do the chores; I help them get their lessons. After they are abed, I wash, iron, or can.

I am 46 years of age, strong and healthy. A contented but anxious mother, I pray for my boys and my Marine brothers nightly, and when I do get in bed around midnight I just die till morning. But at five I am up and at it again. Mrs. C.S., Tex.

Today that young lieutenant is fighting overseas. I have a special reason to be proud of him. He is my son. B.B.M., La.

This is my birthday and I write from my foxhole with a tarp on top to catch rainwater. I can bathe now in as little water as I used to shave with. Lots doing on this island last week: a show by Jack Benny and three girls, including Carole Landis—this little spot in the Pacific catching the stars! Queer place, 143 degrees in the sun sometimes, but the sun never reaches our tents—shade with enormous trees, mostly palm, mahogany, teak, rubber, banyan. Guess you will think we are ex-

travagant but our toilets, walks, benches, etc., are all built of mahogany!

We fish now out among the sharks and barracudas, which are dangerous, but fish are a relief from the dehydrated food. We hang banana bunches in our tents to ripen. As for coconuts, we get tired stumbling over them; they cover the ground. This morning for breakfast a grand surprise: two whole eggs for each man, cold storage, but the first in months.

Such eating and tent-dwelling for a year and a half gets monotonous. What couldn't I do with some fresh vegetables, fresh eggs,

What farm mother isn't sick of nervous exhaustion? Sons away, no help, still trying to send some children to school and care for the smaller children. Raising more food for victory, each day trying to can one extra jar of fruit. Mother of Ten, Mo.

Country Things I Love Most

The sight of my soldier-son home again . . . the eagerness with which he greets all the old familiar pets and animals . . . the pride and contentment settling over him as he helps do the evening chores. I bow reverently to the good, familiar homeland that has nurtured my son to a manhood of high ideals and clean habits and formed in him the passionate desire to preserve the principles for which he stands. Mrs. G.W.G., Tex.

Dear Miss Kate:

I am 7 years old. I live in the Alamo City, where many battles were fought to set this country free. I hope every little school child is doing his share to help win this war. I carry old papers, old silver, and Daddy's old razor blades to school. E.B., Tex.

War on the Cosmetic Front

One young woman suggested that the Army abandon saluting as undemocratic and simply let the enlisted personel greet officers, "Hiyuh, Bud!" That's the same kind of American informality as led the wife of an American mayor to say to the late Queen of Rumania, "You said a mouthful, Queenie." Neither do we think it would be a sound idea for ladies to give up hair-do's and nail polish for the duration, as Miss M.F. proposes, though we do offer to join most heartily in the anti-snood drive. We saw one the other day that looked like a goat's udder with a fly-net on it.

PLAN YOUR VICTORY GARDEN <u>NOW</u>
RAISE MORE FOOD—AND <u>SAVE</u> IT <u>ALL!</u>

FOR YOUR <u>FAMILY</u>—FOR YOUR <u>COUNTRY</u>

Free! "HAVE A VICTORY GARDEN"
84-PAGE BOOKLET LOADED WITH INFORMATION ABOUT VEGETABLE GROWING

You'd expect *International Harvester* to have the best handbook. This is it! Detailed facts on soil, seedbeds, fertilizers, hotbeds, cold frames, planting, cultivating, insect and disease control, harvest, winter storage, etc.

WRITE ADDRESS BELOW FOR YOUR COPY

Shall We Can Nylon Hose?

Does sealing nylon hose in a fruit jar help to preserve them? That is the question of the year, and here is the answer as Miss G.D., home economics consultant of the E.I. du Pont de Nemours & Co., obligingly gives it:

"No, there's no need at all to seal nylon stockings in a fruit jar. It's much better to have put some tomatoes in the jar last summer. Just give the nylons ordinary care as far as storage is concerned. There's no need to keep the jar in the refrigerator either, as a number of women have confessed doing."

Plan Your Victory Garden Now!

Today my neighbor sent seed to her son, stationed on a pin-point island in the South Pacific. He loves the land and hungers to plant again. There was balm for the mother as well as for the son in that packet, for she knows, that if he lives, he will come back to farm. F.S.M., Ga.

Canning Without Sugar

All information obtainable indicates that there will be some sugar allocated for home canning needs. But honey and syrup used judiciously will help stretch the amount of sugar which will be rationed out for canning. Honey is preferred to syrup because the flavor is more delicate and not so apt to absorb or destroy the flavor of the fruit.

Ramblings

Manufacture of radios for civilian use has been prohibited by the Government after April 22, and a program set in motion calling for conversion of the entire radio industry to war production before mid-summer.

Funny men Abbott and Costello last year played to almost 500 service camps, and brought in $100,000,000 in War Bond sales for Uncle Sam.

Shoe ration talk brings this from Bob Burns: "My Uncle Fudd heard they wuz a-goin' to ration shoes, and he wants to know, 'What is shoes?'"

Page 177. Canning the treasure of the harvest had been a necessity in grandmother's day, with many pages of the Progressive Farmer devoted to canning techniques and recipes. During World War I, it was the farmer's patriotic duty to produce as much food as he possibly could and his wife's, to plan and conserve, preaching "the gospel of the clean plate." During World War II, despite a severe labor shortage and lack of repair parts, farm output was prodigious and farm women were again "canning for victory."

Page 178. "Thanks for waiting," said this ad for the 1947 Dodge. During the Second World War, many Americans were making more money than they had in ten, or even twenty, years. Inflation built up as war production and controls created a shortage of goods to buy. After the war, manufacturers quickly turned to consumer goods, with a new emphasis on comfort, smoothness and power.

Page 179. This 1948 ad, portraying teenagers jitterbugging to music from a Westinghouse radio, claimed that "you will get far more enjoyment out of a set that's built up to a standard than you will from one that's built down to a price." Since money was no problem, people were looking for quality, style and status.

Page 180. The coon is "curious, pleasant-smelling, and good to eat," said the Progressive Farmer in an article in October, 1955, for which this cover was done. Over the years, hunters' wives kept complaining about the sport, but one woman wrote in 1963 that she was glad her son was following in his hunter father's footsteps: "Instead of having to worry about drag racing and bad company, I only worry about him finding his dogs."

Page 181. Milking time has not lost its fascination for children since the days of the old "pull and squirt" method. Here is yet another instance of farm children being able to learn, in natural circumstances, about the cycle of life. The last stanza of a poem written to the Progressive Farmer by Lillian Delly puts it perfectly:

It isn't only milk and cream I see,
Brought to my door while I am still asleep—
It is a part of man, of beast, and field;
A portion of their strength is mine to keep.

Page 182. "You can get starting in farming these days," proclaims a 1976 article in the Progressive Farmer. Though initial costs may appear astronomical, a young farmer can start slowly by working for others, renting land, buying used equipment and later expand gradually. This photograph for a Progressive Farmer cover was taken at Kildaire Farm, Wake County, North Carolina, which was established by Dr. W.B. Kilgore, one of the founders of the Progressive Farmer.

The Progressive Farmer

 CANNING FOR VICTORY

JULY 1942

HOLD EVERYTHING...

Did you know, for example, that the new Dodge brakes operate from six hydraulic cylinders instead of four? That's the extra security now being supplied in the smoothest car "afloat."

It's one thing to have such extremes of power and smoothness,—another to have such complete and easy control that (as one enthusiast said) "It's out of this world." You'll see! Thanks for Waiting.

NEW *Dodge*

SMOOTHEST CAR AFLOAT

Westinghouse radios and radio-phonographs are available in a wide variety of models. The one shown here is the 186, which has exclusive Automix record changer, Electronic Feather reproducer, and Rainbow Tone FM. The bow-front cabinet is a Westinghouse classic. Home Radio Division, Westinghouse Electric Corp., Sunbury, Pa.

Listen...and you'll buy Westinghouse

Listen to Ted Malone every morning Monday through Friday ABC

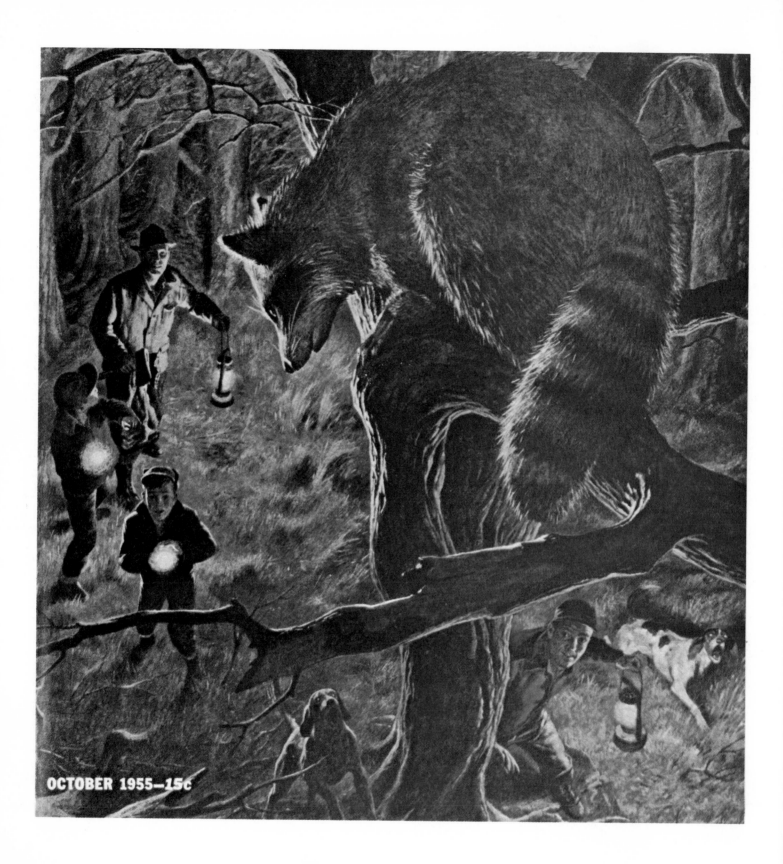

OCTOBER 1955—15c

Once a day...
every day...
enjoy
Campbell's
Soup!

CHICKEN NOODLE SOUP

When a fellow has his good hot soup
GOOD THINGS BEGIN TO HAPPEN

Good spirits happen. Soup's fragrant good broth warms you up, perks you up... it just kind of makes you feel good all over.

Good nutrition happens, too. Have a big bowlful of Campbell's Chicken Noodle Soup. There's good nourishment aplenty in that sunny chicken broth and tender plump chicken and good enriched egg noodles. Satisfying goodness that everybody, old and young, enjoys every day of the year.

By the way... have *you* had your soup today?

The Farm is the Anchor

During the war, farmer sons (and even some non-farmer sons) had dreamed of the land and farmer fathers had ached for their sons return to the farm:

We Plow Together Again

I plow the bottom-land flat.
Bill plows the clay hill,
Curving each cool furrow
That it may cup its fill
Of sweet spring showers
To ease the dry, hot pain
Of summer's shimmering hours . . .

More than his safe return, I sought,
And God's sparing from harm:
I prayed that Bill might love still
The clay-silt, pine-topped farm.
Today is April-sweet, and life's a joy:
We plow together now—me and my soldier boy!

         W.T.P., Mississippi

"Bill" came home to the farm—but as always with dreams—the reality was somewhat different. Farming had become much more complicated. Machinery, expensive and intricate, had been set free by the end of war production. A farmer might invest almost as much in machinery as in the beloved land itself.

By 1949, even Clarence Poe was no longer advising all boys who loved the land to farm. For years, the *Progressive Farmer* had been advocating "two-armed" farming (crops and livestock). Diversification had become essential. Southern farms that had depended on soil-depleting cash crops like cotton must be built up by soil-enriching crops, by putting some land into pasture, by using timber as a crop. The new machines and chemicals must be understood.

But it was even more complicated than that. The farming of land was, it seemed, the most basic industry of all and, as such, the entire nation had some stake in it, much as they must have a stake in the power from their rivers and the gas and oil beneath the earth. Therefore, the people, through their government, must have some say in farming. And there was the rub.

Farming had always been one of the most uncertain of professions. There had always been the uncertain weather. As the world shrank, there had been the uncertainties of world markets. To these now, the uncertainty of government regulation had been added. The chimera of "parity" (the ratio of the return farmers got for their crops in relation to the supplies they must buy, compared to certain specified years) had become an institution. What percentage of profit this ratio should yield and whether price supports should be fixed or flexible (and combined or not with acreage allotments) was now a question that each national administration and Congress must consider. What effect all this would have on their markets, farmers must now try to guess. Moreover, the "farm bill" never seemed to get passed before planting time. The frustration was enormous. It is not surprising that many farmers railed against it and declared that they would prefer to go back to eating potato peelings if they could only cast off government controls. But other farmers, and the *Progressive Farmer*, remembered how cotton had dropped from 40¢ a pound to 10¢ in the space of one year (1919–1920). Whatever frustrations came from government regulation, these farmers agreed that it was better, in the face of so many uncertainties, than no security at all.

However, it seemed to many farmers that government regulations were more in favor of the big-time farmers. The stated aim of

OLD WATER MILL
Woodcut by Clare Leighton

farm plans of some administrations was to drive inefficient farmers off the land, and to reduce the number of farmers in the country by as much as one-third to one-half. But as farmers knew, and national planners often seemed not to know, efficiency could not be measured on farms in the same way as in factories. According to one letter writer, " 'the inefficient' are too often simply those who do not have the land, capital, and other advantages for volume production." Was the small family farm, perhaps, inefficient by government definition? And there was a larger question. As the same man wrote to the *Progressive Farmer* in 1956:

Chicago's slums are recently reported growing by 1600 newcomers each week, mostly small farmers driven from the land by drouth and economic pressures . . .

Those who retire while still able to help themselves could live on very little cash income in many rural areas. A garden, flocks of chickens, pig, cow or goat can provide a large share of the living—not to mention escape from relief rolls and from city smog, traffic, and turmoil.

Farm skills are just manual labor in the cities. The present program of plowing under the small, uneconomic, marginal farmer is a loss and a tax drain upon everyone, urban and rural dweller alike.

But if farmers were leaving the farm for the city at an increasing rate, the city, it seemed, was coming out to meet them. The American commitment to individual transportation in private cars had led to increasingly better roads. Along these roads the city was creeping out to the country. More and more people wanted to escape the problems of the city but still live close enough to work in it. With VA and FHA loans more people could buy houses. House and auto ownership increased dramatically. The suburbs became Suburbia. Farm people looked with

foreboding at this encroachment on their countryside, the wholesale bulldozing of their trees and landscape for tract housing and shopping centers. But worse than the obvious changes were the city temptations drawing ever closer to country youth. How could the feel of loved earth win the battle in a teen-ager against peer pressure to own a four-wheeled steed that would spring at a touch of the fingertips?

These were worrying times, for farmers and non-farmers alike. True, the predicted post-war depression had not occured. On the contrary the economy was booming. There was a plethora of things to be bought—available in such quantities as to satisfy even rationing-starved Americans. Perpetual prosperity may have seemed again (as in the 20's) the reward for being an American. But their very prosperity appeared to some a sign that a conspiracy had been mounted against it. "Communists" (discovered by Senator McCarthy and others) lurked behind every tree. Something was out to get the good guys—just because they, at last, had it so good. The people seemed rootless, seeking, with their new mobility, jobs anywhere—not near the homeplace, whether farm or city, but wherever the job would pay the most. The very tenor of life had changed. One man wrote:

Here in the city every part of a human being is strung up to high pitch all day, and by night, they are too tired and nervous to sleep or rest. We seldom see sunset. We have to pay high prices for everything . . .

Still, the people bought—perhaps to forget their other anxieties. Perhaps dishwashers and TV could blot out those early dawn worries—in 1950 the Korean War and behind it, that infinitesimal creature, the atom, whose infinite force had been liberated to haunt the earth for good or ill.

For the lucky ones, the farm remained. The farmhouse was still big enough to include, and the farm still needed, workers from the extended family. Farm wives were still a vital part of the family enterprise. And the land itself seemed permanent. The land itself, for those that loved it, could be the recompense for the ups and downs of farming. In days awash with nameless fears, the farm, for those who could stay on it, could be the anchor.

Country Voices

I not only love farming; I live it. I tried public work, but the soil I was born on called to me. I love to plow. The smell of turned earth whets my appetite. Out in the field a piece of cold bread and a hunk of meat tastes better to me than dressing and cake do to many.

I go to bed early and rejoice in deep sleep and am up with a leap between four and five to be on my fields again with the rising sun. I love the fresh, clean fruit of my own land and my fine, fresh eggs, milk, butter, vegetables and chicken.

I even like to can. To peel fruit, snap beans, shell peas, etc., is not a chore to me, but a pleasure.
Mr. X., La.

From Korea my brother, Sgt. G.C. of the 84th Engineers, writes: "Sis, I would like to own land. Money has a way of getting away from me, but land wouldn't. It's something to hold onto." Young and single, he goes on to tell me how much money he has saved and how much he could pay a month.

This wanting land is a dream of a child whose parents died when he was seven years old. It must have hurt him even then to stand silently by and watch our father's land sold to strangers, and I believe he has grieved for it ever since . . .

So I have made a down payment on a place, one he always said he wished he owned. Now I'm asking God to keep him safe, so he may live long days on his land and for-

get he has ever been cold, forget his frostbitten hands, forget the wind that howls, as he says "like a Siberian wolf." W.H.C., Okla.

Why does a big business man sit in his office and say, "I'm a farmer," when he never does a day's labor on the land? Driving out on Sunday and footing the bills isn't farming. No, siree! You've got to live on a farm day and night, live with a farm through thick and thin. You've got to get the dirt under your fingernails and be washed with honest sweat. Mrs. H.G., La.

If the big farmer is allowed to evade his taxes by writing off "losses" in income and using that money to grab more land; if the little farmer and the little man in general thus is ousted from holding land in our free-enterprise system—well, it seems to me that the national debt will eventually bleed the country white. That is exactly what the Communists are wishing and waiting for; and this is the only way they can ever hope to conquer us. It will be our own people who will let us down. I do not believe any outsider can do this, if we cling together and help each other, instead of being so covetous and trying to hog more than our share. Mrs. J.W.O., Miss.

What I Like About Our Rural Church

I like the closeness to God I feel in a country church where
. . . the minister preaches what God lays on his heart
. . . people aren't ashamed to kneel and pray
. . . a simple vase of flowers from a member's garden adds warmth and beauty
. . . little children say, "Hello, Mrs. Preacher," not knowing her name
. . . young people, sweethearts, and others sing in the choir
. . . mothers proudly come to Sunday school with their children, with or without new hats . . .

Our main trouble these days is simply this: Too many people in too many cars in too much of a hurry going in too many directions to nowhere for nothing. Mrs. S.M.M., Va.

Who wants to go back to plowing with a mule and one-horse plow? I've seen men come in from the fields absolutely exhausted after such labor. Listening last night to the hum of our tractor . . . I praised God for the noise and for the blessing of modern machinery. My son was doing what used to be a full day's work, easily, happily, and doing it all after school was out. Mrs. F.H., Tenn.

Times have changed. Every day 25 or 30 cars pass by our farm on the way to jobs in town. Many of these people are women who are working in the cotton mills or in the stores. Some of them work only during the winter months and help with the farm work in the summers. Others work the year-round and leave the farm to their husbands.

I wonder about it sometimes. Is this the way farm women should live? Most of the women I've talked with seem to like it. It gives them more money than they ever got off the farm. They can have more modern kitchen equipment to simplify their cooking. They can quit sewing and buy ready-made clothes. They can quit quilting and buy blankets. Mrs. C.V.R., N.C.

What can we farm women do about boredom? We are left so much alone. What started me thinking about this was an argument I heard in which one wife stated that a fox-hunter is as bad as a drunkard. Of course, I don't agree with that; but I do find that most all wives of fox-hunters resent it bitterly. I think it is really a form of jealousy.

Well, the men go off, and you put the kids to bed, and just flop in a chair, too darn tired and ner-

Feather Hill Farm builds on egg profits— This fall's good egg price outlook is a big morale booster for the Tommy Corcoran family, operators of Feather Hill Farm, (quality eggs) Hot Springs, Arkansas.

But a good share of the Corcoran's enthusiasm comes from egg profits already made—profits to build on, even coming out of a period of unfavorable egg prices.

That hanging feeder over the roosts, being checked by Mrs. Corcoran and daughter Susie, is an example of attention to detail that makes egg profits for Feather Hill.

The feeder supplements automatic floor feeding equipment, helps keep feed intake high for hard-working layers. The Corcorans are careful with egg quality, too . . . it's one of the reasons they have egg profits to build on.

And their Nutrena Egg Feed program gets a lot of credit for the success of their operation.

For the 91-day period reported here, 2,383 Corcoran pullets produced eggs at a feed cost of only 14.24 cents per dozen.

The Corcorans feed Nutrena Crumblized Complete Egg Ration—have come to expect heavy-duty, low-cost-per-dozen performance from good birds on Nutrena Egg Feed.

vous to enjoy the paper or radio or anything. Sometimes you think you cannot stand another day of it, and maybe you would be better off if you did just collapse.

If anybody is interested, I have three children, and I've seen one movie in eight years. Mrs. R.R., Tenn.

A man with a wife like that *ought* to give her something to nag about. M.H., Tenn.

We hunt everything we have in South Texas. We've hunted together through the years, and know no happier times than when we sit by the campfire at night in the middle of 10,000 acres, and watch the stars and talk. It's a great life, and our only wish is that we could have more of it. Mrs. I.F.C., Tex.

At the age of 20 we don't care what the world thinks of us; at 30 we worry about what it is thinking of us; at 40 we discover that it wasn't thinking of us at all. W.B., La.

The Best Age?—If I could halt Father Time, I would stay 50. Then the longings and restlessness of youth are passed and we revel in the sweetness of each passing day. At 50 we have reached the

Born on a Farm...
Why I'm Still There

Is farm life the best life? Three people give their views after more than 60 years.

By JOHN McKINNEY

"I WAS born on the farm in 1884. I'm still here. In town you see the same thing every day; you should see my roses. Country neighbors are the best in the world.

"Today I borrowed an old-fashioned maul to drive posts. I manage our 28-cow dairy.

"We raised our three children here—one is a college business manager, another is with the U. S. Army Engineers, and the third, a schoolteacher. I keep farming because I love it."
Mrs. Chester Reeves, Tangipahoa Parish, La.

"IN 1879 I was born on the farm that joins the one where I now live. When I was 24 I worked in town a month and they paid me $40. I quit and came back to my horses.

"When those trees start to putting out—and the birds a-singing—and these grain fields a-waving, oh, man!

"Nobody has worn more patches than I have, but I've stuck with the farm, because I love it.

"On the farm, you never starve. You can tell everybody that."
Charles G. Harris, Augusta County, Va.

"I WAS born in 1891. We were married right here in this room, 50 years ago. We raised 13 happy children and we could never have raised that crowd in town. My children work. On the farm you can teach children to work. Your friends are closer to you out here. I go to the same church my mother carried me to when I was a little baby many years ago. I carried all my children there, 13 at a time. You see, I belong here."
Mrs. R. A. Bedenbaugh, Columbia County, Fla.

mountaintop, and would not go back, but simply see the pines sway in the breeze and the raindrops sparkle and live. Yes. 50 is best. Mrs. W.H.G., Ga.

My old granddad used to say he could take an axe and a woman and find a spring of water and live like Riley.

"It reminds me of opening a new book," Mrs. L.M.H., Arkansas, says of her life since the children grew up. "My husband and I moved to a stock farm. The house is badly run down and in need of repair. He is the carpenter, painter, and plumber. I have the green thumb and a way with chickens. We find the peace and quiet after a moderate day's work a balm for our tired bodies."

My dad will be 80 next year. He makes furniture for the vicinity. He has his land terraced and he himself sowed legumes. He can still sing. Can you? M.F., S.C.

I, too, am old—beyond three score and ten. I live by memories. In the stillness of midnight they flood my soul. My rest tonight was broken by disturbing dreams, so I arose. I have a fire burning and a pot of coffee going on the stove. I sit by the window. The sky is perfectly clear and blue, with bright shining stars.

Beholding the heavens, I thank God for his Son and for all their goodness to me. My heart sings carols: *Silent Night, Holy Night . . .*

Now at 4:30 in the morning, the other members of the family are sleeping, but here by the fire it is snug and warm, and all is peace. I hear the breathing of my sleeping grandchildren, the ticking of the clock, and now and then the baying of a hound far off. I hear the whistle and rumble of a train as it rushes swiftly through the hills and the night. And my spirit goes back through the ages to the wayside inn to face the manger where a Savior is born. "Peace on earth!" M.A.M., Okla.

To improve your figure, your health, and your relationship with your grandchildren, start the record player and dance the rock and roll with them every night. P.W.M., N.C.

Marianna

She worked for Mama 34 years before coming to help me, because Mama had no more babies for her to pet. Never blessed with a child of her own, she loved our children with a passion. When they were punished she went around muttering, with her lips poked out for hours. "Miss Rose, you shouldn't whip those boys. Try to have kindness and teach them."

And now our grief is terrible, for Marianna is dead. Such grief as squeezes and clutches, with a sudden feeling of great faintness, a

bowing of your face into your hands, a murmur to God to "have mercy on her poor soul." John to say, "Muz, I ain't hungry." Joe to say, "I only hoped she would get well enough to sit on her porch in the good sun." Mike to creep into the chimney corner and to cry until he had the jerks.

She suffered a severe stroke yes-

terday and mumbled over and over, "Bring the baby, bring the baby." At sunup Mama and I carried Rose, Jr., down to see her. She knew the baby and kept saying, "Hi, Rose, baby," and each time Rose would say, "Hi, Anna." We only stayed a few minutes and just as we got to the top of the little hill, Bennie called and said, "Miss Rose, she is gone."

Her favorite color was pink and

she was laid away in a beautiful pink shroud. For millions of years she will rock and spoil the babies in heaven.

A letter here before me brings sad news; and I'm talking too much, probably, to put off telling you; but I'm sure that every reader of Voices will want to be told. It is from a far western state, written by a former Southerner:

"Have you heard that our Ben Smith is dead? My last letter to him came back today marked 'Deceased.'. . . Isn't it strange that he should have died in seedtime, just as he said in the first poem of his I ever read—

If I die in seedtime, bury me deep;
   Wrap me in shrouds both strong and
   new
Lest I shall hear the March wind sweep
   The willow branches as it sings
   through.

I have loved the sun, the wind, and the
   rain,
   I would stir like a child in restless
   sleep
If I knew that seedtime were here again
   And other hands sowing—bury me
   deep.

The farm is the anchor that will hold through all the storms that sweep all else away.

Fathers Are Parents, Too

Being a teacher in a rural school I love: Elizabeth bringing a twig with a cocoon bursting into a butterfly . . . Mary clutching a bunch of purple grapes gathered for her teacher . . . little boys coming into classroom from recess with perspi-

ration rolling down their faces in streaks, some carrying balls and bats . . .

That Georgia teacher who complains that country children do not take baths enough has plainly no understanding of what it takes to

Do farmers make better fathers?

The answer is mostly yes. The man who lives close to the soil does live closer to his children. But although he seems to understand his children better, statistics show that the city-dweller protects them better with insurance.

It's the farmer *especially* who needs Living Insurance from Equitable. This kind of insurance not only pro-

vides protection in case of death, but can also provide funds to tide him over a bad year . . . or educate his children . . . or let him take it easy later on. Call The Man from Equitable. ©1959 The Equitable Life Assurance Society of the United States. Home Office: 393 Seventh Avenue, New York 1, New York.

LIVING INSURANCE FROM <u>EQUITABLE</u>

raise a large family on a farm where water has to be hauled in a barrel and baths taken by a stove in the living room. I wonder if she ever crept out of bed in the wee small hours after spending most of the night up with a child crying with earache to prepare several school lunches for other small children—after milking a cow. We do the best we can.

In my community a fine, new consolidated school opens this fall. While I rejoice in the good fortune of this crop of youngsters, I know I had some good things that will not be theirs. I remember a teacher who walked with us along the dusty road from our one-room school and made short the way by reading aloud to us the great poems that have inspired generations. The love of poetry that she inspired in us has remained a comfort through the years.

Junior Poet 1960

Home Land

My land is mountainous,
Vastness,
Cityless,
My land is commonest.
Good land.

My land is apple trees,
Winter freeze,
Bumblebees,
My land is summer breeze.
Fine land.

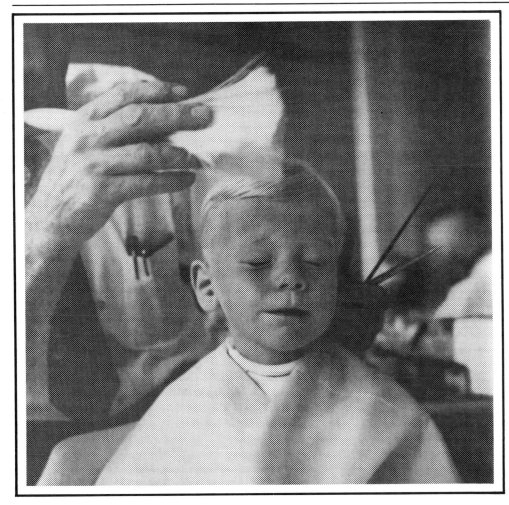

My land is riverlets,
Violets,
Pink sunsets,
My land is work and sweat.
Strong land.

My land has rocks on it,
Weeds on it, friends on it,
My land has tears on it.
Brave land.

My land has songs to sing,
Bells to ring,
Love to bring,
My land's a happy thing.
Home land.

Fathers Are Parents, Too

Recently, I saw a father busy in the field planting potatoes. Behind him, down the long rows, patiently trudged his little four-year-old son. There was something pathetic and lonely about the little figure, bundled up in a heavy coat, a green toboggan cap on his head, following in the footsteps of the big, busy man. Then something happened. At the end of the row the man stopped, and the little figure caught up with him. There was a smile on the man's face, answered quickly with a grin from the boy. They were together.

Vacation months may be a problem for city families with idle children, but summer is when farmers teach their children to farm. The young fellow so taught by helping his father in the field will have a firmer grounding, whatever he does afterward, in these changing times. Mrs. W.A. P., Tex.

Dear Ruth Ryan . . .

Dear R.R.: I'm almost 15 and I weigh 130 pounds. Do you think I'm too young to date boys? A.F.P., N.C.

The boy who calls to ask, "Whatcha doin' tonight, baby?" doesn't really deserve an answer.

To Park or Not to Park

I'll park if my date will, and I'll take her kisses if she hands 'em out—but boy, I've got her number. I'm not the first one she's parked with, and I won't be the last. So she's strictly not for me. I want somebody special. G.C., Md.

I like the girl who invites you in when you drive up instead of the one who runs and jumps on the side of the car and says, "I'm ready. Let's go." R.C.L., N.C.

Pop Comes Across With The Wolf Howl

The teen-agers, bless 'em, are the ones who look good in shorts. I can't blame my husband for whistling softly to himself as they pass. And if these youngsters occasionally wear shorts in inappropriate places, give them time for judgment to ripen.

For me, I wear slacks with reservations. With the right fullness here and the correct length there, they can be as cleverly disguising as a carefully designed dress. For an old worn-out Mom like me, I don't look so bad and Pop always comes across with the wolf howl. He keeps his illusions about the gal he married, and me, I'm flattered. Mrs. M.B., Okla.

I Heard My Father Pray

Once in the night I heard my father pray.
The house was sleeping, and the dark above
The hills was wide. I listened to him say
Such phrases of devotion and of love,
So far beyond his customary fashion,
I held my breath for wonder. Then he spoke
My name with tenderness and such compassion
Forgotten fountains in my heart awoke.

That night I learned that love is not a thing
Measured by eloquence of hand or tongue,
That sometimes those who voice no whispering
Of their affection harbor love as strong,
As powerful and deathless as the sod,
Yet mentioned only when they talk with God.

The Welcome Mat

In pioneer days the man and woman toiled side by side in the fields, in the home, in the manufacture of clothing, crops, and all the essential furnishings of a home. Perhaps we working wives today are pioneering, as our great-grandmothers did, in a different environment. I think our great grand-mothers would approve!

Mrs. R.B., Ala. writes: "I inherited my grandmother's recipe for egg custard, her appliquéd butterfly quilt, and the responsibility for a quaint old tradition known the world over as 'Southern hospitality.'

"In our home there are no 'uninvited guests' . . . but we surely have a lot of 'unexpected company!'. . . When they come, I go right on with what I am doing. I say: 'Come into the kitchen where we can talk while I finish ironing.' "

As Our Mothers Did?

I would like to know the ages of the gentlemen who think we farm women are letting our husbands down by not cooking as their mothers did.

I have memories of my mother getting up early in the morning, grinding coffee to put in the old blue enamel coffeepot, baking biscuits, frying bacon and eggs; yes, and having butter on the table she had churned in the old stone

THIS IS WHAT WE MEAN WHEN WE SAY...

"CHURNS WHILE YOU REST"

churn with a dasher she raised up and down. I can see her poking wood in the old, black, cast iron cookstove.

I would like to say to these gentlemen that we ladies would like to see them plowing with one mule and a double shovel until Saturday noon, then hitching that same mule to a one-horse wagon to take a turn of corn to the mill.

If they would do that and like it, we could do without some mixes to ease our day, if that were the only way happiness could be found.

I am one Southern farm wife who has learned to take shortcuts as long as the meals don't suffer. If I were a flour miller, I would go ahead with the grand mixes, for we will buy them.

Down to Earth

Thank God for petunias and
   salt-rising bread.
They're so down to earth, and
   they keep my soul fed . . .
I wish for my farmer each thing
   he desires—
Good crops, and his creatures
   well fed,
But deep in my heart I wish for
   his soul
What I feel when I'm baking
   good bread.

It makes my heart ache when I see the old, roomy, country homes torn down to make room for these little playhouses of today. Children

Who said Love, Honor and Carry Water?

of today cannot know what farm homes were like, save in the few such farming families that survive. And the children of such homes who have gone out and made homes and started families of their own love to gather back around the old family table and talk over times past. The grandchildren are

welcome and the house is big enough, but not so nice and fancy that they are afraid they will scratch a table or get dirt on the floor.

I love the big, cool bedrooms where there is room enough for an extra chair.

"I believe it's just a matter of time now until air conditioning will be a normal part of the house," H.G.C. of Mississippi told me.

In the past two years I've visited with farmers all across the South who have air conditioning.

Some are like Mr. C. who has a central system. Most, however, are putting in room units—both console and window types. But it doesn't matter which. In every home I've visited, without exception, they have said, "We just wouldn't do without it."

"Air conditioning in our home has become as important to us as any other piece of equipment," C.M. of Texas told us. "We especially enjoy it at mealtime—being able to come in out of the hot weather and eat in cool comfort. Meals taste better. We feel better—more like going back to work after an hour of cool relaxation."

"You're Dealing with Something more Important than H-bombs."

For centuries man has dreamed of having his own "magic globe" into which he could gaze and see happenings in other parts of the world. With television that dream has come true. Man can sit in the comfort and security of his own home and watch on a small screen moving, living pictures of events.

What will it really be like to have a television set in your home? It will be a little like going to the movies. But the screen will be much smaller and the image in black and white only . . . Like radio, television has commercials, but they're lively, animated, and sometimes longer . . .

I remember when instead of going out on winter nights to see some commercial amusement we sat around an open fire and ate parched peanuts, corn, and molasses. When you put on shoes you knew you were going somewhere . . . "Oldtimer," Miss.

To radio and TV chiefs:

You can give us better than this mediocre drivel if you try.
Mrs. P.E.G., Va.

It burns me up to see good TV programs ruined by some snake trying to stimulate drinking. P., N.C.

Please be careful. You're dealing with something more important than H-bombs. There's an eternal soul wrapped in the body of every child you're influencing.

Dragnet

No one has to tell me to hurry with my homework on "Dragnet" night. It is my favorite program and teaches that you can't do wrong and get away with it. It shows what happens to those who try to be "big shots" and makes me appreciate my home and parents more. Joe Friday is brave, kind, understanding, and gives good advice. It makes me want to be a better boy.

Folks tell me there are good things on TV, and I tell them there are good things in the slop bucket, but who wants to pick them out?

When we reach the stage where all the people are entertained all of the time, we will be close to having an opiate of the people.
Carl Sandburg

All Day Singin' 1953

There's an all day singin' at some church in Georgia the year 'round. The singers journey to Mt. Zion, Beulah, New Canaan, Pleasant Hill, Macedonia.

"Trav-el, travel to gloryland, Trav-el the road that leads to glory . . ."

The singing "class" is a group of singers that sits up front and takes the lead, with such volume that the music resounds through the countryside.

A lull comes about noon. Countryfolks invite townfolks to stay for the spread. When they uncover the baskets, the aroma of smokehouse ham and lemon cheese cake makes your mouth water.

The afternoon session gets under way with "There's a Light in the Window," "I'll Meet you in the Morning," "Shake Hands With Mother," "I Heard My Name on Heaven's Radio."

The church is jammed to the doors and windows. Babies whine, a puppy yelps under the benches, children squirm, everyone mops perspiration and fans himself with anything that will stir a breeze. But the singin' never stops.

"Preachin' will end at the grave," declares an 83-year-old farmer from Bethany, "but singin' will go on through eternity. Them that can't sing here will have a new voice when they get over there and will sing a new song."

1960–Present

The Earth is Our Home

The Earth is Our Home

In 1902 farming was the occupation of most people of the world. They labored to bring from the earth what was needed to go into the mouths or on the backs of their families. The earth was the great factory which satisfied (if anything did) the needs of the humans on its crust.

The story of the 20th century has been the story of man leaving the earth, both literally and figuratively. Over and over in the pages of the *Progressive Farmer* since the beginning of the century, we note the editors' (and readers') concern with the lure of the city. Through the years the *Progressive Farmer* has had a dual theme: keep the children on the farm (the most wholesome, most creative place for them to grow up and raise their own families) *and* make the farm life easier so that both children and adults will *want* to stay.

Today in many ways, farm homes are indistinguishable from their city and suburban counterparts. Most farm women have dishwashers, clothes driers and air conditioners. They take their conveniences as much for granted as their city sisters do. In fact, that part of the *Progressive Farmer*'s crusade seems to have been accomplished during these seventy-five years. But the odds of history have appeared to be against the first part—keeping the children on the farm. From a farming country in 1902 we have become a nation of city and suburb dwellers with our farming population now slightly under 4% of the total.

But it may be only now that the last part of the prophecy has been fulfilled that we can see the truth of the former. During the long years of loneliness and hardship on the farm, it sometimes seemed as if the *Progressive Farmer* "doth protest too much." Why, one wondered, if farm life was all the *Progressive Farmer* proclaimed, were so many people living that life not aware of its advantages? Why was the rush away from the farm? It is only now that most of the hardships have been removed that all can see the intangible advantages of farm life so long proclaimed by the *Progressive Farmer:* the sense of permanence in the country, the joy of joining with earth to make things grow, the nearness to the cycles and the core of life, and the creativity and originality needed to "build" a farm.

In the 1920's Clarence Poe wrote a prescient article equating the city with "things" and the country with "life." In the last few years, some suburban parents have been disturbed by their children's acceptance of almost this same idea. Some children have been rejecting their parents' hard-won material gains (gains especially meaningful to parents who were brought up during the Depression) and wanting to return to "country," which their parents had hoped they had left behind long ago. If, in the twenties, parents were trying to keep children within the safety of the known world of the farm, today some parents are worried because of their children's rejection of the safety of the known world of the city and suburbs. But the children are longing for "roots," for meaning, for commitment to more than "things," for "life." Some are looking for it in some form of farming enterprise.

If the trend from the beginning of this century has been away from the land, another trend has been developing almost unnoticed since the early 1960's. While agriculture lost 12.5 million farm people between 1950 and 1968 (a loss of 64%), *rural counties* as a group lost only about half a million people through migration from 1960 to 1966. One woman wrote:

In this small community we used to farm only, but now some member of practically every family is working at a job in town, to keep the family from losing the farm homes so dear to them . . . It isn't easy, but I smile to myself and feel comforted, with our family together under this roof, on yielding land.

In a 1974 article entitled "From the City to the Farm?," the *Progressive Farmer* suggested that if the "usual source of farmers is drying up" (farmers' sons), a non-usual source might be in the offing—"a new means of preserving rural communities." A study of four rural counties showed that "about 60% of farm families get some income from off-farm jobs." The *Progressive Farmer* suggested that "incomes from off-farm jobs have helped to keep the farms strong and intact." It recommended that, since "a large amount of rural land will change hands in the next 10 years," a means should be found of "dividing farmland to be sold into economically-sized parcels to meet the de-

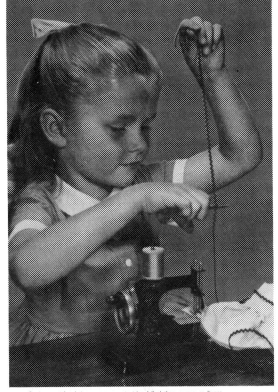

Sewing on rickrack is one easy way to trim doll clothes, aprons, or linens.

To a young girl, sewing
By Elaine V. Emans

It's no occasion to be sad
That you must rip your stitches out
And do them over. Just be glad
That you can rip, and never doubt
That to make a finer, straighter
Seam is excellent advice.
Someday, certainly, years later,
You'll be glad you sewed this twice.

Little girls like sewing

Mothers, what joys your child will know when at first she learns to sew.

mands of these new dual-income farmers."

Despite the fact that farming has become an industry of technology, it is still controlled by *families:* 89.5% of all farms are owned and operated by an individual or a family. Only 1.7% of farms today are controlled by corporations. A new breed of farmer may be emerging.

This farmer, with technology at his side, may not feel the same struggle against the land that his ancestors did. Perhaps he is less likely to feel that total dependence on the land which turns it into a loved (or hated) creature. The new

farmer can take it or leave it. It does not own him. And yet, as one man wrote:

. . . there is something about the felt ownership of land on which a man lives, works and has his home, different from any other kind of ownership on earth.

The age-old call of the land is still being heard. But the farmers' sons, who have grown up with it, also know the difficulties involved in beginning a paying farm business. One farm mother heard her son remark that "there's no way a

She advised him to keep good records and be willing to do without luxuries. And she concluded with her thoughts about his father:

When I go to the top of the hill and look over all the land he has reclaimed from a rundown cotton farm to lush green forage grazed by sleek Holsteins, I know he is truly God's own man, called to one of the oldest and noblest professions known to mankind.

The Mockingbird Still Sings in the Chinaberry Tree . . .

Moneywise, farming has changed from bad to worse. But some things never change. The mockingbird still sings in the chinaberry tree, the hogs grunt with contentment when I rub their sides, and the earth smells good as ever. I shall fight to the bitter end to hold on to my land.

The rural world, rocky right now, is facing toward a recovery of steady and enduring values. Never fear that love of the land will die exhausted, in our young. Voices of the young will be heard; young minds and bodies will put forth strength and force. City jobs won't snatch away the best of our boys and girls. They will stay with us and farm and work and pray . . .
—Ms. A. F., Miss.

young man can get into farming today." She wrote "A Farm Mother's Letter to Her Son," which the *Progressive Farmer* published in 1978. This "Farm Mother" suggested that her son begin farming part time, be willing to start small and work hard. Especially important was to

marry someone enthusiastic about your goal of independence on the farm. It is not enough that she love you to distraction, nor that she be willing to bear your children. She should also be able to mix milk substitute and straddle a three-day-old bovine to force an artificial nipple between reluctant jaws.

Someday a hungry world will be crying for our surpluses. More people and more, until there won't be enough food. Will future writers look back upon our stored bins of corn and wheat and write about a farming age that produced so much farmers had to go out of business?—Jesse Stuart, Ky.

"City farmers"—merchants, bankers, rich men—are responsible for farm surpluses. Take away subsidies and they'll leave farming like fleas from a dead dog.—T. H. T., Tenn.

For years the United States Government has tried to lower farm production to a certain level. And, for years, the Russian Government has tried to raise farm production to a certain level. Before long, people will reach the conclusion that governments do not know how to farm.—J. M., N. C.

Many wonderful advances in science have been announced—such as "seeding" the clouds to make it rain. But when it rains too much, have they found a way to stop it raining?—R. M. W., La.

Quit meddling with the moon.—Mrs. L. A. P., Tenn.

What no one seems to realize is that our open space, our clean, fresh country acres are being gobbled up, desecrated by man's "improvements." When, oh when, will man acknowledge that his original function on earth was, in the words of Genesis 2:15 "to dress it and to keep it?"—Mrs. L. E. T., N. C.

Stolen Calf

In haste I turned from chores and braced my heart. That shattered door filled me with dismay, knowing the ways of first-time

heifer mothers—their primal need to flee the herd and seek deepest seclusion.

How could I trace faint hoofprints in the dust, or be in time to coax her safely home, where veterinary skill might shorten her travail and ease the pain?

I saw the ominous buzzards circling high; then plunged into the thicket of tangling brier, hackberry, and vine; slashing, stamping, kicking, crossing, and crisscrossing acres of wood until my tortured breath and bursting chest brought me to pause and think—and pray.

Then in the hush and quiet af-

termath there came the softly murmured "mother talk" from her I sought praising her newborn son, bidding him rise, to nurse, proudly to stand in this brave new world. —V. A. C., Ark.

When I was young, work mornings started with everything quiet and still. I remember waiting for the sun to shorten the long, ragged pine shadows covering fence rows and hills. My father would use these few minutes to sharpen the hoes. The rhythmic whing-sing of the file across the blades was music, and I never had to look up from my drowsy dreaming to know when he laid one hoe aside and began another.

My father was a self-disciplined artist. Each patch we worked stretched before us in long, curving rows, each identical to the one before it. Each was filled with sturdy cotton plants, uniform in shape and size; the only untidiness was the weeds we were there to chop away. It seemed that even the elements worked with my father in forming these fields of beauty.

He liked us to begin at the beginning, completing each row as we went. Often I would see him glance back over the completed work, his eyes receiving it quietly, like a painter who acknowledges the worth of his canvas.

I worked slowly and meticulously, wearing my father's proudness in the work.

It was only after I had children of my own that I came to realize the lesson I had learned from such simple acts. There had grown a bond between my father and me that belies to this day the use of words.—E. C. A., Tex.

Room for Grandchildren

Aren't we teaching our children to be too comformable? Shouldn't we teach them to refuse to be owned by things and the opinions of others?—Mrs. W. H. H., Ky.

Youth doesn't
Make laws,
Write books,
Shoot pictures,
Make liquor,
Run joints,
Set examples.
Adults, wake up! Children are copycats.—Mrs. J. S., Miss.

Boon companions in the study of nature are Susan Garrett and her grandfather, Julius Benjamin Garrett, of West Feliciana Parish, La.

Three Generations of Farming

A. My grandfather farmed 150 acres by mule. He planted peanuts, cotton, corn, cane, and made syrup. Four Negro families worked the land.

B. My father sold the mules and farms 350 acres with tractors. He plants peanuts, corn, and has 200 acres pastureland on which Herefords graze. In addition, he raises hogs and Shetland ponies.

C. I plan to farm with my brother David, now in ag school. He will farm and I will tend livestock. Our 10 purebred Hereford heifers will be artifically bred this month. We have seeded 125 acres pastureland. In the future, we hope to have a pig parlor for our hogs and a fishpond.—L. W., 13, Ga.

Recently Dr. H. I. Gilmore, 78-year-old physician, delivered his 67th set of twins. Including the

twins, the doctor has brought about 3,000 babies into the world, traveling many miles over hills and hollows, at first by horseback and carriage and then by car to serve his patients. He has been practicing medicine for 55 years in Eastern and Central Kentucky, successfully making the transition from board sidewalks and dirt roads to superhighways. He has no thought of retiring now.—Mrs. L. B., Ky.

It's fun for any child to visit grandparents; but for the grandchildren of Mr. and Mrs. G. G., Miss., it is a special treat—because when the G.'s remodeled their home in 1968 they added a grandchildren's room.

In this room nothing is on the "don't-touch" list; everything is sturdy and easy to clean. The cushions on the sofa and chairs are reversible; one side is plastic—one swipe of a damp cloth removes the jam that sticky little fingers have left there; the other side is covered with fabric for the big folks. The floor is covered in vinyl tile so spills are no problem.

A cupboard at one end of the room holds toys and games. Dolls in one cupboard wait for little mothers' loving hands, and high-heeled shoes and grown-up handbags in another are for playing "lady."

New Outlook for the Old Homeplace

This family has been in the dairy business in and around a little hamlet in northwest Louisiana since the early 1900's. Mr. B., his wife,

"My wife and I believe that the girls should be included in every part of the dairy operation and in the household affairs where they can help," Mr. B. explains. "They are not too young to wash down the calf barn or round up the cows on horseback in the fall . . ."

The B.'s could have . . . moved into the city closer to public schools and commuted to the dairy. They chose to remain on the land, because as Mr. B. expresses it: "We are happy here. We are, after, all country folks—dairy farmers by trade . . . You'd be surprised perhaps, to know that a lot of young folks are returning to the farm, coming back to this area after having lived in the big cities. We're glad to see that trend. We're lucky. We never had to move to the city to find out how good it is to get back to the land."

Homecoming

You cannot rob a house of its housing
spirit,
Though eyes stare darkly from its
weathered face.
Its walls will cling to any succor near it,
To wind or willow, promising a place.

And one day, made more perfect by its
rarity,
Will come two who need pause except a
minute.
Till one will say, with love and not with
charity,
"Let's fix it up. It needs somebody in it."
E. F., Ark.

and their two little girls, 10, and 8, are carrying on the family tradition of dairying.

During the silage season, Mrs. B. drives a tractor from "dawn to 'can't see.' "

She cans and freezes almost everything her family eats. She is on the go all day long, stopping long enough to prepare at least one hot meal for the family. And the children are not exempt from farm chores just because they are girls.